Human Rights
IN THE
Global
Political Economy

Human Rights

IN THE

Global

Political Economy

CRITICAL PROCESSES

Tony Evans

LYNNE
RIENNER
PUBLISHERS

BOULDER
LONDON

*The author would like to thank the Leverhulme Trust for
financial support during the preparation of this book.*

Published in the United States of America in 2011 by
Lynne Rienner Publishers, Inc.
1800 30th Street, Boulder, Colorado 80301
www.rienner.com

and in the United Kingdom by
Lynne Rienner Publishers, Inc.
3 Henrietta Street, Covent Garden, London WC2E 8LU

Library of Congress Cataloging-in-Publication Data
Evans, Tony, 1944–
  Human rights in the global political economy: critical processes / Tony
Evans.
  Includes bibliographical references and index.
  ISBN 978-1-58826-719-1 (hardcover: alk. paper)
  ISBN 978-1-58826-750-4 (pbk.: alk. paper)
  1. Human rights. 2. Human rights monitoring. 3. International economic
relations. I. Title.
  JC571.E852 2010 2011
  323—dc22
                                                        2010018938

British Cataloguing in Publication Data
A Cataloguing in Publication record for this book
is available from the British Library.

For Annie and Seth

Contents

1

Introduction

In 1986 John Vincent published *Human Rights and International Relations,* a work that sought to "bring together in one place an account of the theory of human rights, an examination of the part they play in international relations; and finally, a view of the part they ought to play."[1] The scholarly importance of Vincent's work was immediately recognized and continues to attract attention today. However, since Vincent's book was published, significant changes have occurred, in both the practice of international relations and the academic discipline of international relations, that Vincent could not have foreseen. In the conduct of international relations, a number of events—the end of the Cold War,[2] the impact of globalization,[3] the growth of social movements,[4] changes in international organization for the protection of human rights,[5] a deepening interest in the politics of humanitarianism[6]—contextualize human rights in ways unimaginable in the early 1980s. Similarly, at the level of the discipline of international relations, the recent literature on feminism,[7] poststructuralism,[8] globalization,[9] and neo-Marxism,[10] together with the introduction of aspects of anthropology,[11] sociology,[12] political geography,[13] and legal theory, has broadened the scope of the debate on human rights.

Within the literature generated by commentators, practitioners, and students of human rights, there is a significant and growing level of critique. The distinction between criticism and critique is important here. While criticism is confined to arguments about particular theories, philosophies, beliefs, ideologies, and regimes, critique is more concerned with investigating the ways in which these claims to truth are achieved, legitimated, and presented as the authoritative guide for action. If criticism can be thought of as part of a technical debate, intended to refine particular truths, then critique is concerned with the "politics of truth" itself.[14] As such, critique is concerned with exposing the interests served by the production and maintenance of particular truths, and the processes that enable some forms of knowledge to be accepted as complete and legitimate, while other forms are labeled partial and suspect.

The literature on human rights has always included considerable criticism aimed at organizational and legal issues, in an attempt to improve the quality of implementation and legal rules. More recently, however, the very idea of human

1

rights, together with the principles that underpin current institutional measures created for the protection of human rights, have been subjected to critique. Theorists from many cultural traditions have suggested that the conceptual basis upon which the global human rights regime is built cannot any longer sustain its claim as representing a "truth" to which all peoples should subscribe. This growing attack on a commitment to human rights is motivated by changes in the socioeconomic global order that we commonly term globalization. In particular, technology has enabled faster and more frequent exchanges of ideas, often with those who in the past would not have found a voice. Whereas in the past developments in human rights might have been considered the preserve of developed capitalist states—a one-way street through which the civilized sought to channel morality to the uncivilized—today the cacophony of voices from different cultures, legal systems, polities, and social and class backgrounds impacts on the way we approach all social issues.

The changes wrought by globalization suggest that it is now timely to reassess the project of human rights as an aspect of global politics, rather than the narrower field of international relations that provided the focus for Vincent's work. This book is therefore concerned with bringing together in one place critiques that challenge the dominant theory and practice of human rights. It begins with an examination of recent critiques of the concept of human rights and then moves to critique current practices for the protection of human rights, before finally looking to the future of human rights as a process.

Chapter 2 looks at the ways globalization has eroded the foundations upon which the formal human rights regime is built. Chapter 3 examines theoretical challenges to the dominant theory of human rights emanating from recent developments within Western political thought: postmodernism, feminism, and neo-Marxism. Chapter 4 looks at alternative views of human rights from cultures that are only now finding a voice in human rights talk. In particular, the chapter examines the claims of Islam, Confucianism, and Asian values. Chapter 5 looks at the place and status of human rights within the global political economy, particularly the role played by human rights within the policymaking processes of the World Bank, the International Monetary Fund, the World Trade Organization, and transnational corporations. Chapter 6 argues that if the processes of globalization have changed the nature of sovereignty, as globalization theory argues, then the centrality of the state as the guardian of human rights is in question. Whereas in the past it was assumed that the state was responsible for protecting the rights of its own citizens, the increasing potential for penetrating state borders through cultural, economic, social, and political interactions makes this claim less secure. Moreover, if state sovereignty is transformed under conditions of economic globalization, then the state-centric institutions created to support human rights—international law, for example—may be inappropriate for securing human freedom and dignity.

Recent changes in institutional arrangements for the protection and promotion of human rights provide the focus for Chapter 7. The creation of the International Criminal Court (ICC) and the replacement of the Commission on Human Rights with the Human Rights Council are hailed by some commentators as a sign of further progress. However, the Human Rights Council has already received considerable criticism for its political bias and its propensity to support regional partners no matter their human rights record. Similarly, the early years of the ICC have attracted criticism from those who see its operation as biased toward particular interests. Chapter 8 is concerned with the use of human rights as resistance to the march of globalization. It concludes that in the current struggle between conservatives and radicals—where conservatives seek to present human rights as the moral justification for free market capitalism and radicals as a justification for resisting the social consequences of that system— the dominant view remains that of the conservatives.

The distinction between conservative and radical approaches to human rights remains important in Chapter 9, which casts human rights as a political process rather than an end point defined through the tradition of natural rights. It points to the dynamics of world order and the need to accept that human rights demand continuous reflection and renegotiation if we are to take rights seriously. The never-ending struggle over rights therefore remains central to historic processes of social, political, and economic change.

Before beginning, it is worth stressing three things that this book is not about. First, it is not an attempt to deal a death blow to the whole idea of human rights, although at times this might suggest itself to the reader. Rather, the arguments presented here suggest that in a globalizing world order, the need to create a set of values that protect the dignity and rights of human beings is, if anything, more urgent than ever. That does not mean, however, that the contemporary idea of human rights, which has achieved the status of "common sense" in the minds of many academic and policymaking circles, should continue to proclaim its "truth" in the age of globalization. Nor does this suggest that the current institutions for human rights will serve in the future. Indeed, the social, economic, cultural, and political context of globalization brings changes to all aspects to people's lives that cannot be ignored. Human rights are no different in this respect. What this suggests is the need to stimulate political processes that engage with the new order as it emerges and touches the lives of all humankind.

And this leads to the second thing that this book is not about. It is not about constructing arguments in favor of a particular alternative to current human rights thinking. In an age of rapid change, it is more important to engage with processes that seek to explore alternatives than to establish new sets of values and principles that are quickly outmoded. There is, therefore, no missionary zeal within these pages, if that phrase implies an attempt to tear down the existing order of human rights and to replace it with another. Rather, what is argued is the need to recognize processes of change that make past ideas, values, and principles redundant in the contemporary age. While this approach is well understood by those who accept recently developed theories of globalization, it will, of course, offend those who still cling to the idea of human rights as a natural attribute of humankind that transcends time and space.

Finally, I make no apology for focusing on critiques of the idea of human rights and its associated institutions without reference to, or analysis of, the achievements often proclaimed in the literature. The existing literature cannot be accused of failing to identify shortcomings in the international human rights regime or of lacking courage in offering helpful suggestions for improvements. However, most authors accept the values and principles upon which the existing regime is built, assuming that all the great normative, institutional, and multicultural questions on human rights are now answered, even though some details remain undecided. Rather than engage in problematizing human rights within the context of the contemporary socioeconomic global order, the ethos of most publications is more concerned with celebrating the triumph of the idea. When the literature does nod in the direction of critique, it is often done in a manner suggesting that the author is merely fulfilling an academic or professional obligation to acknowledge alternatives.[15]

Notes

1. R. J. Vincent, *Human Rights and International Relations* (Cambridge, UK: Cambridge University Press, 1986), p. vii.

2. Issa Shivji, "Constructing a New Rights Regime: Promises, Problems, and Prospects," *Social and Legal Studies* 8, no. 2 (1999).

3. David Held et al., eds., *Global Transformations: Politics, Economics, and Culture* (Cambridge, UK: Polity Press, 1999).

4. Neil Stammers, "Social Movements and the Social Construction of Human Rights," *Human Rights Quarterly* 21, no. 4 (1999).

5. Tom J. Farer, "Restraining the Barbarians: Can International Criminal Law Help?" *Human Rights Quarterly* 22, no. 1 (2000).

6. Nicholas Wheeler and Tim Dunne, "Good International Citizenship: A Third Way for British Foreign Policy," *International Affairs* 74, no. 4 (1998).

7. V. Spike Peterson and Laura Parisi, "Are Women Human? It's Not an Academic Quesiton," in *Human Rights Fifty Years On: A Reappraisal,* ed. Tony Evans (Manchester: Manchester University Press, 1998).

8. Richard Rorty, "Human Rights, Rationality, and Sentimentality," in *On Human Rights: The Oxford Amnesty Lectures,* 1993, ed. Stephen Shute and Susan Hurley (New York: Basic Books, 1993).

9. Jan Aart Scholte, "Towards a Critical Theory of Globalization," in *Globalization in Theory and Practice,* ed. Eleonore Kofman and Gillian Young (London: Pinter, 1996).

10. Stephen Gill, "Globalization, Market Civilisation, and Disciplinary Neoliberalism," *Millennium* 24, no. 3 (1995).

11. Richard A Wilson, "Human Rights, Culture, and Context: An Introduction," in *Human Rights, Culture, and Context* (London: Pluto, 1997).

12. Anthony Woodiwiss, *Globalization, Human Rights, and Labour Law in Pacific Asia* (Cambridge: Cambridge University Press, 1998).

13. K. Dodds, "Political Geography: Some Thoughts on Banality, New Wars, and the Geographical Tradition," *Progress in Human Geography* 24, no. 1 (2000).

14. Michel Foucault, "What Is Critique?" in *Twentieth-Century Questions,* ed. James Schmidt (Berkeley: University of California Press, 1996).

15. C. Douzinas, *Human Rights and Empire: The Political Philosophy of Cosmopolitanism* (Abingdon, UK: Routledge-Cavendish, 2007); M. Mutua, *Human Rights: A Political and Cultural Critique* (Philadelphia: University of Pennsylvania Press, 2002).

2

The Idea of Human Rights in the Global Political Economy

Legend has it that in the sixteenth century, as the young, future queen of Spain journeyed from her family home to be married, she was showered with gifts by every town she passed through. In one such town, the merchant class decided that it was appropriate to present her with a pair of silk stockings, a product for which the town was famed. Those accompanying the young woman were horrified at this suggestion, considering it indelicate to mention undergarments, like stockings, let alone to make a public display of such intimate clothing. Rather than insult and disappoint the merchants by refusing the gift and perhaps risk damaging the young woman's popularity, the courtiers announced diplomatically, "The queen of Spain has no legs." Since that time, this phrase has been used as a metaphor for ignoring that which clearly exists or might be imagined to exist.[1] The central theme of this book is that the growing critique of the theory and practice of human rights, like the queen of Spain's legs, cannot be recognized for fear of fatally damaging a set of values and international institutions that provide the moral foundations for contemporary global politics: universal human rights. Before I undertake a more detailed examination of recent critiques of human rights, this chapter asks why these critiques seem to have so little impact on normative and moral discourses today.

Post–World War II Theory and Practice of Human Rights

The claim is commonplace that human rights emerged in the post–World War II period as a reaction to acts of genocide and other atrocities perpetrated during the Nazi era. Although this claim is focused on the creation of the postwar global human rights regime, it is often forgotten that the idea of human rights predates the regime by many centuries. The historical development of the idea of human rights is well covered in the literature and need not be rehearsed here in any detail.[2] However, following Vincent, a broad outline suggests four "stations" that mark the route to the modern idea of human rights. First, the Stoics, who sought to attack the parochialism of the Greek *polis*, proposed instead that all individuals had equal worth, which on rational grounds alone deserved the right to full participation in the wider community. Second, Christian theology developed the idea of individual salvation as a form of deliverance that could be achieved only when certain rights were attached to the individual living in the wider community. Third, while the Renaissance pursued the idea of the individual possessing rights, the Reformation pursued the idea of obligations of conscience, which proposed the right of rebellion against corrupt governments, shifting the established emphasis from duties to rights. Last, in reaction to negative rights and excessive individualism,[3] German romantic thought sort to promote the idea of group rights in an effort to make sense of positive freedoms.[4]

These conceptual movements suggest that the history of human rights is one of innovation and discovery—a continuous, if uneven, discourse of challenge and counterchallenge, of evolution, movement, and process, reflecting the dynamics of social, political, and economic change. As Stammers has argued, while philosophy may be co-opted in the interests of promoting particular rights associated with particular interests, rights claims should be seen more as an integral part of socioeconomic change,[5] exemplified, for example, by the French and American revolutions. In this sense, the history of rights is not therefore the history of struggles to overcome barriers erected by wicked leaders who conspire to deny the existence of rights, although this is the context in which human rights talk is usually conducted.[6] Instead, the history of rights must also be seen as part of a continuous struggle against the dominant contemporary order that seeks to legitimize a moral and ethical code favorable to particular interests. Seen in this way, claims for human rights can be viewed as an ideology of the dominant that attracts resistance, protest, and the assertion of new forms of rights, democracy, and citizenship.[7] Human rights must therefore be seen as both a conservative and radical claim central to many social and political conflicts.

However, with the creation of the modern global human rights regime, the idea of human rights appears to have lost its dynamism. Today, many commentators argue that the global human rights regime, which encompasses a legal framework and institutional machinery, has reified the notion of human rights, performing an act of "closure" that leaves no room for further development. Where in the past, advocates of human rights reveled in a multifaceted discourse, today the "human rights movement is driven by a totalitarian or totalizing impulse," a mission that seeks to transform all societies to "fit a particular blueprint."[8] Within the context of a globalizing political economy,[9] the success of which depends upon establishing a common set of values, the kind of deep reflection and critique that marks the historical development of the idea of human rights has been replaced by a universalizing certainty.[10]

How has the shift from dynamism to closure come about? An examination of the post–World War II negotiations to create a global human rights regime shows that dominant and influential voices asserted the move to "closure" from the beginning. As the most powerful state to emerge from the war, the United States sought to pursue policies intended to extend its sphere of influence, particularly over global markets. Calls for a return to isolationist policies and the swift return of troops from Europe and Asia, immediately hostilities ended, threatened to jeopardize these ambitions. In particular, the long-term maintenance of military bases in many regions of the world was seen as a vital resource for protecting US interests.[11] The pursuit of universal human rights offered a way of countering calls for a return to isolationist policies, while gaining the support of domestic publics for postwar policies aimed at establishing a sustained US global presence. The American people were not being asked to support foreign governments in distant and unknown places, but to take the lead in struggles for the nobler cause of human freedom itself. As Augelli and Murphy have shown, the very rationale for the United States of America, the destiny and identity of its people, is linked historically to universal claims for liberty, freedom, individualism, and liberalism, which the early settlers sought to realize.[12] Thus, if "to be an American is to pursue a view of rights as universal and general,"[13] the United States could not escape the duty to promote these values beyond its borders. Defining human rights as negative freedoms that support ideas of liberalism, the free market, and laissez-faire as the central values for a postwar order was not therefore an option. Rather, it was presented as the fulfillment of American destiny.[14]

The idea of human rights promoted by the United States and its allies was not therefore in question. Only those negative rights that supported the full and unfettered engagement of the individual within a liberal economic order would be promoted vigorously through international law and institutions.[15] The call for including economic and social rights in any international law on human rights was seen as "socialism by treaty,"[16] "un-American," and unacceptable by many influential groups within the United States.[17] For successive postwar administrations, this presented a problem. On the one hand, negative human rights offered an opportunity for legitimating a set of values that supported US ambitions to engage fully in the postwar order and to expand markets. On the other hand, given the context of the ideological struggle that was the Cold War, to adopt an inflexible position on economic and social rights risked losing the support of newly independent states and those that aspired to this status, for whom economic and social rights remained an imperative. For the United States to claim that economic and social rights were not human rights therefore held the possibility of driving underdeveloped states into the arms of the Soviet Union. To avoid this circumstance, the United States was prepared to acknowledge the inclusion of economic and social rights in a nonbinding declaration, while reserving the right not to enter into any treaty that gave legal status to that set of rights.[18] From this position, the United States could continue to promote an ideology of human rights that satisfied the people of the United States while simultaneously rejecting any legally binding obligations that compromised global free market liberalism.

This narrow postwar context laid the foundation for a model of human rights that is often cited today. The model is constructed as three phases: phase one is defined by debates over foundational values upon which human rights might be claimed; phase two concerns standard setting; and phase three seeks to develop institutional machinery for implementation. This model is exemplified by three periods: the 1948 Universal Declaration of Human Rights (UDHR); the period during which all the major pieces of international law were created; and the current period, which is devoted to creating practices to secure the central values and standards agreed in the first two phases. Importantly, it is assumed that this model is built upon a set of abiding and enduring apolitical, neutral, and impartial values, which humankind must pursue for all time. Historical changes in political context, ideology, relations of power, and interests are of little concern when the promotion and protection of human rights is at issue.

However, asserting this model tends to ignore the conflicts encountered at every stage of creating the postwar international human rights regime and its development in later decades. It became clear as early as negotiations for creating the United Nations Charter that general agreement on the idea of human rights would not be achieved easily. Tensions were soon exposed over ideological worldviews, the efficacy of international law as the prime institution for protecting human rights, the philosophical foundations of rights claims, and many other conceptual issues. Later, the different cultural approaches adopted by those engaged in creating the global human rights regime exposed conflicts that served to convince the newly appointed chair of the Commission on Human Rights, Eleanor Roosevelt, that any attempt to resolve them would deflect attention from the primary task of the commission, which she saw as drafting international law.[19] Endless debate about the moral and philosophical foundations of human rights was seen as a threat to achieving this task. However, the determination to shift the debate from conceptual to practical issues, which included avoiding the important issue of how to create institutional machinery for protecting a set of universal values within an international order of sovereign states, each claiming nonintervention and domestic jurisdiction, was sometimes debated but never satisfactorily resolved.[20]

In the immediate years following World War II, few doubted the nation-state's capability to act independently, constrained only by its relative power position within the system of states.[21] States were said to operate within a self-help system, where foreign policy, domestic legal systems, national security, and national economic planning were seen as the exclusive domain of the state. The system of states assumed "community inside [the state], anarchy outside; justice inside, power and, at best, order outside; effective institutions with legislative authority inside, shifting alliances and fragile balancing mechanisms outside."[22] Although the pursuit of universal human rights was recognized as central to the rationale for creating the United Nations, this recognition was understood as freely given by independent, sovereign-state members who reserved the right to domestic jurisdiction and nonintervention. During the discussions that preceded the creation of the Universal Declaration of Human Rights, delegates from all states asserted their country's right to noninterference in domestic affairs, while simultaneously accepting the universality of the rights that the Declaration promised.[23]

Following the period that saw the development of the two major covenants on human rights—one on economic, social, and cultural rights and the other on civil and political rights—the language of international society emerged as an alternative to that of the international system.[24] This alternative language distinguished itself from that associated with the international system by stressing the normative, rule-driven, international-law order that states are said to inhabit. Although this order is qualitatively different from that found within the state, which rests upon some notion of common purpose, international society was assumed to represent fragile relations among adversaries who, unable to persuade others to adopt their own values, agree to adopt international law and the rules of diplomacy as the central means by which global order is maintained.[25] In this formulation, the international law of human rights retains the state as the subject of international law, with the individual as its object, while giving recognition to the need to take the rights of the individual seriously. The sanction for failing to fulfill obligations under international law was ostracism from the society of states, leaving violating states excluded from important economic and political institutions and relationships. By the 1980s, this approach to global order and rights was sufficiently well established that John Vincent was able to argue that a good human rights record had become an additional defining principle of legitimate state sovereignty.[26]

However, despite Vincent's contribution, while noting the attempt to distinguish itself from earlier formulations about the nature of global order, particularly the requirement to act in accordance with international law, the emergence of international society thinking did not necessarily demand action on human rights issues. International law covers a wide range of issues, not only human rights. Under particular circumstances, and in particular periods of history, concerns other than human rights are often given greater weight. In this respect, given that international society thinking emerged during the Cold War years, which focused minds on the ever-present prospect of nuclear war, the maintenance of a peaceful bipolar world order took priority over justice and rights. To criticize friends during the Cold War for their human rights record brought the danger of schism, while to criticize foes might spark diplomatic antagonisms, the escalation of existing conflicts, and, at best, the erosion of the fragile existence of international society or, at worst, catastrophic war.

With the end of the Cold War, many believed that the promises set out in the Universal Declaration would now be realized. The potential threat of nuclear war between East and West, which had dominated the international agenda since the end of World War II, was removed. The collapse of socialist states was portrayed as providing the long-awaited opportunity to place human rights at the center of global politics. Human rights would at last realize its claim as the "idea of our time." Within the space opened by the post–Cold War era, it was assumed that civil society organizations would flourish, creating new social networks devoted to exposing violations and injustices wherever they occurred and thus enable international society to fulfill its promise to promote and protect human rights. In future, it was argued, states would develop and exercise an ethical foreign policy guided by the values found in the human rights regime.[27]

The Era of Economic Globalization

However, as the 2008 report from Amnesty International acknowledges, the promise of human rights remains unfulfilled. The report begins by accepting that while legal and organizational developments at the international, regional, and local level provide evidence that might justify claims of "progress," "the fact remains that injustice, inequality and impunity are still the hallmark of our world today."[28] For Amnesty, while national and international leaders continue with their rhetoric, and never hesitate to put their names to declarations and international law on human rights, narrower political and economic interests continue to dominate global agendas. In the age of globalization, Amnesty argues, the evolution of the formal human rights regime has not been matched by a commitment to act. In short, the Universal Declaration remains an unfulfilled promise. Accordingly, Amnesty claims:

> World leaders owe an apology for failing to deliver on the promises of justice and equality in the Universal Declaration of Human Rights, adopted 60 years ago. In the past six decades, many governments have shown more interest in the abuse of power or in the pursuit of political self-interest, than in respecting the rights of those they lead.[29]

While much time and energy is expended on human rights, a process that has stimulated ever-greater popular interest, the demand for action has often been eclipsed by claims that other, more urgent, needs should take priority. As Tamilmoran has noted, given the conditions of globalization, including the imperative of economic growth and development, when economic, social, political, and cultural rights are violated it is common to offer the defense that society must fulfill its duty to provide for the well-being of future generations—a duty of economic "progress"—even when this means that the current generation must suffer human rights consequences.[30]

The shift in order from an international society of states to one now commonly described by the term *globalization* recognizes processes that were already in motion before the end of the Cold War—most significantly, the globalization of production, markets, and finance. According to recent theory, globalization infers social relations where the social core and periphery cut across existing national boundaries, creating new patterns of economic growth and consumption over which, it is argued, the state has diminishing authority.[31]

While in previous stages of history the state could adopt national strategies for ordering a national economy, including perhaps the nationalization of key industries, today the global organization of production, exchange, and finance means that states "by and large play the role of agencies of the global economy, with the task of adjusting national economic policies and practices to the perceived exigencies of global economic liberalism."[32]

An ideology of modernity underpins the shift to a global economy,[33] which rests upon the twin goals of economic growth and development, defined as global capital accumulation and consumption. The central means for achieving these goals, in both the wealthy North and the impoverished South, is strategic planning at the global level, global management, and the creation of global regimes and agreements. Ideological convergence has the effect of homogenizing and limiting the policy choices of governments. Global management requires adherence to rules that ensure all countries conform to the development model so that the "hidden hand" of the market can operate efficiently. Consequently, responsibility for defining and implementing the rules for international action shifts away from the state to international institutions and regimes.[34] Global governance replaces national government: policy bears on processes designed to further the smooth, efficient maintenance of the global economy.

In recent years many scholars have noted this phenomenon. Panitch, for example, asserts that today the primary function of the state is to create and manage a global order that supports the interests of global capital, not the rights and welfare of citizens.[35] Similarly, Camilleri and Falk argue that the latest stage of modernity has built its foundations upon a universal goal of economic growth, reducing all political and economic institutions "to instruments for the achievement of that goal." As a result, "the world political system, including the system of states, is governed by rules that embody and nurture the logic of market-orientated growth."[36] Decisions made at the national level may disrupt patterns of globalization on occasion, but states cannot ultimately escape its consequences. For Rupert, the power of the capitalist class has never been constrained within the state historically, but under conditions of globalization is at its most effective as the central institution for managing the neoliberal global economy. Capitalism may therefore be "fruitfully understood as a transnational social system which has encompassed the system of sovereign states as well as the seemingly discrete sphere of capitalist economy."[37]

From this perspective, the realization that the global economy, rather than the national economy, exercises greater influence on economic and social well-being, suggests that the state loses its significance as a center of authority through which people can express their preferences. Instead, the focus turns to international institutions and organizations, which assume the task of providing the rules for action. Although governments continue to engage in international politics, governance is conducted by a group of formal and informal organizations, the *nébuleuse*,[38] whose task is to provide and maintain the conditions for capitalist expansion. The move to gain legitimacy for rules that free global capital from all spatial and temporal constraints is significant because "all the noted texts [of international law], confer or hope to bestow a number of rights on transnational capital [but] . . . impose no corresponding duties."[39] The World Trade Organization (WTO) is sometimes seen as the most advanced model for securing the interests of capital because it is the first global organization with the authority to "strike down particular national interests, even when these are enshrined in [national] law or custom."[40] Were the WTO model to be used to create other institutions for global governance, without first developing new forms of global mass participation, existing systems of national democracy would face a serious threat.[41]

The link between government and the governed is therefore weakened, if not replaced, by new forms of governance related to the expansion of the global economy.[42] Over time, the decline in participation, coupled with the maintenance of an order in which the governed are increasingly objectified, ensures that people become more accountable to remote centers of authority, rather than those centers being accountable to people. Giddens has coined the word *distanciation* to capture the phenomenon where "locales are thoroughly penetrated by and shaped in terms of social influences quite distant from them."[43] Distanciation ensures that the relationship between international institutions and populations is not concerned with human rights, human values, environmental degradation, the quality of life, or human dignity, but with technical issues to do with maintaining an order that supports free market principles, economic growth, development, and profit. The program to create intellectual property rights offers a good example here. Such rights are more concerned with the rights of ownership, capital, and the commodification of the environment than with social issues concerning the moral consequences of biotechnology and ethical questions concerning the privatization of life forms.[44]

Furthermore, although globalization theory acknowledges that the development of a global economy is not a new phenomenon,[45] the introduction of new technology, and in particular information and communication technology, that facilitates the organization of production and finance on a global scale accelerates processes of change associated with social integration and disintegration, inclusion and exclusion.[46] On the one hand, access to these technologies has nurtured the formation of new transnational classes whose identities, loyalties, and social bonds owe more to the global political economy than to community, the state, or nation.[47] These new global social formations present a challenge to the beliefs and values upon which traditional notions of community are built, including existing understandings of rights and duties. On the other hand, these same technologies enable the creation of alternative networks for developing strategies designed to resist the move to global homogenization, as social habits, language, belief systems, cultural identities, and norms are challenged. Those who offer critiques of the current human rights regime are among this last group.

The new political context of globalization therefore brings a breakdown in the values embodied in traditional ideas of community, and the rights and duties that describe community. If individuals stand in a variety of relationships with one another, moral conduct is defined by the norms and duties that are widely recognized and respected by the community. In the classical world, for example, the perfection of the individual was achieved within community: the Greek *polis* and the medieval *civitas*.[48] An ethical life, a life of virtue, was achievable only by faithfully performing one's duties. The question of how the citizen stood in relation to "outsiders," where common experiences and regular contact was missing, presented a set of complex and difficult issues. Could one treat "outsiders" as one pleased, including killing them if one wished, or could one appeal to universal values based on natural law for guidance? For Parekh it is therefore unsurprising that "the search for such norms first began in the West with the rise of the Roman Empire, which brought different societies under a common rule and encouraged an extensive movement of goods and peoples across social and territorial boundaries."[49] However, as Douzinas has observed, all this changed radically with the advent of modernity.

> The individual, freed from tradition, history and community, became the foundation and principle of social and political organization. The natural hierarchy of the classical world was replaced by a mobile and dynamic social order in which, in Marx's felicitous phrase, "everything that is solid melts in the air." Duty was replaced by individual rights, and the good was separated from morality. While the classical world defined first what is good and derived moral and legal duties from this definition, for the moderns the good follows right. To be in the right means to act freely, obeying the—moral, state—law in pursuit of self-interest.[50]

In this formulation, the change from an international order represented by discrete state communities to that of globalization suggests a historic opportunity to develop a new normative order forged from the emerging "vague but unmistakable sense" of a global community.[51] To achieve this move would, however, require us to recognize that the ethical and moral dimensions peculiar to the past state-centric order may not fit with the new. In other words, the values and principles developed during the past period, in which the human rights regime was negotiated and agreed, may no longer be as relevant. If authors like Parekh, Douzinas, and others are correct that ethical and moral values are constructed within historical communities, then we should acknowledge the need to take critiques of human rights seriously. At the least, we should interrogate the old categories of international political thought, investigate the construction of identity and community in a globalized order, and question existing distinctions between domestic and international politics, rights, and duties.[52]

In similar vein, Pasha and Blaney deny that consensus already exists on all the major issues in the contemporary global political agenda. They argue that while the notion of global civil society, which is closely associated with the increasing number and activity of international nongovernmental organizations (INGOs), is consistently promoted as evidence for a consensus on universally accepted values—human rights, the environment, democracy—no such consensus exists. Instead, what is promoted as being within the interests of the planet and the "common good" is often a project to sustain global capital, thinly veiled by the moral claims of civil society groups. To merely invoke some vacuous notion of the "common good" presumes that we all share the same vision of what the "common good" is, an assumption that has never been tested. Indeed, Pasha and Blaney argue that no mechanism exists for revealing what the "common good" might be.

> We need only gesture to the contested status of human rights within world politics, to debates about the nature of democracy, or to disputes about who can speak for nature and the implication for the character of the human relationship to the environment, in order to suggest that consensus is mostly lacking. Or we might point to the contested status of the very idea of a cosmopolitan view of justice. Or we might simply ask: how does one know, short of the global democracy that transnational associational life is said to be in the process of creating, that a consensus exists? In other words, advocates of global civil society are quite premature in declaring the existence of a global common good where the deliberative process that could establish such a result are not in place. And, indeed, is it not the lack of consensus, the plurality of interest and visions that justifies resort to democratic processes? What need is global democracy if a few transnationally active NGOs intrinsically possess the vision of the world common good?[53]

From the top-down view, which places the interests of globalization above all other considerations, critiques of the current political economy and its social consequences argue that what is claimed as consensus on the common good emerges from collaboration between capital and the state. Within this relationship, corporate and international financial institutions are interested in creating the conditions for stability, including low transaction costs, control of crime and corruption, economic efficiency, and the consistent application of general norms for economic activity. According to this view, such conditions cannot be sustained if we "continue to tolerate the presence of superfluous billions" who, in the face of the computerization of industry and services, can no longer sell their "muscle power."[54] In this way, citizenship and rights apply to those who have a permanent home, a secure job, and a material future, not to those who are surplus to the needs of economic globalization.[55] With the exclusion of the superfluous, the decline of democratic participation, and decisions that effect local action being made increasingly at the global level, welfare and rights drop down the political agenda. Indeed, Cox argues that today politics is no longer about the struggle for alternative ways of living,[56] but about who is best equipped to manage the "irresistible" and "inevitable" progress of globalization,[57] which is not presented as a political choice but as a "fact."[58] All that is left is "personality" politics that signal the "death of the citizen as the subject of politics, thus the death of politics as the forum for active citizens, and by implication the end of democracy."[59]

The impact of globalization on the moral precepts that play upon individual and group identity suggests a shift away from the state-centric international order upon which the global human rights regime is built. Confidence in concepts like sovereignty, domestic jurisdiction, even central government, which in the past provided an important icon for the construction of identity, are increasingly questioned. In particular, although the global human rights regime is built upon international law, if the international no longer possesses the authority it was once imagined to possess, because power no longer resides exclusively within the state, the much vaunted "progress" in human rights seems misplaced. Thus, a prominent international human rights lawyer is able to claim that the "inability of this branch of international law to make itself felt on the ground is sometimes so complete that one is left wondering why it is called law at all."[60] Furthermore, moral and ethical ideas associated with the dynamics of globalization have established guarantees for the primacy of economic growth and development by "declaring individual (and by extension, corporate) rights as inherent, inalienable, and universal,"[61] no matter the consequences for community, identity, and the social welfare of many groups. Within this new order, human rights talk has become an ever-present aspect of global politics and international relations, but only rarely is it allowed to stand in the way of economic interests.

Globalization and Human Rights

Summing up the movement of human rights from idea to international legal regime, Gearty offers a fourfold model. First, politicized exchanges on the nature of rights embrace a generality of rights talk that cannot be captured through the precise language of law. Debates on rights therefore include many areas of social and economic life, presenting difficult problems when creating legislation. Second, if legal technicalities can be solved, and legislation is eventually generated, the custodianship of human rights moves from the political to the legal sphere of authority. Third, the authority and high regard given to the law in liberal society, coupled with the centrality of negative freedoms in liberal ideology, provides a focus that attracts greater interest in rights claims. In effect, human rights law becomes the "basic" law of liberal society. Fourth, following Hobbes, Locke, and Kant, who saw rights as an antecedent truth, Gearty notes that the legislation of human rights assumes the mantle of a supra- or pre-political idea beyond politics, and thus a set of ideas beyond critique. Thus, for Gearty, "our core or essential human rights are made up of a number of rights that people have which *precedes* politics or which are *above* politics."[62]

In short, although rights might be seen as sustained through politics, there can be no question of engaging in any further serious debates over the nature of rights: the creation of law performs an effective act of "closure." While liberalism boasts tolerance as one of its central virtues, tolerance is not extended to any serious challenge to liberalism's foundational values.[63] Those who fail to embrace liberal values, including what it means for the individual to enjoy rights, are outsiders. In line with liberal principles, tolerance can be exercised only insofar as action does not follow word. In sum, the move to a global political economy, which is in part legitimated by a particular conception of human rights, has seen the creation of a regime for supporting rights associated with particular interests rather than the interests of all.

This view often seems at odds with the popular claim that human rights are the idea of our time: a set of values that act to guide us as we move toward a global community. The reification of human rights within the international human rights regime, which seems to accept the "end of history" conclusion, leaving "humanity stuck at the door of liberalism, unable to go forward or imagine a post-liberal society," asserts that a final truth has been uncovered.[64] Although this thesis is readily accepted by those closest to the center of economic globalization, as discussed above, the technology that enabled the development of global networks of production, exchange, and finance is also available to new forms of political agency. These communities—workers' movements, feminists, environmentalists, human rights campaigners—have taken the opportunity to construct new frameworks for resisting the global economic order and its negative consequences. Gill, for example, has argued that the potential of these new networks inspires a move toward reconceptualizing the idea of human rights, taking account of voices from all parts of the world rather than doggedly asserting the existing human rights regime, which is widely seen as the product of a particular worldview and set of interests.[65] However, despite the many changes in the global political context that have taken place during the sixty years since the UDHR was created, proponents of human rights continue to address the issue as though little has changed during that time.

Given these current critiques of human rights, it is difficult to see how any commentator can continue to argue that the post–Cold War era offers a more propitious context in which to secure human rights. Where in the past the necessity of dealing with known human rights violators was accepted, provided they remained avowedly anti-Communist, in the new order it is argued that human rights will be placed first above all other issues. In the wake of the "triumph of liberalism" and the "End of History," human rights are routinely presented as "the moral wing" of the new order, "valorising individualism, autonomy and liberty, and comfortably occupying the global moral high ground."[66] The struggle to create international law and the institutions for the protection of human rights over many decades will, it is asserted, at last bear fruit.

However, these hopes are not founded upon the values, norms, and principles that describe the age of globalization but upon those that describe the previous period. According to many critics, globalization provides a socioeconomic context in which the protection of human rights is less secure than in the past. This is because globalization structures the transfer of wealth from the poor to the rich, exacerbating existing inequalities within and between states, rewarding capital at the expense of labor, and creating far more losers than winners.[67] Foundational assumptions about human rights, particularly assumptions about the moral responsibility of the individual, have given way to structural violations. Where it was once assumed that state leaders were responsible for gross violations, today the actions of transnational corporations and financial institutions, largely operating within the accepted normative boundaries of globalization, are implicated.[68] With the realization that globalization does not demand any obligations to human rights, in the year 2000 the United Nations Development Programme (UNDP) was able to assert that

> little in the current global order binds states and global actors to promote human rights globally. Many least developed countries are being marginalized from the expanding opportunities of globalization. As world exports more than doubled, the share of least developed countries declined from 0.6% in 1980 to 0.5% in 1990 to 0.4% in 1997. And these countries attracted less than $3 billion in foreign direct investments in 1998. The global online community is growing exponentially—reaching 26% of all people in the United States but fewer than 1% in all developing regions.[69]

With the end of the Cold War and the advent of economic globalization, resistance to liberal rights waned. The matchless preeminence of civil and political rights, which emphasize the freedom of individual action, noninterference in the private sphere of economics, the right to own and dispose of private property, and the principle of laissez-faire, provides the limits of moral action within the globalized world order. The move to reduce support for economic and social programs in all Western countries during the last two decades, a trend that is now accepted as desirable globally, is indicative of the liberal approach to rights. In the current period of globalization, human rights are defined as those rights that require government abstention from acts that violate the individual's freedom to invest time, capital, and resources in processes of production and exchange.[70] Within this order, economic, social, and cultural claims may be legitimate aspirations, but they can never be rights.

Consequently, as a recent report by the Sub-Commission on the Promotion and Protection of Human Rights has noted, there is a "new orthodoxy or ethos about the economic dimensions of globalization that exalts it above all other human values or phenomena, indeed even above the basic conditions of human beings themselves."[71] According to the report, the spread, depth, and strength of this new ethical ethos masks the causes of many human rights violations, which are found to be perpetrated primarily by economic restructuring, trade, and financial liberalization. The authors recognize that existing international institutions were created to promote and legitimate the positive advantages of economic globalization, but this paid little attention to the negative effects these actions might bring, including violations of human rights. For example, the founding instruments of the WTO make only oblique reference to human rights, and they are gender blind. The subcommission's report asserts that

> the assumptions on which the rules of the WTO are based are grossly unfair and even prejudiced. Those rules often reflect an agenda that serves only to promote dominant corporatist interests that already monopolize the arena of international trade. The rules assume an equality of bargaining power between all the countries that engage in trade. They are also designed on the basis of a premise that ignores the fact that the greater percentage of global trade is controlled by powerful multinational enterprises. Within such a context, the notion of free trade on which the rules are constructed is a fallacy.[72]

Accordingly, the measures pursued by the WTO, the World Bank, and the IMF undermine the efforts of global human rights institutions, international human rights law, and the work of progressive advocates of socioeconomic rights. It is also why the relationship between trade liberalization and human rights is frequently overlooked. Even when the linkage is made to civil and political rights, "it is fraught with inconsistencies and national subjective interests."[73]

Four issues follow from the subcommission's report. First, the narrow view of human rights, first established in the early years of negotiations for creating international law, remains widely accepted. While influential voices within the global political economy continue to promote liberal freedoms, socioeconomic claims are viewed as aspirations subject to charity rather than as legitimate rights. Development is understood as industrialization, Westernization, and economic growth, not in broader terms that include the conditions to live a dignified and fulfilling life, welfare security, and political participation. Accordingly, the subcommission's report argues that the negative consequences of the current approach provide a rationale for corporate investment, which is for profit, not to assist in the fulfilment of civil, political, economic, and social rights. While the state's interest may include health, education, access to fresh water, nutrition, and housing, these are not central to corporate interests.[74]

Second, development is always aimed at particular types of production that do not necessarily benefit the socioeconomic needs of the people. Indeed, many larger developments, for example, the construction of dams for electricity and irrigation, directly violate human rights by displacing existing populations, loss of agricultural land, environmental degradation, and the destruction of cultural traditions. As the 1995 UNDP report stresses, some forms of economic development lead to violation of human rights; for example, "that which does not translate into jobs, that which is not matched by the spread of democracy, that which snuffs out separate cultural identities, that which despoils the environment, and growth where most of the benefits are seized by the rich."[75] The UNDP report goes on to note that while economic development often leads to greater national wealth, this is at a cost to many already on the margins, in both advanced and developing economies.[76]

Third, the corollary to the individual as the rights claimant is the individual as the perpetrator of human rights violations. Under the consensus on rights that supports the practices of economic globalization, just as rights reside with the individual, so it follows that responsibility for violating rights also rests with the individual. Drawing on the Judeo-Christian notion of "sin," those who violate human rights are wholly responsible for their actions. Accordingly, the individual is free to act as he or she wills and must be held accountable for all their actions, including violations of human rights.[77] It is rare to find an acknowledgment that the social, economic, and political structures within which people must live their lives has any significance when attempting to discover the causes of human rights violations. Put simply, the notion of individual responsibility masks the potential for exploring structural violations.

Fourth, to minimize the danger of destabilizing revolution springing from the ranks of what Cox has referred to as "superfluous workers," the institutions of global governance have followed a twin-track policy of poor relief and riot control.

> Humanitarian assistance (the poor relief component) has become a top priority of the United Nations and a major activity of a vast range of nongovernmental agencies. Where poor relief is inadequate to prevent political destabilization, then military force (the riot control component) is evoked by the international community. Together, they help to sustain the emerging social structure of the world by minimizing the risk of chaos in the bottom layer.[78]

Through this process, the superfluous are stigmatized for being responsible for all the ills in the world, including their own poverty, overpopulation, pandemics, environmental degradation, drug trafficking, child labor, terrorism, urban violence, population movements, and crime.[79] The state of permanent fear that pervades those who can look forward to a life of full employment stimulates the demand for ever more stringent penalties for transgressions, no matter how minor, and increases levels of intolerance that threatens to reverse decades of achievement to secure civil, political, social, and economic rights. In response, some have suggested the creation of "international citizenship" designed to overcome the democratic deficit brought by the increasing authority of international institutions.[80] While in the past national populations could hope to withhold their consent from decisions made by these international institutions, today this is often not the case, leaving state citizens unable to control their collective lives.[81]

Although this view benefits those whose interests lie in maintaining the existing structures of globalization,[82] because it deflects attention from structural violations, it allows the sites of violations to be confused with the causes. Under conditions of globalization, the decisions of international financial institutions, international corporations, and international organizations, which increasingly shape peoples lives, are more concerned with global planning than with local consequences.[83] Decisionmaking becomes decoupled from people's lives. But if the purpose of human rights is to guarantee the necessary freedoms for the individual to participate fully in economic life, it is necessary also to create and maintain an order that supports this goal. However, while human rights, human dignity, and the quality of life are promoted as desirable goals, the application of strict free market principles as the means for achieving these goals remains categorical.

The General Assembly of the United Nations recognized these problems in a report prepared by Secretary-General Kofi Annan in 2000. While the report acknowledges that globalization is not a new phenomenon it argues that its current manifestation has distinctive features. Among these is the simultaneous movement for integration and disintegration, and social inclusion and exclusion. While some benefit from the opportunities offered by cheap air travel, the World Wide Web, and access to health and education brought by increased wealth through trade and capital flows, others "are being left behind, in poverty, effectively marginalized from the hopes that globalization holds."[84] In particular the report recognizes that "economic growth does not automatically lead to greater promotion and protection of human rights."[85] Furthermore, while structural adjustment programs sponsored by the IMF and World Bank were presented as an economic necessity for growth and development, "their design has generally been motivated by the objective of ensuring repayment of interest on debts owed to international creditor institutions and not by the promotion and protection of human rights."[86] The report also acknowledges the WTO's central role in economic globalization, particularly the removal of trade barriers, which has, the report claims, calamitous consequences for labor in many parts of the world. Not only do jobs disappear, but when wages and conditions improve women are pushed out of the workforce.

The Exclusion of Critique

While the language of human rights continues in the speeches of policymakers, NGOs, and many international institutions, the growing literature on globalization has exposed the inadequacy of that language when theorizing about the moral institutions in the new order.[87] Rather than confronting the new set of problems that spring from the new order, including those that surround the idea of human rights, the old language of rights continues to be used to obfuscate the real social, economic, and political problems that globalization presents. Mutua characterizes this outmoded language as the discourse of "savage-victim-saviour." The "savage" represents a state's ruling elite, who fail to embrace the liberal model of civilization, fervently frustrating the population's clear desire to claim their human rights and exercise liberal freedoms. The "victim" is oppressed by traditional cultural and social relations, a culture that serves the interests of the "savages," and is denied access to the desirable alternatives offered by globalization. Lastly, the "saviour" is the "civilized" liberal state, bent on delivering a moral good in the image of itself to the victim and, in the process, destroying the "savage."[88]

In this schema, the victim is never understood as a casualty of imperialism or past empire, or a consequence of economic globalization, which can act to destroy cultures, social roots, and local knowledge. This history plays no part in contextualizing the present. Mutua therefore argues that the current normative order is "driven by a totalitarian or totalizing impulse, [which is], the mission to require that all human societies transform themselves to fit a particular blueprint."[89] Human rights violations are defined as a "catalogue of abuses committed by the state against liberal values,"[90] where the state acts as proxy for private interests. Through human rights international law, and the machinery set up to implement international law, the United Nations is presented as the grand "neutral" savior, the conscience of those engaged in the noble project of globalization, rather than the "moralized expression of a political ideology."[91] Similarly, nongovernmental organizations often see themselves as "politically neutral modern day abolitionists whose only purpose is to identify 'evil' and root it out."[92]

While Langlois accepts that dialogue on moral issues like human rights might serve as a focus for developing an ethics of globalization, he doubts that such a dialogue would bring the intended results, for two reasons. First, the history of dialogues on global normative issues suggests that conclusions tend toward the "lowest common denominator," which most often means vacuous agreements that all parties can put their name to without need of reflection on existing cultural, social, and economic practices. Second, given the inequalities that exist within the globalized order, any dialogue cannot be a dialogue of equals but must instead reflect the values associated with global capital and its interests. Given these problems, it seems inevitable that "while the language [of rights] is used universally, it does not universally mean the same thing, have the same effect, or aim for the same ends."[93] Similarly, the language of globalization is itself misleading. As Alves has observed, the term *globalization* wrongly invokes images of global markets, global production, and global consumption, all conducted in an increasingly global social order characterized by equality of opportunity. Instead, globalization has become an "ideology of the dominant," a phenomenon that urgently needs regulating if our moral boundaries do indeed include concern for excluded groups.[94]

Although acknowledged rarely today, human rights are not an end in themselves, but a means to an end. The advent of globalization, with its enabling technology, has reignited a more inclusive dialogue about how we should imagine that end. The task to operationalize notions of democracy or human rights should follow this dialogue rather than precede it. To engage in this process demands that we take recent critiques of the theory and practice of human rights seriously. However, these critiques are seen as peripheral or marginal to the project first begun in the immediate post–World War II period to promote a particular version of rights through institutions that describe a past order. The advent of globalization, where "self-regulation and 'Darwinian' competition and survival of the fittest" prevail, are unlikely to inspire conditions under which powerful interests turn against the very norms and values that brought them their success.[95] Nor can we expect those who have devoted their lives to the pursuit of human rights, described by the formal human rights regime, to accept easily the need for engaging in further conceptual struggles.

While critiques of the theory and practice of human rights continue to be generated and widely disseminated through the use of the same technology that has enabled economic globalization, it remains largely peripheral to human rights talk associated with the global human rights regime. Those engaged in the formal human rights regime remain optimistic that technical problems for the full implementation of international law will eventually be resolved. They argue that significant changes in the spatial reach and intensity of social networks will enable reporting of human rights violations, no matter where they occur in the world. The individual freedoms promoted by the human rights regime will continue to support economic development in ways that will inevitably improve the well-being of all. The increased activity and reach of social movements, nongovernmental organizations, interest groups, corporations, financial institutions, indigenous peoples' organizations, and citizens groups engaged in global discourses on every aspect of our social, economic, political, and cultural lives, will act to drive the cause of human rights forward.[96] Therefore, they argue, there is every reason to be optimistic about the future of human rights. We can safely ignore those who critique human rights.

*   *   *

Human rights within the current global order provide succor for optimists and pessimists alike. However, while both optimists and pessimists may share the view that human rights talk has increased in intensity during the past three decades, they part company on claims that the new freedoms found in the processes of globalization offer ever greater opportunities for protecting human rights.[97]

Optimists point to the success found in the generation of international law on human rights, legal outcomes for rights claims brought by indigenous people, trade union legislation created in many states, and the increasing awareness of the rights of women and children.[98] For optimists, the intensity and ubiquity of social networks promises to increase the demand to secure human rights, democracy, and environmental protection for all. While in the post–World War II period of political realism, arguments over sovereignty and the national interest often stood in the way of making progress on human rights, optimists argue that today such arguments are untenable. The greater interconnectedness characteristic of globalization, and increasing demands for transparency, mean that the demand for human rights cannot be circumvented. The vast body of international human rights law created in recent decades is seen by optimists as the formal expression of normative changes that place human rights at the center of global political life. For the optimist, the new order represents "power to the people" insofar as human rights offer the oppressed, the excluded, the victims of tyrannical governments, and those engaged in the politics of identity an opportunity to gain the "moral high ground" in the struggle for emancipation and freedom.

For pessimists, on the other hand, conditions of economic globalization offer an opportunity to exercise "power over people," by promoting particular modes of thought and practice that support the interests of global capital. From this perspective, the freedoms described and "normalized" within the practices of globalization accentuate processes of inclusion and exclusion, equality and inequality, to the detriment of human rights.[99] Pessimists feel vindicated, for instance, when a leading member of a prominent investment corporation, commenting on the possibility of human rights within the current global order, remarks that the "great beauty of globalization is that no one is in control."[100] While the international legal regime of human rights includes a wide spectrum of rights, the values associated with globalization remain the dominant mode of thought that guides political, social, and economic action. The discourse of human rights may have stimulated the creation of international law, but the context in which rights must be promoted denies the possibility of achieving any significant and lasting progress.

Notes

1. For examples of how this phrase has been used in literature, see Michael Quinion at www.worldwidewords.org/qa/qa-que2.htm.

2. For a recent review of the history of human rights, see Micheline Ishay, *The History of Human Rights: From Ancient Times to Globalization* (Berkeley, University of California Press, 2004). See also Olwen H. Hufton, ed., *Historical Change and Human Rights: The Oxford Lectures* (New York: Basic Books, 1995).

3. The distinction between negative and positive rights is well known in the literature. Negative rights refer to those rights that offer *freedom from* (e.g., from arbitrary arrest, torture, slavery, etc.), while positive rights refer to those that offer *freedom to enjoy* certain goods (e.g., food, shelter, association, etc.).

4. R. J. Vincent, *Human Rights and International Relations* (Cambridge: Cambridge University Press, 1986).

5. Neil Stammers, "Human Rights and Power," *Political Studies* 41, no. 1: 70–82.

6. "Human rights talk" is a phrase used by Vincent to mean a complex of philosophical, legal, organizational, and political arguments that surround contemporary human rights practice.

7. Jose A. Lindgren Alves, "The Declaration of Human Rights in Postmodernity," *Human Rights Quarterly* 22, no. 2 (2000): 484.

8. Makau Mutua, *Human Rights: A Political and Cultural Critique*, ed. Bert B. Lockwood, Pennsylvania Studies in Human Rights (Philadelphia: University of Pennsylvania Press, 2002), p. 13.

9. Michael Goodhart, "Origins and Universality in the Human Rights Debate: Cultural Essentialism and the Challenge of Globalization," *Human Rights Quarterly* 25, no. 4 (2003).

10. For a more detailed explanation of the postwar move to establish a particular version of human rights, see Tony Evans, *US Hegemony and the Project of Universal Human Rights* (Basingstoke, UK: Macmillan, 1996).

11. Stephen Gill, "Globalization, Market Civilisation, and Disciplinary Neoliberalism," *Millennium* 24, no. 3 (1995); Barry Gills, Joel Rocamora, and Richard Wilson, "Low Intensity Democracy," in *Low Intensity Democracy*, ed. Barry Gills, Joel Rocamora, and Richard Wilson (London: Pluto, 1993).

12. Enrico Augelli and Craig Murphy, *America's Quest and the Third World* (London: Pinter, 1988).

13. Tracy Strong, "Taking the Rank with What Is Ours: American Political Thought, Foreign Policy, and the Question of Rights," in P. R. Newbert, ed., *The Politics of Human Rights* (London: New York University Press, 1980).

14. For a full analysis of US policy in the postwar years, see Tony Evans, "Human Rights: A Reply to Geoffrey Best," *Review of International Studies* 17, no. 1 (1991): 3–18.

15. The reaction of many influential sections of the US population to the creation of international law for human rights was sufficient to persuade any doubters that "socialism by treaty" would not gain the approval of the American people. See, for example, Frank E. Holman, "Giving America Away" October 1, 1951, *Vital Speeches of the Day*, vol. 16: 748–753, and "The Greatest Threat to Our American Heritage," September 15, 1953, *Vital Speeches of the Day*, vol. 24: 711–717.

16. Dwight D. Eisenhower, *The White House Years: Mandate for Change—1953–1956* (London: Heineman, 1963), p. 278.

17. Prominent among these was Frank E. Holman, president of the American Bar Association. See, for example, Holman, *Vital Speeches of the Day*, vol.16, pp. 248–253.

18. Controversy continues over the exact nature of economic and social rights in US foreign policy. For a recent example of the argument that the United States has always supported economic and social rights, see Daniel J. Whelan and Jack Donnelly, "The West, Economic and Social Rights, and the Global Human Rights Regime: Setting the Record Straight," *Human Rights Quarterly* 29, no. 4 (2007). For a reply to this article, see Alex Kirkup and Tony Evans, "The Myth of Western Opposition to Economic, Social, and Cultural Rights? A Reply to Whelan and Donnelly," *Human Rights Quarterly*, 31, no. 1 (2009): 221–238.

19. See, for example, Eleanor Roosevelt's hand-written notes in Papers of Eleanor Roosevelt, Roosevelt Library, Hyde Park, NY, Box 5487.

20. For a short discussion on this, see Evans, *US Hegemony and the Project of Universal Human Rights,* pp. 64–65.

21. For the classic expression of these principles, see E. H. Carr, *The Twenty Years' Crisis* (London: Macmillan, 1939); Hans J. Morgenthau, *Politics Among Nations* (New York: Knopf, 1985).

22. R. B. J. Walker, "Security, Sovereignty, and the Challenge of World Order," *Alternatives* 15, no. 1 (1990): 3–27.

23. See, Evans, *US Hegemony*. esp. Chapter 4.

24. Hedley Bull, *The Anarchical Society* (London: Macmillan, 1977).

25. Terry Nardin, *Law, Morality, and the Relations of States* (Princeton, N.J.: Princeton University Press, 1983).

26. Vincent, *Human Rights and International Relations*. It should be noted that, although it is widely acknowledged, there is little evidence that ostracism in the name of human rights has ever been exercised.

27. See, for example, UK Foreign Secretary Robin Cook's statements and speeches on ethical foreign policy during 1997; also the House of Commons Foreign Affairs Committee report *Foreign Policy and Human Rights*, HC 100-1 (London: HMSO, December 10, 1998).

28. Amnesty International, "Amnesty International Report, 2008" (London: Amnesty International, 2008).

29. Ibid.

30. V. T. Tamilmoran, *Human Rights in Third World Perspective* (Ithaca, N.Y.: Cornell University Press, 1992).

31. Gill, "Globalization, Market Civilisation . . ." It should be noted that there is little agreement among theorists on the nature of globalization. See David Held, "Democracy: From City-States to a Cosmopolitan Order," *Political Studies* 40 special issue (1992) for one of the best-known surveys of the literature.

32. Robert Cox, "Civil Society at the Turn of the Millennium: Prospects for an Alternative World Order," *Review of International Studies* 25, no. 3 (1999): 12.

33. Of course, many would argue that the process of globalization has multiple causes. For a good overview of this, see D. Held, A. McGrew, D. Goldblatt, and J. Perraton, eds. *Global Transformations: Politics, Economics, and Culture* (Cambridge, UK: Polity, 1999). For an overview of the unidimensional economic causes of globalization, see C. Thomas, *Global Governance, Development, and Human Security* (London: Pluto, 2000).

34. See Christine Chinkin, "International Law and Human Rights," in *Human Rights Fifty Years On: A Reappraisal*, ed. Tony Evans (Manchester: Manchester University Press, 1998); Tony Evans, "International Human Rights Law as Power and Knowledge," *Human Rights Quarterly* 27, no. 3 (2005); Tony Evans and Jan Hancock, "Doing Something Without Doing Anything: International Law and the Challenge of Globalization," *International Journal of Human Rights* 2, no. 3 (1998).

35. Leo Panitch, "Rethinking the Role of the State," in *Globalization: Critical Reflections*, ed. James Mittelman (Boulder, Colo.: Lynne Rienner, 1995).

36. Joseph A. Camilleri and Jim Falk, *The End of Sovereignty? The Politics of a Shrinking and Fragmenting World* (Aldershot, UK: Edward Elgar, 1992), p. 4.

37. Mark Rupert, "Globalising Common Sense: A Marxian-Gramscian (Re)-Vision of the Politics of Governance and Resistance," *Review of International Studies* 29, special issue (2003): 190.

38. Robert Cox, "A Perspective on Globalization," in *Globalization: Critical Reflections*, ed. Mittelman..

39. B. S. Chimini, "Marxism and International Law," *Economic and Political Weekly* 34, no. 6 (1999).

40. Susan George, *The Lucano Report* (London: Pluto, 1999).

41. For a reading of the WTO's activities and their consequences for human rights, see R. Howse and M. Mutua (2000). "Protecting Human Rights in a Global Economy: Challenges for the World Trade Organization," International Centre for Human Rights and Democracratic Development, www.dd-d.ca/sie/publications/index.php?id= 1271&subsection=catalogue; R. O'Brien et al., *Contesting Global Governance: Multilateral Economic Institutions and Global Social Movements* (Cambridge: Cambridge University Press, 2000).

42. Jef Huysmans, "Post-Cold War Implosion and Globalization: Liberalism Running Past Itself," *Millennium* 24, no. 3 (1995).

43. Anthony Giddens, *Modernity and Self-Identity* (Cambridge, UK: Polity, 1990).

44. See Gill, "Globalization, Market Civilisation . . ." for a view of the WTO project to promote intellectual property rights.

45. Paul Hirst and Grahame Thompson, *Globalization in Question?* (Cambridge, UK: Polity, 1996).

46. A. Kirkup, *Exclusion in the Global Political Economy: A Critique of Orthodoxy,* Ph.D. thesis, University of Southampton, 2009.

47. Kees van der Pijl, *Transnational Class and International Relations* (London: Routledge, 1998).

48. Costas Douzinas, *Human Rights and Empire: The Political Philosophy of Cosmopolitanism* (Abingdon, UK: Routledge-Cavendish, 2007).

49. Bhikhu Parekh, "Principles of a Global Ethic," in *Global Ethics and Civil Society,* ed. John Eade and Darren O'Byrne (Aldershot, UK: Ashgate, 2005).

50. Douzinas, *Human Rights and Empire,* p. 35.

51. Parekh, "Principles of a Global Ethic."

52. Gill, "Globalization, Market Civilisation . . ." The term *critique* must be understood in specific terms to mean arguments about the underlying values that support all social formations. The term is defined in more detail in Chapter 3.

53. Mustapha Kamel Pasha and David L. Blaney, "Elusive Paradise: The Promise and Perils of Global Civil Society," *Alternatives* 23, no. 1 (1998): 436.

54. George, *Lucano Report.* This publication is written in the style of a report prepared by proponents of globalization. One of the repeated themes is the need to find ways to legitimate the exclusion of superfluous workers who are neither producers nor consumers.

55. Ulrich Beck, *What Is Globalization?* (Cambridge, UK: Polity, 2000).

56. Robert Cox, "Democracy in Hard Times: Economic Globalization and the Limits to Liberal Democracy," in *The Transformation of Democracy,* ed. Anthony McGrew (Cambridge, UK: Polity, 1997).

57. Prime Minister Tony Blair, speech at the WTO, May 19, 1998.

58. President Bill Clinton, speech at the WTO, May 18, 1998.

59. Cox, "Democracy in Hard Times," p. 64.

60. Conor Gearty, *Can Human Rights Survive?* (Cambridge: Cambridge University Press, 2006), p. 92.

61. Gary Teeple, *The Riddle of Human Rights* (Aurora, Canada: Garamond Press, 2005), p. 17.

62. Gearty, *Can Human Rights Survive?* p. 72.

63. Tony Evans, "The Limits of Tolerance: Islam and Human Rights," *Review of International Studies* (forthcoming).

64. Mutua, *Political and Cultural Critique* p. 3.

65. Stephen Gill, "Constitutionalizing Inequality and the Clash of Civilizations," *International Studies Review* 4, no. 2 (2002).

66. Francis Fukuyama, "The End of History," *The National Interest* (Summer, 1989); Fiona Robinson, "The Limits of a Rights Based Approach to International Ethics," in *Human Rights Fifty Years On,* ed. Evans.

67. Susan George, "Globalizing Rights?" in *Globalizing Rights: The Oxford Amnesty Lectures, 1999,* ed. Matthew J. Gibney (Oxford: Oxford University Press, 2003), p. 18.

68. Steven R. Ratner, "Corporations and Human Rights: A Theory of Legal Responsibility," *Yale Law Journal* 111 (2001).

69. United Nations Development Programme (UNDP), *Human Development Report 2000—Human Rights and Human Development* (Oxford: UNDP, 2000), p. 9.

70. Mary A. Tetrault, "Regimes and Liberal World Order," *Alternatives* 13, no. 1 (1988).

71. J. Oloka-Onyango and Deepika Udagana, "The Realization of Economic, Social, and Cultural Rights: Globalization and Its Impact on the Full Enjoyment of Human Rights" (Geneva: Sub-Commission on the Promotion and Protection of Human Rights, 2000), pp. 3-4.

72. Ibid., p. 6.

73. Ibid., p. 8.

74. Robert McCorquodale and Richard Fairbrother, "Globalization and Human Rights," *Human Rights Quarterly* 21, no. 3 (1999): 735–766. McCorquodale cites the well-known memo written by Lawrence Summers during his period at the World Bank. In this memo, Summers uses the logic of the market to argue that the World Bank should "be encouraging the export of polluting industries to less developed states. The measurement of the costs of health-impairing pollution depends on the foregone earnings from increased morbidity and mortality. From this point of view, a given amount of health-impairing pollution should be done in the country with the lowest wages. I think the economic logic behind dumping a load of toxic waste in the lowest-wage country is impeccable and we should face up to that. . . . I've always thought that under-populated countries in Africa are vastly under-polluted: their air quality is probably vastly inefficiently [high] compared to Los Angeles or Mexico City." For a full report on this memo, see the *Economist*, February 8, 1992.

75. United Nations Development Programme, *Human Development Report, 1995— Gender and Human Development* (Oxford: UNDP, 1995).

76. Ibid. Using a series of measures (health, education, nutrition, etc.), the report demonstrates the growing gap between the haves and the have-nots in both advanced and developing economies; see pages 16–17 for tabulated notes showing this comparison.

77. Johan Galtung, *Human Rights in Another Key* (Cambridge, UK: Polity, 1994).

78. Cox, "Democracy in Hard Times," p. 58.

79. Alves, "The Declaration of Human Rights in Postmodernity."

80. Andrew Linklater, "What Is a Good International Citizen," in Paul Keal, *Ethics and Foreign Policy* (Canberra: Allen & Unwin, 1992).

81. Andrew Linklater, *The Transformation of Political Society* (Cambridge, UK: Polity, 1998).

82. J. Salmi, *Violence and the Democratic State* (Oxford: Oxford University Press, 1993).

83. Giddens, *Modernity and Self-Identity*.

84. UN Secretary-General, "Globalization and the Impact on the Full Enjoyment of All Human Rights" (New York: UN General Assembly, 2000), p. 5.

85. Ibid., p. 3.

86. Ibid., p. 5.

87. Henry Rosemont, "Why Take Rights Seriously? A Confucian Critique," in *Human Rights and the World's Religions*, ed. Leroy S. Rouner (Indiana: University of Notre Dame Press, 1988).

88. Mutua, *Political and Cultural Critique*.

89. Ibid., p. 13.

90. Ibid., p. 25.

91. Ibid., p. 40.

92. Ibid., p. 53.

93. Anthony J. Langlois, "Human Rights: The Globalization and Fragmentation of Moral Discourse," *Review of International Studies* 28, no. 3 (2002): 480.

94. Alves, "The Declaration of Human Rights in Postmodernity," p. 484.

95. George, "Globalizing Rights?" p. 29.

96. Cox, "Civil Society at the Turn of the Millennium"; David Held et al., eds., *Global Transformations: Politics, Economics, and Culture* (Cambridge, UK: Polity, 1999); Linklater, *Transformation of Political Society*.

97. Jan Aart Scholte, "Towards a Critical Theory of Globalization," in *Globalization in Theory and Practice*, ed. Eleonore Kofman and Gillian Young (London: Pinter, 1996); Tony Spybey, *Globalization and World Society* (Cambridge, UK: Polity, 1996).

98. Optimists will cite, for example, the *Convention on the Elimination of All Forms of Discrimination Against Women,* G.A. res. 34/180, 34 U.N. GAOR Supp. (No. 46) at 193, U.N. Doc. A/34/46, *entered into force* Sept. 3, 1981; *Convention on the Rights of the Child*, G.A. res. 44/25, annex, 44 U.N. GAOR Supp. (No. 49) at 167, U.N. Doc. A/44/49 (1989), *entered into force* Sept. 2, 1990; *Convention Concerning Indigenous and Tribal Peoples in Independent Countries* (ILO No. 169), 72 ILO Official Bull. 59, entered into force Sept. 5, 1991 International Labour Organization, Convention No. 87, Convention Concerning Freedom of Association and Protection of the Right to Organize, 1948.

99. United Nations Development Programme, *Human Development Report, 1997—Human Development to Eradicate Poverty* (Oxford: UNDP, 1997); UNDP, *Human Development Report, 1999—Globalization with a Human Face* (Oxford, UK: UNDP, 1999).

100. Robert Hormats, "Globalization and Human Rights" (Washington, D.C.: Public Broadcasting Service, 1998).

3

Challenging the Idea of Human Rights

The assumption that the modern human rights regime has its antecedence in natural rights is a commonplace one.[1] Deriving from ideas of natural law, natural rights are cast as an inalienable attribute of the individual; a set of grand norms when violated represent unimaginably heinous acts against humanity. No person, no social institution, no culture, and no state should take any action that transgresses the natural rights of the individual. Natural rights are such an integral part of what it means to be human that no legal device, contract, or agreement can override them, not even if the individual concerned gives consent. Thomas Hobbes, for example, argued that in matters of self-preservation, the exercise of liberty, including the right not to act, cannot be legitimately restrained by law.[2] Later, John Locke's characterization of natural rights as life, liberty, and property, which are commonly taken as the foundation of modern natural rights theory, informed the American Revolution and the constitutional settlement that followed.[3] In *The Rights of Man,* Thomas Paine looked to natural rights as the foundation for the argument that the people could legitimately overthrow an unjust form of government.[4] In his words, "There never did, there never will, and there never can, exist a form of Parliament, of any generation of men, in any country, possessed of the power of binding and controlling posterity to the "end of time," or of commanding for ever how the world should be governed, or who shall govern it."[5]

Natural rights theory continued to provide inspiration for twentieth-century philosophers. Robert Nozick, for example, argues that the strength of rights claims is so compelling and extensive that the space for the state to intervene in people's lives is almost inconsequential.[6] Taking an altogether different approach, John Rawls starts not with the individual claiming rights but with the need to articulate the principles under which social cooperation can achieve a fair society. From this starting point, he sees the rational outcome for achieving justice is to promote the rights of individuals living together in society.[7]

A feature of natural rights theory that is often noted in the literature is its Western philosophical origin. Although natural rights have received criticism in the past, notably from Karl Marx,[8] insofar as the human rights community feels the need to articulate any foundational claim for human rights, it is to natural rights that they turn. While this has often attracted the attention of critics of human rights writing within a non-Western tradition (which will be examined in the next chapter), during recent years a literature has appeared from within Western philosophy that seeks to mount a further assault on natural rights. It is this literature that this chapter examines.

Keeping in mind the argument in Chapter 2 that economic globalization provides the context for recent criticism and critique of human rights, this chapter looks in greater detail at feminist, neo-Marxist, and postmodernist critiques of the dominant idea of human rights. While other critiques might also be included—for example, those developed in the literature on environmentalism—these three have achieved the greatest attention during the past two decades.[9]

Feminism and the Rights of Man

Historically, feminist critiques have often punctuated dominant contemporary discourses of human rights. From Mary Wollstonecraft's *Vindication of the Rights of Women*[10] to Eleanor Roosevelt's objection to the phrase "the Rights of Man" during preparation for the Universal Declaration, feminists have attempted to highlight the project's proclivity to prioritize the interests of men and to marginalize or exclude those of women. During the past two decades, however, critique of the project for universal human rights has received much greater attention from feminist scholars. The literature generated by this critique, which draws upon contemporary insights into the politics of identity and interrogates assumptions about the universality of human rights, argues that the dominant discourse of human rights remains male-centered, to the exclusion of 50 percent of the global population.[11] Although many branches of feminist thought have been developed in recent decades, they all share a belief that women are largely invisible in mainstream social and political discourses, including discourses of universal human rights.[12] What arguments do feminists offer in defense of this claim?

First, feminists argue that in an age where the increasing spread of economic globalization is widely seen as the only possible future for securing material well-being, where the grip of capitalism is understood as the only true ideology for organizing the satisfaction of human wants, and where liberal political institutions are the only legitimate form of government, women remain on the periphery of almost all social, political, and economic activity. Although the idea of human rights resonates with increasing vigor globally, feminists argue that the attempt to take the global moral high ground is inextricably bound together with the interests of men. From a feminist perspective, the political status of human rights talk, which asserts the equality of all human beings, has achieved the status of "common sense," such that the language of rights obfuscates the real social, economic, and political issues that confront women today.[13] The dominance of liberal rights talk means that alternatives are silenced, so that in the silencing the fact and the acts of silencing also became invisible: without a visible victim, there is no crime, and without a crime there is no perpetrator. And so the history of rights and citizenship examines those who fought for and were successful in obtaining citizenship and rights, rather than the actor and the actors of exclusion and the destiny of the excluded, who form the majority.[14]

The language used in the various treaties that we collectively refer to as the international human rights regime, treaties that serve as the focus for much human rights talk, has attracted the interest of many feminists. Charlesworth, Chinkin, and Wright, for example, have argued that legal reason associated with the practice of international law is conducted in a language that amplifies and intensifies the interests of men. They particularly cite Article 1.1 of the Torture Convention, which outlaws the use of physical and mental suffering as a means of "obtaining from *him* or a third person information or confessions, punishing *him* for an act *he* or a third person has committed" or "intimidating or coercing *him* or a third person" (emphasis added).[15] Gendered language is found in many other human rights declarations and treaties. Article 1 of the Universal Declaration of Human Rights, for example, calls for human beings to "act towards one another in the spirit of *brotherhood*" (emphasis added), and Article 11.1 ensures that "*he* has had all the guarantees necessary for *his* defence" during trials (emphasis added). Additionally, under Article 5, the Declaration appears to link men alone with citizenship when it seeks to guarantee "the right to an effective remedy by the competent national tribunal for acts violating the fundamental rights granted *him* by the constitution of the law" (emphasis added).

Moreover, feminists note the language in the Declaration that assumes a subservient social, economic, and political role for women in relation to men. Beginning with Article 16.3, which states that the "family is the *natural and fundamental group unit of society*," the Declaration then asserts that everyone has the right to "just and favourable remuneration ensuring for *himself and his family* an existence worthy of human dignity" (Art. 23[3]), including the right to "a standard of living adequate for the health and well-being of *himself and his family*," and rights to security in the event of "unemployment, sickness, disability, widowhood, old age or lack of livelihood in circumstances beyond *his* control" (Art. 25[1]). According to feminist analysis, these articles offer the most obvious empirical evidence that the global project for universal human rights is, in fact, a project for the rights of men. The male-headed family is a "natural" social unit in which men are responsible for the security of women and children, including the satisfaction of their material needs. In these articles, feminists argue, the Universal Declaration—widely acknowledged as the single most important statement of human rights—remains silent on the role of women, suggesting that the contribution of women is of only secondary importance—secondary, that is, to that of men. The gendered language found in the Declaration and international law on human rights thus reflects social attitudes that accept male superiority of thought and action on all social, economic, and political issues.

An objection to this argument might be that the gendered language of the Declaration and international human rights law should be seen within the context of its time. In response to this objection, however, feminists argue that the language of rights reveals the extent to which entrenched subliminal meanings have systematically marginalized women's interests, not merely in the global human rights regime but more generally within all social institutions. Through "valorising individualism, autonomy and liberty, and comfortably occupying the global moral high ground,"[16] human rights, as the rights of men, have become the "moralized expression of a political ideology"[17] that is rarely interrogated. Although many states have ratified the major pieces of international human rights law, and have therefore contracted to respect the rights and freedoms of all peoples, for feminists the presumption that contract theory underpins international society, which assumes an inclusive global order, overlooks the male-centeredness of human rights talk and practice. For feminist critics, women become "paradigmatic *alien* subjects of international law" within international society; outsiders in the sense that they are neither full citizens at home or fully integrated within international society abroad.[18]

Second, and following from the above, feminist arguments often focus on the public/private divide, which is presented in liberal theory as a feature of the "natural" social order. In the liberal tradition, liberty is maintained by creating social institutions that provide the widest possible freedom to engage in social, economic, and political activity, limited only by the requirement not to transgress the equal rights and liberties of others. This is the idea of "negative" liberty, where the principle of restraint and noninterference in the lives of citizens legitimately pursuing their individual interests is paramount.[19] For liberal thought, regulation and government intervention cannot be tolerated beyond a minimum role that guarantees rights in the public sphere, a sphere largely occupied by men. The liberal state's responsibility is limited to promoting and protecting the conditions for exercising these "negative" liberties and rights. The private sphere of home and family, which is largely occupied by women, is seen as beyond legitimate state intervention, except perhaps in cases of extreme depravity. Thus feminists conclude that the development of the current international human rights regime reflects the rights of men in the public sphere and excludes those of women confined to the private sphere.

Although this formulation is generally accepted by those closest to the center of globalization, feminists argue that women are excluded from claiming the same liberty as men, including full citizenship and human rights. Indeed, Charlesworth argues that an underlying assumption of international human rights law is that the public/private divide actually exists in the sense that people do, in fact, understand their lives as two distinct spheres. However, for feminists, it "is an ideological construct rationalizing the exclusion of women from the sources of power."[20] International law therefore contributes to maintaining repressive social control over women's lives through its focus on the public sphere, where the formal institutions of human rights operate. In response to this criticism, and following intensive lobbying during the UN Decade for Women,[21] the United Nations (UN) created the Convention on All Forms of Discrimination Against Women (CEDAW). However, CEDAW has been criticized for the number of reservations entered by signatory state parties,[22] which has further weakened the already feeble language and poorly conceived provisions. Furthermore, although the rationale for CEDAW was discrimination, it is now seen as a corrective for violence against women.[23]

For feminists, however, international human rights law reflects much broader, deeper, and entrenched social attitudes about the characteristics that liberal society assigns to female roles. While men are portrayed as endowed with reason, decisiveness, independence, and strength, attributes to which society gives high status, women are portrayed as possessing characteristics in exact opposition: as muddleheaded, capricious, dependent, and weak.[24] Walker notes that the lower status given to women's assumed attributes is evident in the works of Machiavelli, where he argued that society naturally prizes *virtue* (maleness) over *fortuna* (femaleness), because of its superior qualities in matters of security and politics.[25] Indeed, Machiavelli warned that men must resist the distractions offered by *fortuna*, and the beguiling comfortable life that *fortuna* promises, and instead devote themselves to the pursuit of manly *virtue* found in the public spheres of politics and economics. Thus, for feminists, the rules of social behavior that flow from the internalization of the distinctive capacities claimed for men and women are far-ranging, including physical appearance, language, work, economic and social expectations, and social role. In most societies, the normative context in which women live their lives, where they discharge their primary responsibilities, and attain status, identity, and recognition, is within the institution of the family, the private sphere in which public authority should not interfere.

This leads to a third criticism leveled by feminists, which also concerns the family. The legitimation of the divide between the public sphere of men and the private sphere of women is often reinforced with arguments over childbearing and women's capacities for childrearing. The reproductive role of women, it is said, "confines" women to the family and home, where their "natural" talent for nurture is best exercised and where they can be protected by men from threats emanating from the insecurities found in the outside world.[26] This biological rationale, coupled with Machiavelli's assertion that men possess greater intellectual powers than women, permits the construction of gendered social roles. While the attributes of men are said to be more suited to engaging in the public world of politics and economics, women are better suited to the reproductive role of home and family. Following from this reasoning, feminists argue that the reproduction of family relations assigns to women a set of "sentiment-based non-contractual obligations" founded upon an assumed "natural" social order,[27] where "the family is a powerful regulatory mechanism of a female's productive abilities, reproductive capacity, sexuality, and participation in other social contexts."[28] No matter the existence of universal human rights, for women citizenship and rights are "mediated through the patriarchal family structure, their primary duty being to bear and raise children" and to provide for the needs of men.[29] Moreover, Peterson and Parisi note that the global human rights regime serves only to reinforce and naturalize heterosexist family relations, and thus reaffirms the role of women within the family as isolated, inferior partners with little to contribute to the public sphere.[30]

Liberal theory thus confirms the family—defined as a heterosexual couple and their children—as the essential and "natural" foundation upon which the liberal order is built. The family is sustained not by the coercive force of law but by social conventions that flow from natural social relations. Accordingly, feminists argue, the family has achieved the status of a sacrosanct, fundamental social institution to the extent that to "introduce the language of rights is to acknowledge that the "emotional bonds of compromise and sacrifice have failed."[31] Legitimate state intervention is confined to the public, not the private sphere. The state must therefore remain cautious about meddling with family issues, confining the limits of its responsibilities to a few exceptions: sexual deviance, birth-rate patterns, property transactions, women's reproductive rights, and issues concerned with family form. Domestic violence, for example, is rarely defined as a violation of human rights but as a social issue deserving of social rather than legal solutions. The state may therefore be seen as both the protector of human rights in its role within the public sphere and a violator of human rights in its failure to protect women in the private sphere. Thus, the claim that human rights law is inclusive is unsustainable because it does not offer protection on equal terms to both men and women. As MacKinnon has concluded, "what were called individual rights have become, in life, the rights of men as a group over women individually and as a class."[32]

Fourth, research into the political economy of women's rights demonstrates that women's work is undervalued, both within the home and in the world of paid work. For many feminists, the role of the political economy, locally, regionally, nationally, and globally, serves to promote and maintain gender inequality and thus deny women access to their economic and social rights. In the private world of family and home, in which the productive and reproductive labor of women is mostly located, male superiority is exercised and sustained by material relations of inequality. Steans notes that these inequalities are reflected in national and global institutions—for example, in policies for welfare and pensions, inheritance, labor regulation, taxation, wage structures, and global institutions.[33] The 1995 UN Development Programme report, for instance, shows how in developed countries men devoted two-thirds of their work time to paid activities and one-third to unpaid activities, while for women the reverse ratio was found.[34] In developing countries, market economic activities occupy more than three-quarters of men's working time, while the nonmarket, unpaid work assigned to women is conducted in the home. Moreover, women are routinely paid between 30 percent and 50 percent less than men for equal work. Since status within a globalized economy is often related to income-earning capacities, and men receive a comfortably greater share of income, women remain unrecognized and undervalued. However, if the unpaid work of women were to be properly valued, women would emerge in most societies as the major breadwinner. The UNDP estimates that in 1995 the "non-monetized, invisible contribution of women is $11 trillion a year."[35]

Feminists have also noted that the image of the male as breadwinner influences the rights of women in industrial relations. Although unions would argue that they seek to represent all workers regardless of sex, the status of women in the workplace and the barriers that women encounter in gaining entry to traditional male jobs suggests that the state, employers, and unions all accept that women's jobs are secondary to those of men. Forrest, for example, argues that government officials, employers, and working men all share the understanding that women are second-income workers, whose primary role is located within the home. This assumption is now so well entrenched that the image of the male as breadwinner and head of the household informs many state policies that are unreflectively presented as gender neutral, while women's economic contribution is seen as a mere supplement to that of men.[36]

A further example that strengthens feminist arguments over the inferior status of women in the sphere of economics is given by Young, Fort, and Danner. They note that although in traditional societies women have assumed responsibility for agricultural production, as societies become mechanized it is men who tend to take control of agricultural machinery. Consequently, women are stripped of their status as important contributors to food security. Moreover, as traditional knowledge of agricultural production quickly becomes redundant and forgotten, women are further marginalized and disempowered.[37]

Similar observations on the lower status given to women's knowledge in the economic sphere are revealed in the UN Food and Agriculture Organization's attempt to introduce new agricultural technologies. Although expectations for increasing production were high, the programs did not achieve their goals until development workers consulted women, encouraging them to build upon their traditional skills and technology in conjunction with the new. Furthermore, while in the early phase of the programs men sought to acquire technology as the means for providing greater security for themselves and their immediate families, women gave greater importance to forms of production that benefited the whole community.[38]

For many feminists, under conditions of globalization women have suffered ever-greater increases in their work burden and further deprivations of rights. The pervasiveness of liberal principles, specifically that of noninterference, has seen the state withdraw from providing vital services in health care, education, and the care of the elderly, adding further to the work conducted within the home, and thus to the workload of women. International Monetary Fund and World Bank structural-adjustment programs (SAPs), which routinely include demands for the state to reduce its contribution to welfare, health, and education, are therefore implicated in questions of inequality.[39]

There are, however, two important problems with the feminist approach to human rights, both of which flow from the charge of its "Western" bias. The first concerns the charge that feminists are prone to ignore the differences between women, both across and within any particular social tradition or culture. While this may be a serous criticism for some branches of feminist thought, particularly liberal feminists, postmodernist feminism has attempted to offer a solution. Nash, for example, turns to the work of Richard Rorty and his argument that value judgments and social norms are always ethnocentric because they emerge within the context of particular social attitudes, desires, and sentiments that are integral to moral self-identity. Since Rorty claims that there are no moral universals against which to make moral judgments, the moral claims of all societies are always ethnocentric. However, Rorty argues that this need not necessarily be a barrier to promoting moral ideas. Although the dominant conception of human rights was historically developed within only a narrow social context peculiar to Western Europe and the United States, so long as that conception is extended to all peoples, including women, promotion of ethnocentrism is acceptable. In Rorty's view, although this opens the West to the charge of cultural imperialism, it is preferable to not attempting to promote the idea of a rights-based society.[40]

While this seems to offer a solution to the problem of ethnocentrism, at least viewed from the West, it appears to leave universal human rights as little more than an aspect of power. While postmodernists may have no difficulty with this view, which is discussed further below, it does nothing to answer the critiques of human rights emanating from outside the West. More specifically, critiques of women's rights point to the second charge often leveled at feminist approaches to human rights, that of essentialism.

The essentialist critique of feminist arguments concerning human rights is an attempt to deconstruct the assumption that the category "women" has some intrinsic qualities that are found within all societies. If identities are always socially constructed, including gendered identities, why should we accept the category "women" as universal? The whole feminist critique is that the human rights regime is not inclusive. Why then should we accept the assertion that "women" are an inclusive category, possessed of essential characteristics shared by all women globally?

These questions of cultural relativism raise important issues for feminist critiques of human rights. Although human rights talk has achieved a central place on the global political agenda in recent years, it has not succeeded in making the transition from a transnational project to the local, non-Western tradition and culture. For the human rights community, the global is afforded greater legitimacy than the local, so that custom is seen as a barrier to implementing the full range of rights. In this sense, the "global-local divide is often conceptualized as the opposition between rights and culture, or even civilization and culture."[41] There is a tendency to understand culture in terms of reified, unchanging social institutions, which defy all attempts to imagine new futures. As Merry observes, in this sense there is a "whiff of the primitive" about this approach that suggests a global confrontation between the "civilized," who inhabit a globalized world, and the "uncivilized," who remain locked into some kind of time warp.[42] If, on the other hand, culture is conceptualized as a dynamic process, contextualized in the current period by the conditions of globalization, then the potential for change is embedded within global power structures. The promotion of human rights then becomes a function of globalization, as a way of reconceptualizing justice within a global framework. To defend, say, violence against women as an aspect of culture then becomes unjustifiable.

Furthermore, the methods for implementing human rights are also conditioned by culture, religion, and tradition. The attempt at "transplanting" developed states' legal institutions into traditional cultures, often without any knowledge of existing cultural norms and mores, inevitably leads to failure.[43] As Coomaraswamy notes, the corpus of international human rights law, including the Women''s Convention, is based upon Enlightenment principles that stress nondiscrimination rather than empowerment. In many countries, particularly those where the role of women is sharply differentiated from that of men, the concept of the autonomous individual possessed of an ability to gain access to the law is not extended to women. Attempts to change such traditions often meet with antihomogenizing, local resistance, accusations that the state is giving way to Western values or colluding in destroying traditional ways of life.[44]

Noting the issues discussed above, most feminists conclude that the inclusive claims of the international human rights regime are a fiction. Consequently, "exclusions, constraints and abuses more typical of women's lives are neither recognized nor protected by human rights instruments."[45]

Marxism and the Political Economy of Human Rights

Although there are few published works taking a specifically Marxist perspective on human rights, a number of authors have returned to the ideas of Karl Marx when trying to explain aspects of international human rights law and the philosophy and politics of rights.[46] The move to revisit Marx and Marxist writings demonstrates a growing dissatisfaction with the mainstream human rights discourse, which is also reflected in the feminist and postmodernist critiques. Questions about the foundations of human rights, political power, the principles of international law, the failure of the mainstream literature to address the political economy of rights, and the "Westernization" of human rights have all come under scrutiny from a Marxist standpoint. Although mainstream human rights discourse has not so far shown signs of fully engaging with the Marxist critique, the literature has attracted greater attention in the post–Cold War era.

The materialist conception of history is fundamental to all of Marx's work. Marx argued that social formation was not the outcome of intellectual developments achieved through the application of reason to particular social issues but, rather, the product of the material conditions of life.

> The prevailing mode of production of material life conditions the social, political, and intellectual life process in general. It is not the consciousness of men that determines their being, but, on the contrary, their social being that determines their consciousness.[47]

Thus, both the emergence of human rights as an intellectual project, as developed by liberal philosophers since the time of Hobbes and Locke, and rights discourse as a central principle for social order, most clearly seen in the French Revolution, should be understood through the prism of historical materialism. As expressed in the Communist Manifesto,

> Does it require deep intuition to comprehend that man's ideas, views, and conceptions, in one word, man's consciousness, changes with every change in the conditions of his material existence, in his social relations, and in his social life?
> What else does the history of ideas prove, than that intellectual production changes its character in proportion as material production is changed? The ruling ideas of each age have ever been the ideas of the ruling class.[48]

Following from this, the key to understanding the role of human rights within a capitalist order is an understanding of civil society. Marx argues that "so-called human rights, the rights of *droits de l'homme* in contrast to *droits de citoyen*, are nothing but the rights of members of civil society."[49] Since civil society represents the private sphere, a sphere intended to guarantee the liberty necessary to pursue private satisfactions, particularly those associated with relations of property, human rights describe the egotistic, atomized, isolated individual, separated from community. The exercise of human rights is thus the right to property. It is the individual's

> right to enjoy his possessions and dispose of the same arbitrarily, without regard for other men, independent of society, the right to selfishness. It is the former individual freedom together with the latter application that forms the basis for civil society. It leads man to see in other men not the realization but the limitation of his own freedom. Above all it proclaims the right of man "to enjoy and dispose at will of his goods, his revenues and fruits of the work and industry." (quoting from the French Constitution 1793)[50]

In such a society, a society where the concept of liberty does not indicate social relations between individuals but the separation of individuals from one another, the possibility of developing the necessary emotional ties associated with community are severely constrained.[51] However, to maintain social order there remains a need to create an imaginary space, the state, in which to fabricate the institutions of unity, including those associated with citizenship, equality, and individual freedom. Human rights therefore offer support for the egotistic individual, "withdrawn behind his private interests and whims and separated from community." All that is left to hold people together is "natural necessity, need and private interests, the conservation of their property and their egotistic person."[52]

For Marx, rights do not create the conditions within which human emancipations can be achieved. On the contrary, the legitimation of rights talk has more to do with protecting the social relations of the existing capitalist order, which is best achieved when liberal rights are accepted universally. Rights therefore act to mask class interests by offering the false claim that a rights-based society can deliver a universally fair, objective, and just distribution of social costs and benefits. For Marx, the moral principles found in liberal rights, which are promoted as the means for regulating conflicting claims and interests, placate class conflicts, postpone the revolutionary moment, and arrest the dawn of a new form of social relations that has no need of rights. Once the illusion of rights is recognized, the cause of present injustices and inequalities can be removed, making way for a form of social organization that has no need of rights.[53] The call to abandon the project of human rights, like Marx's call to abandon religion, is the call to overturn relations of power that necessitate illusions as the means for furthering class interests.

Bringing these ideas together in the Communist Manifesto, Marx and Engels express cogently the global consequences of capitalist expansion. In a passage that encapsulates many of the elements that appear central features of economic globalization today, Marx and Engels acknowledge the increasingly "cosmopolitan character" of exploitation, production, and consumption. In the future, they argue, national systems of production will be replaced by "industries whose products are consumed, not only at home, but in every quarter of the globe." Consequently, in "place of the old local and national seclusion and self-sufficiency, we have intercourse in every direction, universal interdependence of nations." In parallel with the growth of material production, ideas also become increasingly globalized.

> The bourgeoisie, by the rapid improvement of all instruments of production, by the immensely facilitated means of communication, draw all, even the most barbarian nations into civilization. The cheap prices of its commodities are the heavy artillery with which it batters down all Chinese walls, with which it forces the barbarians' intensely obstinate hatred of Foreigners to capitulate. It compels all nations, on pain of extinction, to adopt the bourgeois mode of production; it compels them to introduce what it calls civilization into their midst, i.e., to become bourgeois themselves. In a word, it creates a world after its own image.[54]

Reaffirming the relations of property to rights, Frederick Engels reiterates this approach to human rights in the *Anti-Duhring*.[55] In this volume he argues that all moral claims are the product of particular socioeconomic formations.

Since the history of the world is one of class struggle, morality must be seen as class morality, used to justify the dominance of the ruling class, legitimating class interests, providing a sense of moral superiority and, thus, affirming a right to exercise authority and leadership. All claims to universal verities, ethical laws, and timeless moral dogmas are characteristic of class domination and should be rejected. The claims of bourgeois philosophers to have "discovered" rights through reason should be seen for what they are: the product of particular socioeconomic conditions at the service of the dominant class.

> We know today that this kingdom of reason was nothing more than the idealized kingdom of the bourgeoisie; that this eternal Right found its realization in bourgeois justice; that this equality reduced itself to bourgeois equality before the law; that bourgeois property was proclaimed as one of the essential rights of man; and that the government of reason, the Contrat Social of Rousseau, came into being, and only could come into being, as a democratic bourgeois republic. The great thinkers of the eighteenth century could, no more than their predecessors, go beyond the limits imposed upon them by their epoch.[56]

If all claims to moral truths are expressions of class interest—reflected in the predominant means of production and the stage of material development achieved in any historic period—then, as Heller argues, it is absurd to think that moral discourse can create the means for change, since "all moral and intellectual concepts *belong to* the very society which has to be changed."[57]

In the age of capitalist expansion, the demand for new markets leads to inevitable demands for the freedom to engage in unconstrained trade on a global scale.[58] The growth of global trade, in particular, brings demands that "equality should assume a general character reaching out beyond the individual state, that freedom and equality should be proclaimed *human rights*."[59] Once established, this demand could not be contained within bourgeois society alone, but of necessity had to be extended to all human beings. For the proletariat, who have only their own labor to sell, human rights as individual possessions provided moral equality, but did nothing to redress economic and social inequalities. Indeed, as noted by Marx, human rights reinforce the notion of the isolated individual, left to his or her own devices, including the freedom to sell his or her own labor and suffer the consequences when failing to do so.[60] The rights associated with the capitalist market system were therefore negative rights of forbearance, which offered a justification for free trade on a global scale. The legal expression of rights is one of formal equality but capitalist exploitation, where labor has no option other than to accept the rules of exchange that support the interests of capital.[61]

The successors of Marx and Engels continued to build upon this critique of human rights. Lukes, for example, notes that at times both Lenin and Trotsky reiterated Marx's approach to human rights. Lenin argued that the class struggle had no time for "eternal morality," stressing that it was the duty of Communists to "expose the falseness of all the fables about morality." Similarly, Trotsky claimed that human rights had little to do with equality, and more to do with protecting the social relations of the existing order, which, he argued, is secured through the universal acceptance of rights associated with capital.[62]

What are the mechanisms of power that sustain the widespread illusion of universal human rights? The Italian Marxist Antonio Gramsci sought to clarify the relationship between class domination and moral universals through the concept of hegemony. According to Gramsci, the long-term prospects for class domination depended upon creating a consensual order to which the general populace subscribed. While control over coercive forces remains a vital necessity for sustaining the interests of the dominant class, Gramsci argued, coercion alone cannot guarantee a hegemon's longevity. Consequently, as a complement to coercion, the hegemonic class must foster a consensus around a set of values that support its own interests. Hegemony is therefore sustained in two ways: first, *externally*, by administering rewards and punishments, and secondly, *internally*, by providing "intellectual and moral leadership" that shapes the beliefs, wants, opinions, and values that reflect interests associated with the hegemon.[63] Order is maintained through a "common social-moral language" that expresses a singular vision of reality, "informing with its spirit all forms of thought and behaviour."[64] The highest form of hegemony is exercised when the hegemon's values are universally accepted as "common sense."[65] When this is achieved, subordinate actors have completed the process of socialization that binds the ruler to the ruled in a consensual order that legitimates the authority of the hegemon.[66]

In this reading of hegemony, the emergence of universal human rights post-1945 represents a vital ingredient in developing the global reach of capital. The global ambitions of capital are served by values attendant on human rights—most importantly, the idea of the autonomous individual claiming rights and freedoms that legitimate economic engagement on a global scale, the free market, and property. Since 1945, global institutions claiming to act neutrally have been created to support these values—the World Trade Organization, the World Bank, and the International Monetary Fund, for instance.[67] While the United States is often cited as the post–World War II actor most heavily engaged in supporting global capital, from the Gramscian perspective the hegemon should be understood as the emergence of a global capitalist social class that cannot be defined by territory. Ellen Meiksins Wood is thus able to argue that the institutions of global governance represent a particular network of social relations, which "does not simply stand in opposition to the coercive policing and administrative functions of the state but represents the *relocation* of these functions, or at least some significant part of them."[68]

Reaching similar conclusions concerning the sociohistorical context for rights, Alasdair MacIntyre famously argues that "the truth is plain: there are no such rights, and belief in them is one with belief in witches and unicorns."[69] Noting that no expressions of "a right" are found in Hebrew, Greek, Latin, Arabic, or any Asian language before the fifteenth century, MacIntyre argues that the discovery of human rights as an attribute of all individuals was historically anomalous. MacIntyre's explanation for the discovery of human rights looks to the failure of the Enlightenment to replace the old, secure, eternal, and divine truths of the past with an alternative, widely accepted, understanding of moral agency. Accordingly, although the Enlightenment's dynamic, philosophical project to find new foundations for moral authority proposed several possibilities, it failed to produce any decisive conclusions. Since, for MacIntyre, moral rules "come into existence in particular historic periods under particular social conditions," and "are in no way features of the human condition,"[70] there remains a gap between the meaning of moral expressions and their use. For "the *meaning* is and remains such as would have been warranted only if at least one of the philosophical projects had been successful; but the *use*, the emotivist use, is precisely what one would expect if the philosophical project had all failed."[71]

MacIntyre's argument suggests that although the Enlightenment project on the nature of rights failed, the image of human rights retained its importance in political discourses. The politics of human rights, the emotive use of the term in support of specific actions, remains a feature of global politics today. This is seen in contemporary foreign policy, which promotes human rights as the rationale for undertaking overseas adventures. To recall Mutua's imagery encountered in Chapter 2, the popular view of human rights is captured in the "saviour-victim-savage" model, where the savior rescues the human rights victim from the savagery of governments that refuse to fully engage in the global political economy.[72] In the so-called war on terror, for example, the victim is often depicted as veiled women, who are denied education, equal economic, social, and political rights, access to adequate health care, and political participation. Such representations not only provide the savior with a sense of moral superiority, albeit as an expression of colonial patronage over the ignorant savage, but also reinforce socially constructed gender identities concerning male oppression of women. However, as Fernandes argues, the garnering of public opinion in support of international action has more to do with economic and strategic interests than with concern for human rights or fulfilling responsibilities under international human rights law.[73]

The revitalization of Marxist scholarship following the move to economic globalization, the end of the Cold War, and the collapse of the USSR has brought a reexamination of human rights from the perspective of hegemony, exploitation, social control, and illusion. For the majority, rights over property extend only to consumer goods, where large items are often bought on credit, notably in the purchase of housing. However, legal protection for property is more concerned with corporate rights—rights that are further protected by state intervention through the use of police and military, should individuals use their universal rights to challenge corporate power. Gary Teeple, for instance, argues that under conditions of contemporary capitalist social formation, "control over the realization of most civil rights has passed into corporate hands."[74] Moreover, freedom "of speech has been all but appropriated by corporate control and the self-serving use of the media in film, radio, television, and book, newspaper, and magazine publishing."[75] The recent expansion of the rules that legitimate the actions of global capital, notably those connected with the World Trade Organization, confer or hope to bestow rights on transnational capital, but "impose no corresponding duties."[76]

Similarly, Douzinas states clearly that "human rights do not belong to humans and do not follow the dictates of humanity; they construct humans."[77] For him, the postwar move to promote a rights-based global order is indicative of the loss of community, characteristic of economic globalization, where consumerism and the demand for the protection of property rights play a central role in creating social identities. Human rights law therefore reflects the values that describe existing socioeconomic structures—in the current period, those structures that support the global expansion of capital, most prominently negative freedoms set out in the international human rights regime. However, no legal or other mechanism exists for addressing the ethical and moral validity of property rights, leaving the law an empty vessel that cannot address the social structures in which people must live their lives.[78] Consequently, Douzinas argues that since existing human rights law describes people of a particular type and kind, there is considerable potential for the law to infuse the individual with ideas and values that serve the dominant interest of capital. Thus, the international human rights regime, which recognizes that all human beings possess civil and political rights, but sees economic and social rights more as aspirations, sets out agreed global moral standards that provide the ethical rationale for corporate activity based upon private property and exploitation.

Picking up on the assertion that private property rights are central to contemporary social formation, some authors writing from the Marxist perspective have stressed the distinction between virtue and rights. The civil humanism of past generations gave greater attention to public goods and the polis, rather than rights and legal means for enforcing rights. The virtuous person was one who possessed sufficient wealth to be freed from daily struggles associated with satisfying basic wants. Released from the daily round, the virtuous life was achieved through devotion to public work, where the formal structures of the state offered a framework for engaging in the great ethical, social, and political questions of the day. According to Eagleton, this is in contrast to today, where virtue has been replaced by rights, notably property rights, legally defined to provide the ethical boundaries of action. In the age of economic globalization, ethical and moral reasoning is thus conducted in the language of law and rights, where the individual is a rights-bearer and proprietor, an isolated, private individual concerned with the protection of private property, rather than a virtuous citizen fulfilling civil duties. While it is often argued that Marxists have little interest in human rights, the Marxist tradition does claim an interest in virtue, provided that the means to conduct the virtuous life are available to all citizens, a situation that cannot be achieved in a capitalist order defined by property rights.[79]

The role of the state in maintaining this order has also attracted Marxist analysis. Rosenberg shows how the modern state emerged within the context of particular economic conditions, demonstrating that the Realist idea of continuity from the classical city state to the modern state is a fiction.[80]

Following this argument, the task of the state within the current order is to undertake the political tasks associated with creating and maintaining the public sphere, leaving the private sphere of business, finance, and trade unhindered. Reiterating the work of Marx and Engels, Rosenberg asserts that within global capitalist society human rights claims assume equality between those engaged in exchange relations, an assumption that not only ignores the possibility of an unequal distribution of power but also denies any duty to respond to calls for help outside exchange relations. The role of the Universal Declaration is to articulate the ethical ground norms upon which global capital legitimates its expansion—ground norms that give primacy to inherent, inalienable, and universal rights, most prominently those associated with property rights and economic activity.[81] The conceptualization of the "human" in human rights is also reflective of the dominant mode of production. If rights are limited to exchange relations, then the participants in those relations are the rights holders. Since capitalism is a historically specific order, and rights are associated with property and market relations, the claim that rights are universal remains questionable.[82]

A recent example of the role played by the modern state is that of South Africa's transition to democracy, where the new postapartheid constitution protects property rights—most importantly, land. The protection of those interests, which was a major issue during negotiations that preceded the transition to majority rule, severely constrained the possibility of undertaking land reform. The long campaign to achieve majoritarian rule in South Africa focused upon civil and political rights, without regard for land reform that would address apartheid's inbuilt asymmetrical power relations. Although changes in the law during the 1990s did remove racial barriers to property ownership, the majority were far too poor to take advantage of new property rights without government intervention. What the new constitution did, ironically, was to preserve and legitimate the privileges of those associated with the old order—mostly, white males. Consequently, when the state agreed to retain the status quo over property rights, it "gave the stamp of approval for an unjust and unfair society" and thus was unable to address the central issue that Marxists argue stands in the way of achieving equality.[83]

In cases where the illusion of rights and democracy fails to maintain social order, states have devised new strategies for coping with potential threats to the capitalist order. These new strategies have been categorized by Cox as "poor relief" and "riot control," concepts previously encountered in Chapter 2.[84] The growing number of nongovernmental organizations committed to humanitarian aid, to which the United Nations has given the highest priority, offers the most tangible evidence of the "poor relief" element. Should such action fail to prevent further political and economic destabilization, governments resort to employing force as the means for "riot control." Recent examples of this are seen in the "Battle in Seattle"[85] and the brutality carried out against the Ogoni people in Nigeria.[86] Thus, "poor relief" and "riot control" "help to sustain the emerging social structure of the world by minimizing the risk of chaos in the bottom layer."[87] Claims for human rights, and the institutions of democracy, are of limited interest when social unrest threatens the smooth continuation of practices that define the global capitalist system.

In sum, the Marxist critique of universal human rights provides a political-economy analysis to which recent scholarship has turned in the attempt to explain rights in contemporary global politics. From the Marxist view, rights are limited to civil and political claims—claims that secure a sphere of freedom in which the egoistic individual pursues economic interests. If some groups choose to use the freedoms offered by civil society to challenge, say, the class, gender, ethnic, or race inequalities underlying the formal equalities of citizenship, the state intervenes, in most cases within the implementational constraints of a system of law or, if this fails, through direct action by the police and military.[88] When such events do occur, civil society attempts to negate that which it has produced by appeal to the state to defend the existing order. To paraphrase Marx, the rights represented by civil society are extended to those who want to receive the freedom of property or the egoism of trade, not to those who desire to free themselves from property and trade. The role of political life is to secure the purpose of civil society, which is the separation of the egoistic individual from the community, to secure the individual's liberty in the private sphere, and to legitimate the suppression of any challenge to an order that supports the economic interests of the dominant group. In short, it is civil society that constitutes the limits, form, and extent of rights, not the state.

To elevate economic "aspirations" to the level of rights would, Marxists argue, threaten core capitalist values and the whole purpose of the postwar human rights regime, which is to gain legitimacy for free market, laissez-faire practices and the expansion of the capitalist economy on a global scale. To implement economic and social rights in full would infringe on "natural" liberties and private-property rights. It is for this reason that "there is rarely any constitutional guarantee of social rights, or any state obligation to provide them."[89] Economic and social rights are achieved only following political struggles, not because they are recognized as human rights, valued in the same way as civil and political rights. To retain those economic and social rights already conceded by capital during past struggles requires constant vigilance because, as concessions, they are subject to changes in political leadership, economic cycles, ideological contestation, and the narrow self-interest of those best placed to take full advantage of the conditions of globalization.[90]

While the creation of the human rights regime may mark a defining moment in human history, from the Marxist view it reflects the dominant values associated with capitalism. However, the advent of economic globalization has served only to expose existing tensions, contradictions, and anomalies within the regime, which suggest that the Marxist view of rights cannot be achieved within a global capitalist order.[91] Lukes, for example, argues that from the Marxist perspective, those who currently exploit and oppress by exercising their "legitimate" rights to property, their liberty, and their freedom to pursue personal economic gain, do not deserve "soft-hearted" treatment during the political struggles for emancipation.[92]

The Marxist critique of human rights should not, however, be taken as a complete rejection of human rights. Ellen Meiksins Wood, for example, argues that the dominant construction of rights certainly marks a shift toward achieving a level of equality that has not been enjoyed by previous generations. But, for Wood, the current regime defines and promotes a particular set of rights that mask the "exploitative power of capital" expressed both inside and outside the workplace, "through the mechanisms of the market, the compulsion of competition, accumulation, and profit-maximization, which regulate social activity and take precedence over any other human goals." Moreover, Wood argues that the often-heard boast that the emergence of democracy as the only legitimate form of government capable of securing human rights overlooks the way that many advanced capitalist states claim that changes in, for instance, the rights of unions are often justified as defending the democratic rights of citizens from "collective oppression."[93] Following recent terrorist attacks in several advanced capitalist countries, those who defend human rights are increasingly concerned that the introduction of new legal restrictions on liberty are eroding those rights previously won in earlier political struggles. The UK's Prevention of Terrorism Act, for example, which permits the home secretary under certain circumstances to derogate from rights conferred by human rights law, is often seen in this light.[94]

Postmodernism and the Question of Universal "Truths"

Like Marxists, postmodernist analysis concludes that claims of universal human rights are a fiction. However, in contrast to Marxist thought, postmodernism rejects the idea that universal social truths are generated by powerful interests associated with capital. Rather than seeing power as residing in a dominant capitalist class, postmodernists see it as suffused through all social relations, with the movement going from the bottom up, rather than from the top down.[95] Not only are there no universal human rights, but there are no universal "truths" of any kind. What passes for "truth" is merely an aggregation of historic ideas, subject at all times to change through the dynamics of social existence. As Beck notes, in the postmodern world, the universalism discovered by the scientific rationality of the Enlightenment, including those associated with universal human rights, are now exposed as "nothing other than the voice of 'dead old white males,' who had trampled on the rights of ethnic, religious, and sexual minorities by absolutizing their own partisan meta-narrative."[96] Claims that universal human rights are a foundational and unqualified characteristic of human nature are therefore rejected by both Marxists and postmodernists: Marxists because human rights represent part of the processes of oppression, and postmodernists because all absolutes are a discursive fiction and a hostage to history.[97]

It is common to see the claim that human rights are the "idea of our time." What this optimistic view hopes to convey is the notion that international society has at last come to recognize an eternal, abiding, and revealed "truth," which now sits at the center of the emerging global order. In this way, human rights are presented as a symbol of "progress," which is now pursued enthusiastically and ubiquitously. However, the eagerness and passion that the idea of human rights attracts has often ensured that the idea remains largely free of reflective critical comment.[98] For postmodernists, however, the phrase "idea of our time" should be taken at face value, not as an idea possessing transcendental qualities but as an idea characteristic of a particular historic social configuration. This is not to suggest that the literature consistently fails to engage in criticism of the international human right regime. On the contrary, criticism is not hard to find, particularly that aimed at the failure of international society to solve the problems associated with compliance and implementation. Yet these criticisms are commonly concerned with refining, polishing, and elaborating currently accepted norms and standards, in an attempt to make the regime more elegant, sophisticated, imposing, and magisterial. As one commentator has observed, it is criticism undertaken by committed human rights experts, resolutely "advancing the faith."[99]

From the postmodernist perspective, what this approach conceals is a lack of critique. While criticism is confined to arguments about particular theories, philosophies, beliefs, ideologies, and regimes, critique is more concerned with investigating the ways in which these claims to truth are achieved, legitimated, and presented as the authoritative guide for action. If criticism can be thought of as part of a technical debate, intended to refine particular truths, then critique is concerned with the politics of truth itself.[100] As such, critique is concerned with exposing the interests served by the production and maintenance of particular truths and the processes that enable some forms of knowledge to be accepted as complete and legitimate while other forms are labeled partial and suspect. In this sense, critique occupies a limited space within the human rights literature.

The reason for the absence of critique, according to the postmodernists, can be found in the practices of discourse and discipline. Postmodernist arguments about "truth" begin by looking at "discourse," which refers to the argument that language is not merely a means for describing external reality, providing nothing more than a technique for labeling objects, but acts to signify generalized, socially constructed categories of thought to which important social meaning, beliefs, and values are attributed. These attributes act as a guide for social action within the prevailing social environment by defining and promoting the parameters of moral thought and behavior. In this sense, discourses lend structure to our experiences, to the meanings we give to our experiences, and the judgments we make about our own and others' actions. For example, when we use the term *lawyer,* we are not describing a person by professional category alone but also invoking a bundle of other meanings, expectations, and understandings that go far beyond mere empiricism. Included among these are assumptions about authority, fairness, social class, punishment, justice, integrity, legitimacy, erudition, and social order. Discourses therefore provide sets of values and beliefs that inform our social responses and actions, often unselfconsciously.

As discourse emerges as a generalized system for framing a particular social issue, professional, intellectual, and interest-based groups take the opportunity to institutionalize particular norms and values, effectively "privatizing" a discourse by introducing a specialized language, images, and concepts that act to exclude the uninitiated.[101] In this way, the veracity, reliability, integrity, and authority of discourse "experts" is reinforced, while other voices from outside the discourse are marginalized, derided, excluded, and sometimes prohibited.[102] Discourses therefore act as the meeting place for power and knowledge.[103] Foucault, for example, rejects the liberal notion that knowledge can flourish only in the absence of power. Instead, he argues, there can be no knowledge without power or power in the absence of knowledge.[104] To gain an insight into the truth-claims emanating from discourse must therefore include an inquiry into power relations. However, such an investigation does not imply that the generation of truth is necessarily corrupted by power, but that the social world described by discourses always involves power relations. In this sense, liberal concerns that power can be defined in terms of legitimacy and illegitimacy misses the important point that even the legitimate exercise of power also excludes, marginalizes, silences, and prohibits alternatives.

Some authors engaged in the critique of human rights talk suggest that dominant voices within a discourse can be described as "speech communities."[105] Although most human beings possess the power of speech, and are therefore equipped to enter a speech community, the capacity to engage with a discourse does not imply an entitlement to exercise that capacity. Lyotard, for instance, observes that "capacity does not legitimacy make."[106] He warns us that to confuse these two concepts offers a false vision of freedom and equality, based upon reciprocity, which slips seamlessly from fact to value and word to deed. The work of Amnesty International, for example, focuses upon the right of prisoners to be granted the freedom to speak within the framework of liberal notions of tolerance, which are expressed in the provisions of public law. However, for Lyotard, "this legality conceals confusion between capacity and aptitude to speak, and the legitimacy and authority to speak."[107] The claim for a universal right to speak therefore passes through a prism of tolerance that shifts the focus from capacity to capability, a process that permits some voices to be heard and others to be silenced or overlooked. Furthermore, access to a speech community may be controlled by violent means (torture and imprisonment) or nonviolent means by simply labeling alternative voices as "mad."[108]

The playwright Harold Pinter has also argued that language is often used as a means of social control. In his acceptance address for the Nobel Prize in literature, he took the opportunity to attack prevailing wisdom on global politics, arguing that although global leaders adopt the language of humanitarianism in defense of their actions, it is often a way to "keep thought at bay" so that the truth is never sought or reflected upon.[109] As an example, he pointed to the community of critics devoted to documenting the tyranny of East European Communist states during the Cold War, whose main purpose was to demonstrate the moral superiority of the West. However, Pinter argued, the tyranny of the West during the same period remains less well documented, and he pointed to, for example, President Reagan's assertion that democracy prevailed in Nicaragua while at the same time funding the Contras to perform atrocities against innocent civilians. A more recent example might be found in military action taken in Iraq, which was in part conducted in the name of human rights, while the United States simultaneously maintained the camp at Guantanamo Bay, exercised "extraordinary rendition," and extradited detainees to other countries while knowing that their subsequent arrest would lead to torture. For Pinter, there "are no hard distinctions between what is real and what is unreal, or between what is true and what is false," for a "thing is not necessarily either true or false; it can be both true and false."[110] Pinter's effort to describe the confusion over assertions of "truth" reflects postmodernist inquiries that have sought to explain how "truth" is manufactured and sustained, including the assertion of universal human rights.

What form does discipline take in the current global order? The "truth" of human rights can be thought of as part of a program for disciplining global order.[111] Foucault uses the term *discipline* to refer to a mode of social organization that operates without need of coercion. It is a form of power that imbues the individual with particular ways of thinking, knowing, and behaving, thus instilling modes of social consciousness that make social action predictable. Discipline is learned and practiced in the day-to-day complex of social life, where notions of correct and incorrect behavior and thought are clearly delimited. "Common sense" is achieved when a particular mode of thought and conduct is unquestioningly accepted as normal.[112] This is not to argue that discipline cannot be defined as a system of rules, but these are not necessarily the rules articulated within the pages of international law. Instead, these rules are concerned with the norms, values, and beliefs that act to reproduce social life and to "normalize" it.[113] In this sense, the disciplines, which are the domain of global civil society, operate without compulsory obligation, while continuing to exert collective pressure that brings objective results by instilling particular modes of thinking and acting.[114]

The maintenance of disciplinary power is conducted through systems of surveillance: the processes of data collection through observation, recording, measuring, inspecting, reporting, and monitoring, which today are more easily facilitated by systems of electronic data collection.[115] Data accumulated from the observation of large numbers defines the "normal," opening the possibility of specifying the attributes of "acceptable" and "unacceptable" behavior within the values, terms, and language of dominant discourses of truth. Those who violate the norms of acceptable behavior are therefore identifiable, enabling appropriate sanctions to be applied, while those who conform are rewarded. Foucault argues that the form of disciplinary power operating within the contemporary world order emerged during the eighteenth century, noting ironically that "the Enlightenment, which discovered the liberties, also invented the disciplines."[116]

From the perspective of disciplinary power, critics of liberal notions of power have argued that the institutionalization of discourse, which produces and promotes truth-claims, obscures and conceals the processes of domination that lie beneath normal social practice.[117] Gill refers to the most prominent of the disciplines within the current global order as "market discipline," which stresses economic growth and development, deregulation, the free market, the privatization of public services, and minimum government.[118] Market discipline describes a set of normative relationships with a global reach, supported by discourses of truth, and widely accepted as "common sense." These relationships are manifest at both the domestic and global level; for example, in national and international economic planning, market-based solutions for environmental degradation, the move to privatize social-welfare provision, and the move to privatize life itself, seen in the scramble to patent the genes of both human and nonhuman life-forms. Surveillance is undertaken by international and regional agencies; for example, the World Trade Organization (WTO), the World Bank, the European Union (EU), and the North American Free Trade Agreement (NAFTA). Each of these is understood as the authentic voice of market discipline and each exercises systems of surveillance and data collection on a global and regional scale.

Within the remit of market discipline, as opposed to that of international law, human rights are conceptualized as the freedoms necessary to maintain and legitimate particular forms of production and exchange. These are a set of negative rights associated with liberty, security, and property, which offer a moral and normative foundation for justifying actions within the current global political economy. Although the global legal human rights regime is said to embrace the unity of all rights, including economic, social, and cultural rights, market discipline pursues only those rights necessary to sustain legitimate claims for liberal freedoms. The catalog of rights associated with market discipline therefore describes human beings as individuals and agents of a particular kind and type. For postmodernist critics, the human rights regime is partial. Despite the mechanisms of self-discipline at the center of market discipline, there remains a need for authoritative, expert pronouncements and idioms when norms are transgressed.[119] This is a central role of international law, which itself reflects self-discipline through the international legal principle of reciprocity, and articulates the "neutral" rules of conduct that describe the "natural" global order as presented by market discipline.

If we accept these arguments, then there is no possibility of establishing transcendent "truths," no possibility of discovering the moral foundations for universal human rights, and consequently no reason to believe that any "truth-claim" offers greater certainty than an other "truth-claim." As the central moral claim in the globalizing order, universal human rights become little more than an assertion supported by a particular configuration of power relations. Richard Rorty supports this conclusion when he argues that the so-called universal desire to discover eternal truths is no more than the universal desire for justification. For Rorty, the only way to transcend a current social practice is to create another social practice, just as the only way to transcend a current discursive strategy is to create another discursive strategy aimed at achieving a better goal.

> But because I do not know how to aim at it, I do not think that "truth" names such a goal. I know how to aim at greater honesty, greater clarity, greater patience, greater inclusiveness, and so on. I see democratic politics as serving such concrete, describable goals. But I do not see that it helps things to add "truth" or "universality" or "unconditionally" to our list of goals, for I do not see what we shall do differently if such additions are made.[120]

Following the earlier assertion that critiques of human rights have been largely ignored, it is appropriate to conclude this chapter with the postmodernist critique of human rights. This critique attempts to offer an explanation for the exclusion of alternative versions of all claims to universal "truth," noting that liberal society is not so tolerant as to tolerate intolerance of its core values.[121] In Rorty's argument, discourses are concerned with justification wrapped up as "common sense," which passes for "truth." All alternative claims and critiques are excluded from the discourse.

*   *   *

The theoretical critiques of human rights discussed here draw largely on Western political thought. Feminists, Marxists, and postmodernists all frame arguments for understanding human rights within particular, historic relations of power. Feminists reach this conclusion by presenting analysis of the Universal Declaration and international human rights law, which is seen as male-centered, reflecting male interests and male dominance. Most centrally, according to feminists, these instruments describe a role for women that confines them to the private sphere of the home, family, and the important task of biological and social reproduction. Marxists and postmodernists direct their critique at the particular interests served by human rights: Marxists claiming that capital looks to civil and political rights for legitimating global capitalism and postmodernists claiming that any dominant discourse should be seen as describing a social order tied to particular time and place.

Notes

1. For a well-known analysis of natural rights, see J. M. Finnis, *Natural Law and Natural Rights* (Oxford, UK: Clarendon Press, 1980).

2. Thomas Hobbes, *Leviathan*, ed. Michael Oakeshott (Oxford, UK: Blackwell, 1945).

3. John Locke, *Two Treatises of Government*, ed. Peter Laslett (Cambridge: Cambridge University Press, 1960).

4. Thomas Paine, *The Rights of Man* (Oxford, UK: Woodstock, 1992).

5. Quoted in David Powell, *Thomas Paine: The Great Exile* (London: Hutchinson, 1985), p. 182.

6. Robert Nozick, *Anarchy, State, and Utopia* (Oxford, UK: Blackwell, 1974).

7. John Rawls, *A Theory of Justice* (Cambridge: Cambridge University Press, 1971).

8. Karl Marx, "On the Jewish Question," in *Karl Marx: Selected Writings*, ed. David McLellan (Oxford: Oxford University Press, 2002).

9. A. Light and H. Rolston, eds., *Environmental Ethics* (Oxford, UK: Blackwell, 2002); W. Sachs, "Environment and Human Rights," *Development* 47, no. 1 (2004): 42–49; J. W. Nickel and E. Viola, "Integrating Environmentalism and Human Rights," *Environmental Ethics* 16, no. 3 (1994): 265–274.

10. Mary Wollstonecraft, *Vindication of the Rights of Women* (London: Penguin, 1982).

11. Michael Walzer, *Spheres of Justice: A Defence of Pluralism and Equality* (Oxford, UK: Blackwell, 1995).

12. Georgina Ashworth, "The Silencing of Women," in *Human Rights in Global Politics*, ed. Tim Dunne and Nicholas J. Wheeler (Cambridge: Cambridge University Press, 1999).

13. Fiona Robinson, "The Limits of a Rights Based Approach to International Ethics," in *Human Rights Fifty Years On: A Reappraisal*, ed. Tony Evans (Manchester: Manchester University Press, 1998).

14. Ashworth, "Silencing of Women," p. 261.

15. Art 1.1, Convention Against Torture and Other Cruel, Inhuman or Degrading Treatment or Punishment, GA resolution 39/46, December 10, 1984, entered into force June 26, 1987.

16. Robinson, "Limits of a Rights Based Approach," p. 58.

17. Makau Mutua, *Human Rights: A Political and Cultural Critique*, ed. Bert B. Lockwood, Pennsylvania Studies in Human Rights (Philadelphia: University of Pennsylvania Press, 2002), p. 40.

18. Celina Romany, "State Responsibility Goes Private: A Feminist Critique of the Public-Private Distinction in International Human Rights Law," in *Women's Human Rights*, ed. Julie Peters and Andrea Wolper (London: Routledge, 1995).

19. I. Berlin, "Two Concepts of Liberty," in *Four Essays on Liberty* (Oxford, Oxford University Press, 1969).

20. Hilary Charlesworth, Christine Chinkin, and Shelly Wright, "Feminist Approaches to International Law," *American Journal of International Law* 85, no. 4 (1991): 629.

21. Jill Steans, *Gender and International Relations* (Cambridge, UK: Polity, 2006), pp. 428–454.

22. Ashworth, "Silencing of Women."

23. Upendra Baxi, *The Future of Human Rights* (Oxford: Oxford University Press, 2002).

24. Steans, *Gender and International Relations*.

25. R. B. J Walker, "Gender and Critique in the Theory of International Relations," in *Gendered States: Feminist Revisions of International Relations Theory*, ed. V. Spike Peterson (Boulder, Colo.: Lynne Rienner, 1992).

26. Catharine A. MacKinnon, "Crimes of War, Crimes of Peace," in *On Human Rights: The Oxford Amnesty Lectures, 1993*, ed. Stephen Shute and Susan Hurley (New York: Basic Books, 1993).

27. Ibid.

28. Araati Rao, "Home-Word Bound: Women's Place in the Family of International Human Rights," *Global Governance* 2, no. 1 (1996): 250.

29. Jill Steans, "Engaging from the Margins: Feminist Encounters with the 'Mainstream' of International Relations," *British Journal of Politics and International Relations* 5, no. 3 (2003): 428–454. See also Terry Eagleton, "Deconstruction and Human Rights," in *Freedom and Interpretation: The Oxford Amnesty Lectures, 1992*, ed. Barbara Johnson (New York: Basic Books, 1992).

30. V. Spike Peterson and Laura Parisi, "Are Women Human? It's Not an Academic Question," in Evans, ed., *Human Rights Fifty Years On*.

31. Rao, "Home-Word Bound," p. 245.

32. MacKinnon, "Crimes of War."

33. Steans, *Gender and International Relations*.

34. UN Development Programme: *Human Development Report, 1995—Gender and Human Development* (Oxford, UK: UNDP, 1995).

35. Ibid., p. 6.

36. Anne Forrest, "Securing the Male Breadwinner: A Feminist Interpretation of PC 1003," *Relations Industrielle* 52, no. 1 (1997).

37. Gay Young, Lucia Fort, and Mona Danner, "Moving from 'the Status of Women' to 'Gender Inequality': Conceptualisation, Social Indicators, and an Empirical Application," *International Sociology* 9, no. 1 (1994).

38. den Bernard Ouden, "Sustainable Development, Human Rights, and Postmodernism," *Philosophy and Technology* 3, no. 2 (1997).

39. See William Felice, "The Viability of the United Nations Approach to Economic and Social Human Rights in a Global Economy," *International Affairs* 75, no. 3 (1999); J. Oloka-Onyango and Deepika Udagana, "The Realization of Economic, Social, and Cultural Rights: Globalization and Its Impact on the Full Enjoyment of Human Rights," (Sub-Commission on the Promotion and Protection of Human Rights, E/CH.4/mb2/2000/13, 2000); Chris Simms, Mike Rawson, and Siobhan Peattie, *The Bitterest Pill of All: The Collapse of Africa's Health System*, www.eldis.org/vfile/upload/1/document/0708/doc8889.pdf (2001). See also Caroline Thomas, *Global Governance, Development, and Human Security*, ed. Caroline Thomas, Human Security and the Global Economy (London: Pluto Press, 2001).

40. Kate Nash, "Human Rights for Women: An Argument for 'Deconstructive Equality,'" *Economy and Society* 31, no. 3 (2002); Richard Rorty, "Human Rights, Rationality, and Sentimentality," in *Oxford Amnesty Lectures, 1993*.

41. Sally Engle Merry, *Human Rights and Gender Violence* (Chicago: University of Chicago Press, 2006), p. 6.

42. Ibid. See also Eva Brems, *Human Rights Quarterly* 19, no. 1 (1997): 136–164.

43. See, the electronic journal *Theoretical Enquiries in Law,* which has a number of articles on "transplants" of Western systems of law into non-Western cultures: http://www.bepress.com/til.

44. Radhika Coomaraswamy, "To Bellow Like a Cow: Women, Ethnicity, and the Discourse of Rights," in *Human Rights of Women: National and International Perspectives*, ed. Rebecca Cook (Philadelphia: University of Pennsylvania Press, 1994).

45. V. S. Peterson and L. Parisi. "Are Women Human? It's Not An Academic Question," in Evans, ed., *Human Rights Fifty Years On*, p. 132.

46. For examples of international law, see B. S. Chimini, "Marxism and International Law," *Economic and Political Weekly* 34, no. 6 (1999); China Mieville, *Between Equal Rights: A Marxist Theory of International Law* (London: Pluto Press, 2006); for examples of theory, see Terrell Carver, *The Postmodern Marx* (Manchester: Manchester University Press, 1998); Eagleton, "Deconstruction and Human Rights"; for politics, see Tony Evans, *The Politics of Human Rights: A Global Perspective*, 2nd ed. (London: Pluto Press, 2005); Gary Teeple, *The Riddle of Human Rights* (Aurora, Canada: Garamond Press, 2005).

47. Karl Marx, "Preface to the Critique of Political Economy," in *Marx: Selected Writings*, ed. McLellan, p. 425.

48. Karl Marx and Frederick Engels, "The Communist Manifesto," in *Marx: Selected Writings*, ed. McLellan, p. 260.

49. Kark Marx, ed., *Early Political Writings* (Cambridge: Cambridge University Press, 1994), p. 44.

50. Marx, "On the Jewish Question," p. 60. Marx uses male-gender language throughout his work, reflecting the period in which he worked.

51. Kees van der Pijl, "Transnational Class Formation and State Forms," in *Innovation and Transformation in International Studies*, ed. Stephen Gill and James Mittelman (Cambridge: Cambridge University Press, 1997).

52. Marx, "On the Jewish Question," p. 61.

53. Steven Lukes, "Can a Marxist Believe in Human Rights?" *Praxis International* 1, no. 4 (1982): 243.

54. Marx and Engels, "The Communist Manifesto," pp. 248–249.

55. Frederick Engels, *Anti-Duhring: Herr Eugen Duhring's Revolution in Science* (London: Lawrence & Wishart, 1975).

56. Ibid., p. 26.

57. Agnes Heller, "The Legacy of Marxian Ethics Today," *Praxis International* 1, no. 4 (1982).

58. For arguments on the development of the human rights regime and its relationship with markets, see Tony Evans, *US Hegemony and the Project of Universal Human Rights* (Basingstoke, UK: Macmillan, 1996).

59. Engels, *Anti-Durhring,* p. 127 (emphasis in original).

60. Marx, "On the Jewish Question."

61. Mieville, *Between Equal Rights.*

62. Lukes, "Can a Marxist Believe in Human Rights?"

63. Antonio Gramsci, "Selections from the Prison Notebooks," ed. Quinton Hoare and Geoffrey Smith (London: Lawrence & Wishart, 1996), pp. 57–58.

64. J. Femia, *Gramsci's Political Thought: Hegemony, Consciousness and the Revolutionary Process* (Oxford, UK: Clarendon Press, 1981).

65. Gramsci, "Selections from the Prison Notebooks," pp. 419–425.

66. G. John Ikenberry and Charles A. Kupchan, "Socializaiton and Hegemonic Power," International Organization 44, no. 3 (1990): 283–315.

67. Evans, *US Hegemony and the Project of Universal Human Rights.*

68. Ellen Meiksins Wood, *Democracy Against Capitalism* (Cambridge: Cambridge University Press, 1996), p. 254 (emphasis in original).

69. Alasdair MacIntyre, *After Virtue: A Study in Moral Theory* (London: Duckworth, 1981), p. 67.

70. Ibid., p. 65.

71. Ibid., p. 66.

72. Mutua, *Political and Cultural Critique.*

73. Leela Fernandes, "The Boundaries of Terror: Feminism, Human Rights, and the Politics of Global Crisis," in *Just Advocacy? Women's Human Rights, Transnational Feminism, and the Politics of Representation*, ed. Wendy S. Hesford and Wendy Kozol (New Brunswick, N.J.: Rutgers University Press, 2005).

74. Teeple, *Riddle of Human Rights,* p. 37.

75. Ibid., p. 38.

76. Christine Chinkin, "International Law and Human Rights," in Evans, ed., *Human Rights Fifty Years On*, p. 339.

77. Costas Douzinas, *Human Rights and Empire: The Political Philosophy of Cosmopolitanism* (Abingdon, UK: Routledge-Cavendish, 2007), p. 48.

78. Johan Galtung, *Human Rights in Another Key* (Cambridge, UK: Polity, 1994).

79. Eagleton, "Deconstruction and Human Rights," p. 122.

80. Justin Rosenberg, *The Empire of Civil Society: A Critique of the Realist Theory of International Relations* (London: Verso, 1994). See also Mieville, *Between Equal Rights.*

81. Teeple, *Riddle of Human Rights.*

82. Eagleton, "Deconstruction and Human Rights."

83. Mutua, *Political and Cultural Critique,* p. 151.

84. Robert Cox, "Democracy in Hard Times: Economic Globalization and the Limits to Liberal Democracy," in *The Transformation of Democracy*, ed. Anthony McGrew (Cambridge, UK: Polity,1997).

85. J. Bhagwati, *Free Trade Today* (Princeton, N.J.: Princeton University Press, 2002).

86. Abdul Rasheed Na'allah, *Ogoni's Agonies: Ken Sara Wiwa and the Crisis in Nigeria* (Trenton, N.J.: Africa World Press, 1998).

87. Cox, "Democracy in Hard Times," p. 59.

88. Hugh Collins, *Marxism and Law* (Oxford: Oxford University Press, 1990).

89. Teeple, *Riddle of Human Rights,* p. 15.

90. Paul Patton, "Foucault's Subject of Power," in *The Later Foucault: Politics and Philosophy,* ed. Jeremy Moss (London: Sage, 1998).

91. Teeple, *Riddle of Human Rights,* Chapter 7.

92. Steven Lukes, "Five Fables About Human Rights," in *Oxford Amnesty Lectures, 1993.*

93. *New Socialist,* interview with Ellen Meiksins Wood, "Democracy and Capitalism: Friends or Foes?" http://www.newsocialist.org/magazine/01/article08.html.

94. "The Prevention of Terrorism, 2005," see http://www.opsi.gov.uk/ acts/acts2005/ukpga_20050002_en_1.

95. Michel Foucault, "Two Lectures," in *Critique and Power: Recasting the Foucault/Able Debate*, ed. Michael Kelly (Cambridge, Mass.: MIT Press, 1994).

96. Ulrich Beck, *What Is Globalization?* (Cambridge, UK: Polity, 2000), p. 5.

97. Jose A. Lindgren Alves, "The Declaration of Human Rights in Postmodernity," *Human Rights Quarterly* 22, no. 2 (2000); Eagleton, "Deconstruction and Human Rights."

98. Chimini, "Marxism and International Law."

99. Quoted in David Chandler, *From Kosovo to Kabul: Human Rights and International Intervention* (London: Pluto, 2002).

100. Michel Foucault, "What Is Critique?" in *Twentieth-Century Questions*, ed. James Schmidt (Berkeley: University of California Press, 1996).

101. Herman and Peterson show that the moral claims for recent humanitarian interventions use the utterances of intellectual "experts" to support and justify military ac-

tion. See Edward S. Herman and David Peterson, "Morality's Avenging Angels: The New Humanitarian Crusaders," in *Rethinking Human Rights*, ed. David Chandler (Basingstoke, UK: Palgrave, 2002), pp. 196–216.

102. Alan Hunt, *Explorations in Law and Society: Towards a Constitutive Theory of Law* (New York: Routledge, 1993).

103. Michel Foucault, *Discipline and Punish*, trans. A. Sheridan (New York: Pantheon, 1977).

104. David Cozens Hoy, "Power, Repression, Progress: Foucault, Lukes, and the Frankfurt School," in *Michel Foucault: Critical Assessments*, ed. Barry Smart (London: Routledge, 1995).

105. Jean-Francois Lyotard, "The Other's Rights," in *Oxford Amnesty Lectures,* 1993.

106. Ibid., p. 49.

107. Ibid., p. 114.

108. James Keeley, "Towards a Foucauldian Analysis of International Regimes," *International Organization* 44, no. 1 (1990).

109. Harold Pinter, "Nobel Prize for Literature Acceptance Speech," *Guardian*, August 8, 2005.

110. Ibid.

111. Tony Evans, "Disciplining Global Civil Society," *Studies in Social Justice,* 1, no. 2 (Autumn 2007): 108–121.

112. Gramsci, "Selections from the Prison Notebooks."

113. Foucault, "Two Lectures."

114. For further reading on poststructuralism and civil society, see David Chandler, *Constructing Global Civil Society* (Basingstoke, UK: Palgrave, 2004).

115. Stephen Gill, "Finance, Production, and Panopticanism: Inequality, Risk, and Resistance in an Era of Disciplinary Neo-Liberalism," in *Globalization, Democratization, and Multiculturalism*, ed. Stephen Gill (Basingstoke, UK: Macmillan, 1997).

116. Foucault, *Discipline and Punish,* p. 222.

117. Duncan Ivison, "The Disciplinary Moment: Foucault, Law, and the Reinscription of Rights," in Moss, ed., *The Later Foucault*.

118. Stephen Gill, "Globalization, Market Civilisation, and Disciplinary Neoliberalism," *Millennium* 24, no. 3 (1995).

119. C. G. Prado, *Starting with Foucault: An Introduction to Genealogy* (Boulder, Colo.: Westview, 1995).

120. Richard Rorty, "Universality and Truth," in *Rorty and His Critics*, ed. Roper R. Brandon (Oxford, UK: Blackwell, 2000), p. 7.

121. Ibid. See also Tony Evans, "The Limits of Tolerance: Islam as Counter-Hegemony," *Review of International Studies* (forthcoming 2010).

4

Non-Western Concepts of Human Rights and Dignity

In recent years, questions of cultural relativism have gained ground within the discourse of human rights. This is not a new phenomenon, historically.[1] The post–World War II period is, in this respect, no exception. From the Dumbarton Oaks Conversations on International Organization to the creation of the two major covenants on human rights and beyond, philosophical and conceptual concerns over promoting a set of universal values within a multicultural world order were occasionally raised but never seriously pursued.[2] The failure to engage with questions raised by cultural relativism, to establish a clear philosophical basis upon which to build future human rights law and institutions, meant that from the early days of the United Nations human rights regime, the discourse "largely pirouetted around a missing centre."[3] During the early years of the regime, when states from a Western, natural rights, liberal democratic tradition dominated the discourse of rights within the United Nations, all talk of cultural relativism was seen as little more than an irritant that threatened to stand in the way of "progress."[4]

Today, however, with the growth of social, economic, and cultural globalization, the context in which rights discourse is conducted has changed radically. As we saw in Chapter 2, the emergence of a new global political economy has brought transformative forces to bear on the old Westphalian order of states. Some have argued that this has transformed the terrain of political struggles, shifting its focus from poverty, egalitarianism, and scarcity to that of identity, difference, and exclusion.[5] The new politics of identity is often couched in the language of cultural relativism, which assumes a "clash of civilizations" in the struggle for moral dominance.[6] At the heart of cultural relativist arguments is the assumption that any claim for moral universalism is fundamentally flawed because it fails to acknowledge that the validity of rights is derived from the cultural context in which it is asserted. Thus, all claims to universality are false, "because the history of the world is the story of the plurality of cultures."[7] From this perspective, those who promote universal human rights are open to the charge of imperialism, understood in the current period as the moral arm of the United States and its allies. For many less-developed states, universal human rights should therefore be treated with deep suspicion, if not downright rejection.

However, in the current period it is a mistake to understand the new politics of identity as a reaction to imperialism, if this is seen as an attempt to generalize the moral values of a particular social, cultural, and moral tradition. Instead, the new politics of identity should be seen as emerging in the wake of changes to the global socioeconomic context within which people (and peoples) must live their lives. In the age of economic globalization, the demand for changes in systems of production and exchange have seen the emergence of new forms of social relations that challenge existing social habits, moral ideas, and cultural identities. In many locales, these changes instigate feelings of anomie and social disintegration, as traditional knowledge is replaced by the new.[8] As we saw in Chapter 2, the increasing grip of economic globalization therefore provides the context for political struggles that may threaten those whose interests are most closely associated with the move to a new global order characteristic of recent decades.[9]

To accept the cultural relativist argument is to accept "that moral judgments deriving outside a culture being judged can have no validity, [making] morality a slave to custom [where] the 'ought' loses its transcendental power over the 'is.'"[10] While such an approach is unthinkable for proponents of universal human rights, it is as well to remember that the majority of the world's peoples do not define themselves as rights-bearing individuals but as bearers of duties to kin and community. As globalization enables us to gain a greater knowledge of other traditions of rights and duties, the claims of European political philosophy to have discovered the foundations of human rights seems less secure. Moreover, as we have come to doubt the works of John Locke, Adam Smith, and their successors, we have simultaneously developed an interest in the work of scholars from other cultures.[11] Of particular interest today is the approach adopted by Islam and Confucius, which is the focus of the present chapter.

Islam and Human Rights

As Antony Black has asserted, the distinction between reason and revelation as philosophical method is key to understanding all aspects of Islam.[12] Whereas Western political thought constructed the idea of universal human rights through the application of reason, for Islam human rights are revealed in the word of God.[13] Following from the Islamic premise that the earthly realm is God's creation, all human capacities and capabilities are God-given, constituting a "divine sovereignty" that demands religious devotion. The revealed word of God, which the Prophet recorded in the Quran fourteen centuries ago, sets down moral truths as a guide for building a just social order within which all Muslims can find both material and spiritual security. These truths include the duty of the individual, the family, and the wider Muslim community *(ummah)* to participate in creating and sustaining social relations for realizing God's design.[14] In this sense, revelation serves to bridge the divide between the earthly and the heavenly realms, where the former is characterized as the day-to-day struggle for survival and the satisfaction of physiological and material needs and the latter as a transcendent realm beyond earthly desires, which satisfies psychological and spiritual needs.

From the perspective of revelation, it follows that any attempt to separate the physiological and material from the psychological and spiritual aspects of human existence, which is central to Enlightenment thought, must be rejected. Qutb, for example, explains this rejection through his critique of Thomas Hobbes, whom he claims emphasizes reason and the acquisition of knowledge at the expense of revelation. In Qutb's reading of Hobbes, knowledge of the natural world opens the possibility of imagining a future where the failure to satisfy natural appetites is less likely. Reason therefore offers the potential to satisfy physiological needs through the exploitation of nature to generate surpluses.[15] However, the state of nature determines that others may attempt to satisfy their own physiological needs through appropriation. Hobbes therefore proposes a social contract in which citizens surrender some liberty to a "leviathan" in exchange for security defined by rights over property. Accordingly, Qubt argues that the role of the secular state is limited to the physiological needs of citizens.[16] Sociopsychological needs remain a private matter of faith and religious devotion, a sphere of social life in which the state has little interest and, therefore, no legitimate claim to interfere.[17] Thus, Qutb claims that Hobbes explicitly rejects the need for the state to engage with issues of religious belief and instead focuses exclusively on the material world.[18]

For these reasons, the secularist turn found in most advanced capitalist economies, which separates the state's duty from duties associated with religious observance and assigns religion to the private world, is rejected by Islamic scholars. For Islam, the social world must be investigated as a "unity between worship and work, ideology or creed and behavior, spirituality and materiality, economic symbolic value, the world and immortality, heaven and earth."[19] In Islamic thought, the development of distinctive disciplines in economics, international relations, politics, philosophy, sociology, law, and theology, each with its own language, methodology, and normative context, brings only confusion, partial truths, and conflict. While Enlightenment thought encouraged a methodology that seeks "truth" through an examination of every facet of society in isolation, Islam adopts a holistic approach: an "Islamic spirit" that is realized only when the individual's consciousness is awakened by submission to the will of God.[20] In short, many Islamic scholars argue that the Enlightenment project to abandon holistic thought, its preference for a methodology that focuses upon the parts rather than the whole, and its rejection of God as the source of "truth" creates a social order that fails to satisfy either the physiological or psychological needs of humankind.[21] For many proponents of Islam, the schism between physiological and psychological needs is the major cause of decadence found in developed capitalist states, where the instances of family breakdown, drugs, violent crime, and social dislocation threaten the collapse of social order.

Although from the perspective of Enlightenment thought, Hobbes's rationale and ambitious program offers an optimistic view of human progress, viewed from Islam it offers the prospect of a socioeconomic order that fails to deliver spiritual and moral guidance. By contrast, the Islamic version of the social contract is said to actively assert a normative foundation that seeks to go beyond the mere satisfaction of physiological need by extending that satisfaction to the psychological, spiritual, and moral needs of the whole community. As Judy explains, it is a contract that seeks to awaken the individual's consciousness to Allah's guidance on the nature of the universe and humankind's place within it. Any claim to knowledge that fails to accept the "truth" of Allah's guidance, or otherwise preempts the possibility of engaging that "truth," is seen by Islamic scholarship as the very definition of ignorance *(Jahiliya).*[22] Consequently, the struggle to gain a greater knowledge of the material world alone must fail if it produces a disconnected and temporal form of knowledge that cannot provide the foundations for creating forms of community based upon social justice and a stable moral order.

The opposition between knowledge as reason and knowledge as revelation provides the foundation for many disagreements between those who see a prosperous future through the values embedded in the neoliberal global political economy and those who reject the allure of materialism and seek fulfillment through the traditions of Islam. As Hoogvelt has noted, it is an ontological difference theorized in a self-serving contrast of identity and progress, where capital is cast in the role of economic dynamo *"because* it [is] universal, rational, pluralist and secular," while the "Orient [is] economically stagnant *because* it [is] particularistic, traditional, despotic, wallowing in religious obscurantism, and therefore stagnant."[23] While neoliberals claim to focus on the satisfaction of material needs, personal security, and secular forms of government and society, Islam claims to emphasize both material and spiritual needs, security for the community, and forms of earthly government that fulfill Allah's moral vision for humankind. For Islam, a philosophy that rejects revelation can lead only to social formations full of decadence, moral decay, illegitimate laws, and corrupt government. Marshaling the values that spring from revelation in order to mount a counterhegemonic movement is therefore a central concern for Islam.

The Rights of the Individual

The distinction between knowledge and truth derived from the application of reason and that derived from revelation brings consequences for values associated with the global human rights regime. The success of human rights associated with market discipline, which was the focus of Chapter 2, can be seen in claims that in "virtually all regions of the world . . . there is broad acceptance of the triad of human rights, free markets and democracy as desirable, attainable policy objectives."[24] Of course, the rights referred to here assume a partic-ular conception of rights, defined as the freedom of the individual to invest time, capital, and resources in processes of production and exchange.[25] They are the rights that are said to release the creative potential of humankind in the pur-suit of wealth, benefiting all sections of society through the so-called trickle-down mechanism.

However, while it may be possible to claim that all peoples throughout the world do now, as a matter of fact, embrace the concept of human rights, there can be no certainty that the particular conception of human rights associated with the current global order has achieved universal acceptance. To reiterate the argument of Pasha and Blaney encountered in earlier chapters, the effort to promote particular notions of civility, by proclaiming the "truth" and "univer-sality" of a particular conception of human rights or democracy, may add to the "sense of grievance that motivates a politics that transgresses civility."[26] This sense of grievance is at the root of Islam's objections to the current dominant discourse of human rights. As many Islamic scholars argue, while the domi-nant human rights discourse emphasizes rights and the individual, Islam favors duties and community.

Islam claims to have no difficulty in entering a discourse of universal human rights.[27] As noted above, Islamic thought looks to revelation as the foun-dation on which to build its moral framework, including notions of universal human rights. Accordingly, since God created humankind, and rights are an at-tribute of humankind, rights are God-given and therefore attract the utmost re-spect. As Mayer explains, this revelation inspired Islamic scholars to create a discourse of rights in the early days of the ummah.[28] Although these early schol-arly works originated through different branches of Islam and from different cultural traditions, Mayer argues that it is still possible to identify dominant human rights themes throughout Islamic thought. In particular, she cites the work of al-Farabi in the tenth century and Ibn Rushd (Averroës) in the twelfth century, whom Mayer claims come closest to acknowledging the application of reason in pursuit of rights, truth, and justice.[29] However, these earlier dis-courses on justice and rights served only to reinforce the prevailing view that justice should be garnered from divine revelation found in the Quran and *sharia* law, which embody God's wisdom and will.

Following the conclusion reached in these historic debates has encouraged many religious leaders to argue that the Islamic system of ethics and rights is not in need of further revision.[30] Ayatollah Khomeini, for example, asserted that rights established through reason (natural rights) were a fiction, and that be-lievers should therefore submit to the word of God, where the limits of justice and rights were securely rooted.[31] More recently, in a Friday sermon delivered in the Holy Mosque, Mecca, Shaykh Salih Bin Abdullah Bin Humied argued that the debates on rights and justice conducted many centuries ago represented the first instance of a rights regime in world history. Muslims should therefore be confident in entering the contemporary global human rights discourse because "it was Muslims who exported the principles of Human Rights to other nations, then these rights [were] re-exported to us, as if they were a new human revealing that we have never known before, just like rainwater that falls from he sky, stays in the ground, to reappear afterwards, as a strong spring or a running well."[32] However, while Islamic scholars often acknowledge the concept of human rights as a significant global issue, such that it is now "ugly and abominable to stand against human rights,"[33] the conception, construal, and elucidation of human rights is very different from that found in the dominant neoliberal global discourse.[34]

The priority given to the needs of the ummah over those of the individual, in contrast to the valorization of the individual in neoliberal thought, has already been mentioned above. Contrary to the claims of the human rights associated with market discipline, Islam claims to unleash the creative potential of humankind, not as isolated individuals freely exploiting labor and the natural world, but within the social context of the ummah. Community and exploitation are incompatible.[35] Since the full expression of human capability and capacity requires the prior satisfaction of both material and spiritual needs, which can be achieved only when social order is maintained, claims of individual rights and freedoms make no sense.[36]

Given the social context of the ummah for economic activity, the interests of the individual are inextricably fused with those of the community. It is therefore legitimate to curtail individual freedoms when the security of the ummah and the collective interests of its members are threatened. These interests, which include the maintenance of minimum levels of welfare, housing, education, and medical care, take priority over the rights of the individual to secure self-serving accumulation.[37] Any state based upon the precepts of Islam may therefore limit the rights of the individual, including the exercise of property rights, when sustaining such a claim might harm the community. The duty of the Islamic state is to establish and maintain the principles, norms, and values of Islamic society, not to ensure the rights of individuals in pursuit of personal wealth. States that claim a constitutional affinity with Islam, but fail in their duty to fully implement policies directed at protecting and promoting Islamic values, and populations that fail to hold such states to task, are apostate.[38] In short, while market discipline is expressed in the language of individual rights, the language of Islam is duties to and within the ummah.

The long tradition of emphasizing duties over rights in Islam asserts a hierarchical social order ordained by God, which remains stable only when each accepts his or her social role. Soroush expresses this neatly when he asserts that a "knowledge of duties is as marginal to modern law as that of rights is to traditional religious law."[39] Indeed, many Islamic scholars cite the "cult of individualism" as a primary cause of social instability, which is said to generate arrogant, haughty, and inflated attitudes about self-worth and personal capabilities, attitudes that are presented as deserving greater rewards than the rest of the community.[40] This was perceived many centuries ago when Ibn Khaldun argued that the "cult of individualism" creates a miserable, unhappy, destabilized, and unfulfilling life that must be rejected in favor of duties to Allah and the ummah.[41] There is no place for the individual in the sense suggested by the state of nature and natural rights, which provides the foundations for the dominant conception of human rights. Rather, individualism is seen as a disturber of the collective harmony and is therefore abhorrent.[42] For Islam, by accepting one's social lot, and not behaving as though one is above the fray, all members of the community achieve contented and rewarding lives. Freedom is therefore realized by accepting Allah's order and by each member of the community fulfilling his or her duty to God and the ummah.[43]

The contrast here between Islam's approach to rights and that now widely accepted as universal is clear. For Islam, a neoliberal claim that there is only one legitimate conception of rights demonstrates to many Islamic scholars a level of ignorance that makes any global discourse on rights impossible. Why, some scholars ask, should Islam accept the truth of a Declaration of Human Rights when Islam has had no voice in its construction?[44] Islamic scholars and commentators therefore argue that in view of Islam's historic validation of human rights, there is an urgent need for the world to acknowledge deficiencies in the current human rights regime and to work toward finding a closer fit with Islam, rather than persist in claiming that Islam must be modernized to fit with human rights.[45] Given the context of economic globalization, the failure to accept the need for processes that enable a constant reassessment of dominant values and norms adds to existing feelings of discontent.

Put another way, the more vigorously global civil society promotes market discipline and its associated human rights values, the greater the resistance, creating a "periodic and irresolvable problem of policing the non-civil in civil society."[46] Those who adhere to the norms of "civility" and aspire to the ends promoted by market discipline are included, while those who offend against the "normal," either through critique, reflective alternatives, direct action, or a stubborn refusal to participate, are excluded, including the poor found in many Muslim societies. Disapproval may be registered by the agencies of international society in a number of ways; for example, by including aid conditionalities that emasculate government decision-making powers, by threatening intervention, by simply labeling alternative voices "mad,"[47] or by asserting that the excluded do not possess the moral capacity to engage fully in decision-making processes about their own best interests.[48]

Many Islamic scholars therefore reject the current human rights regime because it describes only one kind of person, valorizes the individual over the community, does not pay sufficient attention to the religious and spiritual nature of human existence, and relies too exclusively on legal rather than social processes for promoting and protecting human rights. Article 18 of the Universal Declaration, for example, on freedom of thought, conscience, and religion, is often seen by Muslims as a form of rampant individualism that threatens to legitimate polytheism and a return to pre-Islamic society.[49] For these reasons, Soroush argues that while Islam must engage with the secularizing pressures that accompany the move to modernization, it is necessary to confront both a Universal Declaration that is "oblivious to religion and the rights of the creator" and the demand to abandon the "truths" found in revelation.[50] Moreover, the demand that all states must now accept liberal democracy as the only legitimate form of government creates tension and conflict between secularist modernizers and religious traditionalists who remain suspicious that the "invitation to democratization of the religious government will ineluctably eviscerate any religious content."[51]

Again, Humied's Friday sermon on human rights is instructive here. In this, Humied asserts that the market-discipline conception of human rights is little more than a shabby arm of imperialism, a political tool in the campaign to convert the world to a soulless, utilitarian belief system that has no room for God and spirituality. Accordingly, "human existence will never enjoy rectitude" if people are deprived of the rights proclaimed by the Prophet and the reformers, who fought for establishing and fixing these rights.

> Don't you see that hundreds of millions of human beings are forced to blaspheme God, receive an education that disdains religion, and causes damage to sacred things. All over the world, there is a gloomy imperialistic and fanatic colonization that steals food and creeds, poisons the thought, and seeks to divert the attention of nations from their beliefs. The world is looking forward to a Declaration of Human Rights in which the sound mind agrees with the Divine Revelation. When such a Declaration is formulated, it can be supported and respected.[52]

While the concept of human rights has gained greater credence within global politics during the last six decades, the neoliberal conception of rights is far from universally endorsed. Islam's alternative notion of human dignity, which emphasizes duty and community rather than rights and the individual, therefore represents a potential counterhegemonic threat to cherished beliefs associated with the globalizing neoliberal world order. Most central to this threat is Islam's definition of property rights, to which we now turn.

Property

Islam's understanding of property begins by recognizing that "God gave dominion over all the assets of the world, including the sun and moon, the sea, animals, the firmament."[53] However, from the earliest days of Islam, these principles were not unconditional. In the decade following the death of the Prophet, for example, Abu Dharr argued that any wealth created by individuals beyond the needs of subsistence, including wealth created through the exploitation of labor and nature, should be used to fulfill the command of God, which was to further the spiritual and material well-being of the ummah. In fulfillment of this duty, it was prerequisite for those engaged in any form of wealth-creation to acknowledge a duty to provide for those unable to secure the basic necessities of subsistence through the application of their own skills and talents.[54] To reinforce this limitation on wealth, the starving and destitute were permitted to take whatever was needed to sustain life, without fear of punishment. *Zakat*, the duty to give charity, is one aspect of this restriction on wealth and property.[55]

A more recent manifestation of Islamic principles relating to property was articulated by Habubullah Peyman, following the Iranian revolution of 1979. Peyman argued that there is no prohibition on the ownership of private property. Neither does the Quran denounce the inequalities that derive from an unequal distribution of wealth, the ownership of the means of production, nor the pursuit of profit and the use of wage labor. However, since all material assets are a gift from God to the Muslim world, resources must be made available to any Muslim who wants to apply his or her creative labor to those resources.[56] This is the Islamic doctrine of "peoples ownership," which, in line with John Locke, begins by asserting that one has legitimate ownership only over the goods produced by one's own labor. Unlike Locke, however, property rights under Islam are limited by a "sufficiency principle," which ordains that property rights are restricted to satisfying one's own needs and those of one's family. Muslims therefore have a duty to freely redistribute excess wealth beyond their own needs to those who are unable to provide for themselves through their own endeavors. Crucially, since labor is the only legitimate means for creating wealth, receiving wages, and a share of profits, there is no legitimacy in a shareholding corporation, where the exploitation of labor is separated from rights to take profits.[57]

Against a background of growing resentment over conspicuous wealth, accumulation, the increasing gap between rich and poor, an awareness of structural exclusion on a global scale, and the erosion of time-honored approaches to social welfare as the market demands cuts or the abolition of transfer payments, Muslim societies often reject neoliberal principles of property and turn instead to those offered by Islam. In some cases, this has opened the space for Muslim socialists to promote the economic principles expressed in the Quran. In the 1970s, for example, Ali Shariati wrote extensively on an Islamic version of historical materialism, which sought to offer a radical reading of Shiism. According to Shariati, the central teachings of Islam offer the oppressed, the poor, and the excluded the means to achieve emancipation from social and political oppression, including the resources to assert economic and social rights. Most significantly, and of particular concern for the capitalist global economy, Shariati argued that the abolition of all institutions associated with property would lead to a more just and classless society.[58] These arguments found a sympathetic ear in the People's Mujahedine and other Muslim organizations dedicated to promoting a political economy that generated further movement toward achieving a particular kind of social order, which they claimed was revealed in the sacred texts.[59]

For many interpretations of Islam, therefore, wealth-creation is not concerned solely with investment, profit maximization, and personal aggrandizement. Indeed, under Islamic economics, the duty to use surplus wealth for the good of the ummah demands that investment and production activity include social-utility calculations before proceeding. This could, for example, include the goal of delivering economic and social rights through full employment, environmental protection, health provision, poverty alleviation, social welfare, and social housing.[60] The aim of profit maximization is not, therefore, concerned solely with increasing personal wealth, although this is not prohibited, but must also be concerned with increasing the well-being of the ummah. In short, and by definition, legitimate economic activity is concerned with both wealth-creation *and* social justice. Accordingly, "before entering the market place and being exposed to the price filter, consumers are expected to pass their claims through the moral filter."[61] This reflective process is intended to sift out socially harmful investment and production activities and to act as a guide for consumer choice. Thus, according to the Islamic view of property, the moral and price filters satisfy both spiritual and material needs within a socioeconomic order that seeks to satisfy the physiological and psychological needs of the community.

An attempt to express these principles is seen in the constitution of the Islamic Republic of Iran. The preamble states that the purpose of the economy is to make provision for the material needs of the population, which is not an end in itself but a means for attaining the ultimate goal of living by Islamic principles and norms. This is contrasted with the prevailing global orthodoxy, and materialist schools of thought, where the economy is seen as an end in itself, "so that it comes to be a subversive and corrupting factor in the course of man's development."

> From this viewpoint, the economic programme of Islam consists of providing the means needed for the emergence of the various creative capacities of the human being. Accordingly, it is the duty of the Islamic government to furnish all citizens with equal and appropriate opportunities, to provide them with work, and to satisfy their essential needs, so that the course of their progress may be assured.[62]

From the perspective of an Islamic approach to property rights, the efficient allocation of resources does not exclude the possibility of private property or the self-serving activity to create wealth. However, the well-being of all members of the ummah is the central purpose of economic activity, and this cannot be achieved in an environment that fails to promote socioeconomic justice. While the market does contribute to the efficient allocation of resources, competition within markets alone does not meet the moral standards expected to achieve Islamic socioeconomic justice. In contrast to the "culturally approved behavior model for a neo-liberal market society based on private property and competition," which remains the dominant order in the global economy, Islamic economics rejects the rational economic actor model in favor of one that gives central place to social welfare and justice.[63]

Consequently, although the individual does have a duty to strive to create wealth, when this choice is made it cannot be realized other than within the context of the ummah. Without the stability and predictability provided by the rules and norms that describe the ummah, the avaricious individual must lead an isolated, atomized, egotistic existence separated from the community. To engage in economic activity merely to generate wealth dedicated to one's own enjoyment, personal aggrandizement, or the craven satisfaction of a lust for power as sanctioned by the global neoliberal order is to exploit the ummah in ways that are morally repugnant. It is this that motivates Islam's claims for ethical superiority over neoliberal hegemony, as practiced under conditions of globalization. Crucially, the spiritual dimension in Islam's economic thought, and the existence of a moral community whose boundaries do not coincide with the state and the modern state system, provides an alternative image of globalization that is unacceptable to neoliberalism and its proponents.

Government, State, and the Ummah

Resistance to modernization, which includes resistance to moral values and principles alien to the tradition of Islam, can be seen in the tension between government and the ummah. According to Islamic principles, the role of government is to "construe the phenomena of God's sovereignty because God's will is embodied in His legislation," which takes priority over the will and orders of all social or political institutions, including the democratic will of the people.[64] The clearest expression of this is seen in the application of sharia law, which must be obeyed not because it is the command of the state but because of its authority as the voice of God. While at first take this seems alien to mature liberal democracies built upon the rule of law, Vaezi insists that in all ideologies and belief systems, including liberalism and socialism, one finds a constitution that proscribes the actions of governments who violate the fundamental beliefs and abiding principles that describe the social and cultural context in which political institutions are embedded.[65] Democratically elected governments, for example, cannot legitimately undertake actions or make decisions that breach fundamental democratic values, even though the majority may support such actions or decisions. In this respect, many scholars argue that the Islamic state is no different from the liberal democratic state, for no majority can overthrow any of the principles and values of Islam.

Accordingly, the starting point for looking at all social, political, and economic issues, including human rights and democracy, is to recognize God's sovereignty. In contrast to the modern secular state, where material and physiological needs provide the focus for government and where the moral and ethical authority of religion is not formally enshrined within a constitution, the purpose of the Islamic state is to act as the guardian of religious values, rather than those said to be guaranteed by international law. In contrast to contemporary global politics, which emphasize rights and democracy, Islam emphasizes the duties of the ruler and the ruled as ordained by God. The state may enact laws and create institutions for regulating the actions of citizens in social, economic, and political affairs, but these remain subject to the guiding norms and laws found in the Quran and sharia law. As noted previously, the constitution of the Islamic Republic of Iran is presented as an attempt to operationalize this principle.[66]

Consequently, it is common to find Islamic scholars arguing that the preferred model of democracy, particularly the notion of majority rule, is "absolutely incompatible with Islam."[67] According to Ahmed Vaezi, when the liberal democratic state abandons the authority of God, relocates moral questions in the private sphere, beyond the limits of government, and seeks legitimation through democracy and rights, society has experienced social and moral decay, typified by welfare-induced sloth.[68] In place of procedural democracy, which seeks legitimation through periodic elections, it is the duty of all Muslims to remain permanently and fully vigilant to ensure that government does not transgress the core principles of Islam. In the current world order, this includes guarding against the importation of values that may be antithetical to Islam.

The duty of the state leader is to see that God's justice is done, not to create a version of justice constructed through reason and rights. The Prophet's message was religious, concerning spiritual guidance, not a message from God on the correct form of government a society should adopt. This message describes a community of the faithful, not a state, its duties, and responsibilities. The spiritual and moral health of the ummah must at all times prevail over the rights of the citizen. For these reasons, many scholars argue that in contrast to values found in secular societies, where the legitimate actions of government are limited by outlawing any interference in the spiritual, private, moral, and social world of the individual and the family, under Islam these are the very issues that are in need of guidance.[69]

Given the impetus for change brought by the forces of economic globalization, changes that touch the lives of all people, governments in states where Islam is the dominant belief system are caught between competing demands. Those who make these demands are often categorized as "modernizers," "reformers," and "neofundamentalists." While "modernizers" pursue the goal of full integration within the global political economy, "reformers" and "neofundamentalists" present a challenge to the neoliberal order.

Modernizers seek to reform and rationalize Islam in an attempt to bring it in line with neoliberal thought and the needs of economic globalization. This is a call for engaging fully in the processes of globalization by accepting the norms, values, and conditionalities of neoliberal global order, including the legitimacy of the global human rights regime. It is also a call to develop a modern secular state capable of developing an efficient administrative role for promoting global capital.[70] For this group, modernization is the "process of progressive complexity and differentiation of institutions and spheres of life," the expansion of the neoliberal global economy, and the further incursion of capitalist market values. Secularization is recognized as an instance of modernization, which differentiates religion from economic and political institutions and the church from culture and conscience.[71] The shift from a theocratic society to a secularized society is seen by modernizers as an inevitable consequence of economic globalization; a shift from action guided by religious tradition to action guided by the needs of a modern economy. Consequently, modernizers argue that neither the material nor the spiritual needs of the ummah can be satisfied by looking to an Islam developed many centuries ago. Instead, modernizers argue that the tensions between the values that describe the new global political economy and those of Islam can be resolved only by constructing a new theology for the twenty-first century and beyond. For modernizers, such a theology must come to terms with the reality of economic globalization and its social consequences, including the secular state and form of government. If that means that Islam must embrace universal human rights, so be it.

The reformers also look to develop a state and form of government that engages with economic globalization. However, while modernizers call for the separation of church and state, reformers seek a synthesis of Islam and the dominant global political economy, in an attempt to "Islamize" some aspects of modernity. In this way, reformers recognize the duty of all cultures to contextualize cherished traditions and values within the emerging, globalized social, economic, and political order. Soroush, who was an important intellectual influence during the early years of the new Islamic Republic of Iran, argues that the only realistic way to overcome existing social and economic deprivations is to engage with economic globalization. However, for Soroush such an engagement does not imply an inevitable corruption of Islam. Indeed, he argues that globalization offers an opportunity to provide the space for greater levels of reflection upon the moral and spiritual world—a process, he notes, that has already begun in the developed world, as signified by feminism, postmodernism, and environmentalism. The Islamic state's engagement with economic globalization therefore offers an opportunity to overcome social deprivations while also contributing to reflections on the vices characteristic of the global political economy from an Islamic perspective.[72] In this way, the state fulfills two roles: first, by improving the social conditions of the people; and second, by playing a facilitating role in new ethical and moral discourses with Islam.

Both the modernizers and reformers are opposed by what Hoogvelt refers to as neofundamentalists, religious leaders who see globalization as an irredeemably corrupting process that should be rejected by all and any available means.[73] Neofundamentalists reject all attempts to engage with the contemporary world of market discipline, where individualism and rights take priority over the ummah and duty.[74] For neofundamentalists, the move to embrace modernization may permit some groups to gain access to technological, scientific, and industrial goods, and services that increase material well-being, but this cannot be achieved without also embracing social values hostile to Islamic thought. Instead, in the face of calls by some groups to accelerate the state's drive toward modernization, neofundamentalists call for a "return to the past" and the reestablishment of sharia law and Islamic social traditions. While it is often assumed that the advanced economies offer the most obvious target for neofundamentalist opposition, this group see the main culprit as "quasi-Islamic" governments who collude with interests associated with economic globalization and thus promote market disciplinary values and "infidel ways."[75] For example, Arkoun argues that "Islam has given humanity an ideal code for living a fulfilled and moral life, which confers honour and dignity on humanity and eliminate(s) exploitation, oppression, and injustice." Since God is the author of laws designed to protect the moral identity of the ummah, "no leader, no government, no assembly or any other authority" can legitimately violate the social and moral foundations of Islam.[76]

Seen in this light, neofundamentalists argue that modernization has encouraged Islam to take a wrong turn. Governments in so-called Islamic states may display all the ritual that is expected of Islam, but their association with developed states suggests that they are apostates who have abrogated the holy law by embracing foreign values, customs, and laws.[77] The removal of such leaders is therefore a legitimate and essential precursor to recapturing an authentic Muslim society. As Mernissi points out, historically, leaders who fail to fulfill the duty to govern through God's law have been assassinated.[78] While neofundamentalists often express anti-Western rhetoric, pointing to the corrosive effect that Western values have on Islam, the elimination of existing leaders remains central. Noting this, Bernard Lewis points to the overthrow of the shah of Iran in 1979 and the assassination of President Sadat of Egypt in 1981, acts that are seen by neofundamentalists as a necessary process of "inner cleansing," before establishing a true Islamic state forged from the values found in sharia law and the rights and duties described in the Quran.[79] Crucially for neofundamentalists, responsibility for achieving a return to the past and for recapturing the spirit of Islamic unity is not solely the responsibility of the citizens of any particular Muslim state but that of the global ummah as a whole. For neofundamentalists, the state and the modern state system take second place to the preservation of the ummah.

It is in the interface of modernization, reform, and neofundamentalism that questions of women's rights emerge. For neofundamentalists, inequality between men and women, or for that matter Muslim and non-Muslim, is not part of a political discourse on rights and citizenship. Instead, these inequalities are part of divine revelation found in the holy scriptures, putting them beyond question, and thus not subject to constitutional inquiry into the nature of citizenship. Therefore, there is no injustice in constitutional rights that reflect the different,

God-given, attributes of men and women. Equality must be judged not by whether men and women share identical rights, but as the equal application of the law to their different roles. Provided a constitution secures the different roles filled by men and women, justice is done.[80]

For reformers and modernists, on the other hand, the continued suppression of women through the invocation of holy scripture is little more than a "mask" for vested interest, constructed on the claim that Islam and economic globalization are so incompatible that the choice is between one or the other, but never both at once. The justification of this claim, which must be sustained if the exploitation of women in both the private and public sphere is to be maintained, requires a justification that would be difficult to construct under conditions of economic globalization. However, by pointing to the past, to interpretations of the holy scriptures undertaken many centuries ago, those who seek to legitimate and justify women's inferior status in Muslim society may be accused of manipulating sacred texts and scholarly works that are inappropriate for today's globalized world order. And, as Mernissi argues, since social and political power has been legitimated by religion since the seventh century, the tradition of inequality between men and women is sustained through the fabrication of false traditions.[81]

Caught between reason and revelation, modernization and tradition, governments have often tried to follow the path of reformists, claiming a correspondence between God's word and their own policies for improving the material needs of the people. However, such policies often open up opportunities for a relatively small group of educated, mostly urban-dwelling citizens, while the less-well-positioned population continue to suffer social and economic deprivations.[82] Fearing that they have been "forgotten by their own people, who have found another identity and are involved in other networks, especially those very strong ones that create profit on an international scale," the majority seek comfort and consolation elsewhere.[83] Alternatively, governments seek to appease the demands of religious leaders and devout followers, reject the values of modernization, and jeopardize the prospect for fulfilling the material needs of the people.[84] In both cases, governments face uncertainties and instabilities, generated by frustrations over the failure to improve social and economic conditions or to protect Islam from the corrupting influence of economic globalization.

Asian Values and Confucianism

The emergence of "Asian Values" as an alternative to the principles expressed in the global human rights regime shares many of the values found in Islam.[85] First, family and community ties are seen as the foundation upon which social harmony and order are built. Such ties call for responsibilities to one's immediate community, not the wider community, and certainly not to some notion of a global moral community. Second, through the mechanism of family and community ties, social order is maintained through moral injunctions that describe the correct way for thinking and acting. While in the West legal injunctions are seen as the primary means for maintaining social control, in Asia social taboos, shame, and dishonor serve to discipline society. Third, social harmony is maintaining when individuals perform their duties to the best of their abilities, a task that takes priority over all concern for self. Rights are defined by the role the individual is allotted within the social order, not through abstract claims like universal human rights and freedoms. Fourth, conflicts of interest must be resolved through processes for building consensus, not through adversarial processes of law. Fifth, as the Chinese sage Mencius argued, political rule must be sanctioned by the "Mandate of Heaven"; however, because Heaven itself cannot speak, the only way we can know the Mandate is to consult the people. Thus, government is legitimated only through the consent of the people, although this is limited by the objective of social harmony.[86]

For most Asian countries the origin of these principles is found in ancient wisdom, rather than in religious texts or the revealed word of God. The foundations of modern Asian Values discourse can be traced back to the work of the social philosopher Confucius (551–471 BC), who developed a system for moral government, justice, and social order that is still taught in many Asian countries today. Like Islam, ancient wisdom asserts that the state should not remain neutral over moral issues but must instead adopt policies toward creating a virtuous society. For many Asians, the failure to promote and protect these ancient principles, and to acquiesce to claims for the universal rights of the individual, leads only to the neglect of duty, ineffective government, and social decay.[87] Indeed, the absence of any equivalent term for human rights in many Asian languages is often seen as evidence that the philosophical traditions of Asia have no use for the language of rights. For example, it has been noted that the Chinese word *Ren* implies human happiness through the love of our fellows, rather than rights as freedoms associated with the global human rights regime.[88] Similarly, in Japanese no term for human rights existed until the nineteenth century. In the 1870s, the movement for human rights adopted the term *minken* as a way of claiming the right and liberty of the people to make claims against the government. In time, the term *jiyu minken undo* (movement for freedom and people's rights) came to be understood specifically as meaning the rights of groups to oppose the government, rather than the rights of the individual.[89]

The Rise of Asian Values

An Asian challenge to the dominant idea of human rights was formally articulated during the 1993 Bangkok regional conference, held preparatory to the United Nations Vienna conference on human rights. The declaration that emerged from the Bangkok meeting affirmed the sovereign authority of the state as a bulwark against the West's proclivity for meddling in the internal affairs of Asian states. The promotion of universal human rights was seen as a significant part of this intrusion. However, while the Bangkok Declaration accepted the universality of human rights, it sought to promote a conception founded on a set of explicitly Asian values. These values, it was argued, stress the importance of Asia's regional particularities; the historical, cultural, social, and philosophical context in which the conception of human rights emerges and the means for implementation are created.[90]

The political context of the Bangkok Declaration offers an insight into existing discourses of human rights. The rise of the "Asian tiger" states during the 1980s and early 1990s was achieved by what Davies had called "market preserving authoritarianism,"[91] an approach to the political economy that stresses strong leadership and social discipline rather than democracy, rights, and individual freedoms. In this view, the success of Western democracies was achieved following economic growth, not, as Mahbubani has argued, by placing the "democratic cart before the economic horse."[92] Asian leaders argued that economic development in the West preceded rather than followed social and political development. For the leaders of many less-developed states, the attempt to promote democracy and human rights in advance of economic development therefore represented a naïve misunderstanding of history. In the face of criticism by some Western INGOs (international nongovernmental organizations), and occasionally Western governments, the tiger states' economic success fostered a growing confidence that their particular approach represented a viable and winning formula. Bangkok offered an opportunity to develop this formula—to assert Asia's growing confidence, to establish an identity distinct from that of the West, and to answer those who sought to disparage Asia's successes.

The context for developing arguments in favor of Asian values was, in part, a reaction to the colonial past. Asian states accused the West of failing to acknowledge the legacy of colonialism, which caused not only delays in economic development but also contributed to the impoverishment of populations.[93] From the perspective of Asian populations, intervention in the name of universal human rights looked like an attempt to concoct a legitimate reason for denying self-determination and the continuation of colonial control over internal affairs by other means. Applying human rights conditions to aid and the conditions of trade was seen as a particular example of postcolonial intervention.

Furthermore, Asian leaders accused the West of failing to acknowledge that the social pathologies now confronting them—illegal drug usage, rising rates of divorce, dysfunctional families, single-parent families, high crime rates, welfare-induced sloth[94]—signaled the onset of social decay. According to some Asian leaders, this decay was clearly evident in the West's fetishization of the individual and material life at the expense of community and social interactions that provide the foundation for leading a fulfilled and happy life.[95] Prime Minister Mohammed Mahathir asked Malaysians to reject Western democratic values, which he claimed were the root cause of moral decline, "homosexual activities, single parents and economic slowdown because of poor work ethic."[96] The link between moral decay and economic decline was a regular theme for Mahathir, who would often stress that to give in to the most modest demands for Western freedoms was the prelude to ever-greater demands that would destroy the existing, economically successful, social order. As a bulwark against the serious shortcomings of Western capitalist development, Asian leaders sought to resist the worst excesses of capitalism by differentiating Western values from Asian values. In short, Asian leaders sought to promote an alternative vision of human rights that supported Asian states economic and political interests and provided a defense against external interference in the internal affairs of states growing in prosperity and confidence.

The Foundations of Asian Values

What is the foundation for Asian values? Following the works of Confucius and his later followers, proponents of Asian values promote social harmony as an essential prerequisite for leading a full and fulfilling life. Confucius argued that it was a grave error to build social order upon religious beliefs, which taught that individual appeal to a deity could alter the will of heaven. Since we cannot have complete knowledge of a supernatural deity, Confucius argued, our only alternative was to devote ourselves to gaining an intimate knowledge of our immediate social world and its problems. A thorough understanding of history was a necessary step along the path to creating a harmonious society that enabled government to discharge its responsibilities for welfare and the conditions for happiness.[97] At the heart of this objective is filial piety *(xiao),* which includes ancestor worship (past relationship), reverence for one's parents (current relationships), and the necessity for descendents (future relationships). Thus, if one worships one's ancestors, reveres one's parents, and has children, continuity and harmony are achieved.

According to Confucian thought, harmony is achieved when all members of society practice appropriate manners, ways of acting, and modes of thought. The failure to adopt these practices disturbs social harmony and thus represents a potential threat to the security, well-being, and happiness of all. Every individual therefore has an obligation to fulfill the social tasks assigned to them as an attribute of their particular status.[98] Put another way, the duties that describe a particular social role exhaust the limits of possible claims against others. Roles are placed within a hierarchical social structure, creating an interdependent social order that is at its strongest when every role-holder performs his or her duties to the highest level.[99] In this schema, the space for self-expression, deviance, and the exploration of alternative ways of thinking and acting is severely limited.[100] The individual is defined by the totality of his or her social role and associated duties. Rosemont expresses this clearly when he argues that in the Confucian social order, we are not autonomous individuals, free to act within our own best interests. Rather, summed up by Rosemont:

I am the totality of the roles I live in specific relation to others. When they have all been specified I have been defined uniquely, fully, and altogether, with no remainder with which to piece together a free, autonomous self.[101]

Given the centrality of duty over rights, and the obligation for citizens to discharge their responsibilities fully, attention to personal achievements, ambition, and self play a limited role in building and maintaining a harmonious society. From the perspective of Asian values, the excessive individualism that characterizes the march of economic globalization must be rejected in favor of the interests of communal harmony. In the words of Prime Minister Lee Kuan Yew, the "Confucian view of order between subject and ruler helps in the rapid transformation of society . . . in other words, you fit yourself to society—the exact opposite of the American rights of the individual."[102] Social, economic, and political decisions should be reached by consensus as a means to maintaining the ethos of Confucian "oneness" and community, rather than the competitive struggle over policy that is characteristic of Western capitalism.[103] Furthermore, the hierarchical order that structures society built upon Asian values demands loyalty to one's superiors, which the idea of individual rights challenges. Consequently, any move to prioritize the rights of the individual over those of the community should be seen as an antiestablishment threat to the hierarchical order that brings social harmony. In the postcolonial period, where state-building, economic planning, and the need to forge a single national identity are central issues, any claim for the rights of the individual appears as a challenge to the authority of government.[104]

It is clear from Confucian teachings that reference to the individual is more concerned with the roles and social attitudes of men than with those of women. Confucianism sets down five fundamental relationships without which the goal of social cohesion and harmony fails. These relationships are: father-son, husband-wife, elder brother–younger brother, older friend–younger friend, and ruler-ruled. In each of these relationships the first of each couplet is accepted as the superior, because of longevity, experience, and the greater wisdom that age brings. All of these relationships are concerned with men. Women get an explicit mention only in the husband-wife couplet, and then only as the inferior partner. Indeed, Billington observes that Confucius himself problematized women, stating that they get out of hand if one is too friendly, and resentful if one is too distant.[105] While it is permissible for the subservient partner to question his superior about actions that might bring consequences for what Confucians called *jen* (love of man, benevolence, care, community interests), and even refuse to follow the wishes of a superior who errs, this risks weakening the five fundamental relationships themselves. Given the centrality of harmony through observing duty and the five fundamental relationships, questioning one's superior is seen as a grave step, and one that should be taken rarely.

This is in contrast to Western liberal attempts to define universal human rights. The work by John Rawls, for example, is seen by Confucians as fundamentally flawed because Rawls begins with assumptions about the presocial individual living under a "veil of ignorance," whose rights are independent of any particular culture or society. For Confucians, human beings only become truly human by experiencing life within society.[106] To express one's humanity outside this context is absurd because it assumes that the extant society has no ancestry, entrusting the conceptualization and creation of the moral society to "thoroughgoing amnesiacs."[107] Moreover, in response to liberal arguments that freedom can be exercised to the extent that it does not harm others, Confucians argue that the concept of harm offers a too-restrictive limitation on a society that is defined by moral rather than legal injunctions. From this perspective, it is said that some actions are so immoral that restrictions on the freedom of the individual are legitimate; for example, a ban on the creation and sale of pornography even by consenting adults.[108]

The distinction between moral and legal injunctions is an important characteristic of Asian values. Since social harmony is achieved through each and every individual performing in accordance with the prevailing moral and ethical order, the emergence of rights as legal injunctions is seen as a failure to exercise due diligence in performing duties. More specifically, in the case of national leadership, the demand for rights implies that leaders have failed in their duty to create and maintain a harmonious institutional framework in which citizens can discharge their duties, a situation that proponents of Asian values see as inconceivable for Asian society. The Western approach, which uses legal means to achieve social order, is seen as a poor alternative, because it encourages the search for legal loopholes that legitimate transgressions, dispelling any sense of shame and freeing the individual from the ethical code that describes Asian values.[109]

The Political Economy of Asian Values

The economic context for introducing and developing Asian values in the global human rights discourse has already been mentioned above. Asian values reflected sustained economic success and a sense of difference and independence from past colonial power. This success was not built entirely upon the foundations of Western-style capitalism, which stresses individualism, rights, and competition. In place of these Western values, it drew upon aspects of Confucianism, which stresses loyalty, hierarchy, harmony, duty, and responsibility. The potential for utilizing dedicated, loyal, committed, and educated workers, characteristics that were transferred from the traditional focus of the family and village to the corporation, offered Asian business interests an opportunity to play a full role in processes of economic globalization. The success of "Confucian capitalism,"[110] a nonindividualistic account of capitalist expansion, challenged the dominant Western liberal version, where rights play a central role. The discourse of Asian values might therefore be seen as providing the philosophical rationale for a new economic model, not for developing some new notion of the "good life" but for exercising social control and the management of exploitative labor relations.[111]

Many influential Asian business interests argue that their role is central to the phenomenon of economic globalization, as capital seeks to open new markets and systems of production. For many industrial leaders, Asian states play a full and central role in the rapid deepening and widening of economic globalizations, which in its earliest contemporary form dates from the late 1970s. Given this central role, Asian states and business interests expected "status parity" as an integral player within a rapidly globalizing world.[112] It was therefore inappropriate for Western states to openly criticize Asian states for their human rights record, still less to use political and economic sanctions as a way of forcing compliance with the international human rights regime. Given the legacy of colonialism, Asian governments argue that what is needed is a period of strong government to deliver economic security before the full range of rights can be considered. What the West saw as authoritarian government was merely a reflection of Asian culture, a set of values that may be very different from those that describe Western culture, but nonetheless an equally valid approach to achieving the "good life," based upon deeply embedded Asian traditions and social beliefs.

However, from the perspective of the politics of human rights, such claims do not necessarily live up to close interrogation. Takeda, for example, has noted that reference to the Confucian tradition played an important role in disciplining workers from the earliest days of Japanese industrialization, and remains central today.[113] The notion of the "corporate family," which provides economic security, health care, housing, and education, stood in the way of developing strong independent trade unions and the pursuit of labor rights. The grip of "company absolutism," which demands long working hours and a singular devotion to the interests of the employer, is seen in the high incidents of suicide when workers feel shame for not working hard enough and letting down both the company and fellow workers. The Japanese term *karoshi*, which is now internationally recognized, indicates those who suffer a permanent disability or death through overwork. In this sense, the promotion of Asian values is seen less as a necessary expression of a particular cultural tradition than as a response to economic interests in a globalized setting.

If Confucian values are used to excuse the paucity of workers' rights, the sanctions threatened by Western states in the name of protecting human rights are no less cynical. The rationale for imposing sanctions on Asian states is often presented as a commitment to international human rights standards by compelling those who fall short to comply. However, some have argued that the accusations of developed states over the poor human rights record in Asia have more to do with economic protectionism than a concern for humanity. As Stoltenbery argues, with US imposition of sanctions on Southeast Asian states, ostensibly because of these states' poor record on unionization and labor standards, "one could plausibly ask, with some degree of cynicism, whether the real driving force is genuine concern for suppressed Southeast Asian workers or pressure from domestic union interests to exclude cheaper imported goods."[114] The call for human rights emanating from Western liberal states, and the Asian-values response, might therefore be understood as "guided not by theoretical or scholarly considerations, but by the needs of international trade and politics."[115]

Cultural Tradition, Economic Aspirations, and Human Rights

As with Islam, questions arise over whether it is possible to represent Asia as a unified entity, possessed of a common moral outlook. Malaysia, for example, can claim both an Islamic and Asian heritage, and the influence of Confucianism in other states is not always clear. However, while not all Asian states fully endorsed the assertions of Asian values, most were receptive to ideas that overturned the last vestiges of colonialism by drawing a clear identity separate from that of the West.[116] Many Asian states also saw expressions of Asian values as defining a particular moral philosophy from which their future economic prosperity would flow.[117] The expression of both economic and postcolonial identity was a central rationale for convening the 1997 meeting of the Association of Southeast Asian Nations (ASEAN) foreign ministers. This meeting provided a platform for ASEAN leaders to enhance the self-esteem of their countries by expunging old colonial attitudes that held Asians to be somehow "lesser beings in a Western universe."[118] Although this meeting was overshadowed by economic crisis in several Asian countries, the original intention was to celebrate the rapid economic success of the region and its capacity for regional cooperation free of Western interference.[119] Most importantly, from a human rights perspective, the meeting was intended to reinforce the cultural commonality of ASEAN countries and to promote their major religions and belief systems as morally equivalent to those of the West.

It should also be noted that enthusiasm for Confucianism has waxed and waned during the recent period of rapid development. In the 1960s and 1970s, developed capitalist states claimed that Confucian values presented a major barrier to achieving economic development. It was argued that the emphases on community rather than individualism, harmony rather the competition, duty rather than rights, and moral rather than legal injunctions, were at odds with the values that had delivered liberal economic success in Western states. Following the rise of the Asian tigers, Confucianism in the guise of Asian values made a virtue of the differences, capitalizing on the obedience and loyalty of Asian workers and the acceptance of hierarchical and patriarchal work methods reflecting traditional social relations. At the level of global and international politics, Asian values were invoked in claims for "status parity," an expression of independence and partnership that demanded an equal voice in global economic and political decisionmaking. Following the 1997 economic crisis, Confucianism was used as a symbol of unity, strength, continuity, and stability, which sought to reinforce ideas of social solidarity during periods of social stress.[120] Today, Confucianism is once again seen as the foundation upon which to build a new economic future. China, for example, has reintroduced the study of Confucianism to the school curriculum for the first time in many decades.

Throughout the modern period, however, shifts in emphasis on Confucianism were motivated by the economic interests of those closest to the apex of the hierarchical social order.[121] While the discourse of human rights centering on the global human rights regime was not dismissed summarily by those who promoted Asian values, fulfilling the obligations of the international human rights regime was not the prime concern of Asian governments. Instead, Asian governments, like other governments of less-developed states, were more concerned with economic development than with rights and democracy. The defense for this position was that, historically, developed states had followed the path of economic development over many decades before responding to demands for rights and democracy. Less-developed states should therefore be left to take the same path. In the current period, it was necessary for governments to act decisively, even at the cost of human rights, if nations were to break out of the "vicious circle of poverty" sustained by past social structures opposed to changing the status quo.[122]

Liberal democracy and rights are not therefore high on the agenda of Asian countries. A political culture with its foundations in Confucianism is more concerned with democracy understood as social harmony, rather than as a mechanism through which citizens express civil, political, and economic rights and preferences. Mauzy, for example, notes that many Asians believe that individualism, rights, and liberal democracy produce weak government and social destabilization.[123] For proponents of Asian values, politics should be concerned with providing the conditions for seeking collective, consensual solutions to social and economic problems. While liberals see rights as antimajoritarian, as a bulwark against the tyranny of the majority, Asian values prefer nonconflictual processes that move toward consensual agreement along the path to socioeconomic development and order.[124]

*   *   *

Both Islam and Confucianism are subject to many subtle interpretations that potentially lend support to many political regimes and political actions.[125] The two belief systems discussed here have been selected because of their growing and future influence on global politics. While accepting this, this chapter has sought to identify the central common characteristics of Islamic and Asian thought. Each of these traditions offers a critique of the international human rights regime while also offering an alternative guide for a future regime. Other belief systems might have been included—Buddhism, for example[126]—which also have the potential for challenging the existing human rights regime and its conceptual underpinnings. While each alternative approach would no doubt argue that it, and it alone, has the key to defining and securing rights and duties, there is no reason to believe that any will offer a more inclusive regime. The critiques offered by non-Western political thought, like those offered by recent Western political thought, should therefore be seen as a consequence of the forces of globalization, as actors respond to the new and still emerging socioeconomic contexts.

Notes

1. For a good discussion of cultural relativism, see Michael Freeman, *Human Rights* (Cambridge, UK: Polity, 2002).

2. See Tony Evans, *US Hegemony and the Project of Universal Human Rights* (Basingstoke, UK: Macmillan, 1996).

3. Moses Moskovitz, *International Concern with Human Rights* (Dobbs Ferry, N.Y.: Oceana Publications, 1974), p. 161.

4. Typical of these disagreements is the "tea party" that Eleanor Roosevelt hosted on the Sunday following the first meeting of the commission. At that gathering, deep disagreements emerged between C. P. Chang (vice-chair of the commission) and Charles Malik (rapporteur). Chang urged Malik and others to read Confucius before making any decisions on the foundations of human rights. Roosevelt, who saw the task of the commission to be to "complete a draft Bill in two weeks time," saw no useful purpose in pursuing such philosophical arguments. See box 5487, papers of Eleanor Roosevelt, Roosevelt Library, Hyde Park, New York.

5. Nancy Fraser, "Rethinking Recognition," *New Left Review,* no. 3 (May–June, 2000).

6. Samuel P. Huntington, *The Clash of Civilizations: Remaking of World Order* (New York: Touchstone, 1997).

7. R. J. Vincent, *Human Rights and International Relations* (Cambridge: Cambridge University Press, 1986).

8. J. Salmi, *Violence and the Democratic State* (Oxford: Oxford University Press, 1993); Kees van der Pijl, *Transnational Class and International Relations* (London: Routledge, 1998).

9. Susan George, *The Lucano Report* (London: Pluto, 1999).

10. Stephen A. James, "Reconciling International Human Rights and Cultural Relativism: The Case of Female Circumcision," *Boethics* 8, no. 1 (1994): 4.

11. Henry Rosemont, "Human Rights: A Bill of Worries," in *Confuciansim and Human Rights*, ed. William Theodore De Bary and Tu Weiming (New York: Columbia University Press, 1998), p. 64.

12. Antony Black, "Classical Islam and Medieval Europe: A Comparison of Political Philosophies and Culture," *Political Studies* 41 (1993): 58–69.

13. The term *reason* is not used here in the Orientalist sense, which contrasts Western rationality and its application to science, philosophy, and social organization with non-Western irrationality and ignorance. Instead, reason and revelation are understood here as equally valid modes of rationality, each dedicated to discovering truths about the natural world and humankind's place within it. The will of God revealed through Islamic theology is as rational for Muslims as the empirical world revealed through scientific method is for Western thought.

14. Ali Mohammadi, "The Culture and Politics of Human Rights in the Context of Islam," in *Islam and Encountering Globalization*, ed. Ali Mohammadi (London: RoutledgeCurzon, 2002), pp. 111–130.

15. Of course, neoliberal political economy does not satisfy the material needs of all. Rather, it meets the needs of those who possess the purchasing power. It cannot

therefore be claimed that neoliberalism provides security in the broad sense of the term, which includes economic security.

16. Ronald A. T. Judy, "Sayyid Qutb's *Fiqh al-waqi'i,* or New Realist Science," *boundary* 2, no. 31 (2004): 113–149.

17. J. Plamentaz, ed. *Thomas Hobbes: Leviathan* (London: Fontana, William Collins, 1969).

18. Secularism does not imply that a society lacks religious conviction, as is seen in the United States, with its millions of "born-again" Christians. Instead, secularism implies the separation of religious beliefs from the political, social, and economic decisionmaking. For example, Article 1 of the US Bill of Rights states categorically that "Congress shall make no law respecting an establishment of religion, or prohibiting the free exercise thereof; or abridging the freedom of speech, or of the press; or the right of the people peaceably to assemble, and to petition the Government for a redress of grievances." Article 4 of the US Constitution states that "no religious Test shall ever be required as a Qualification to any Office or public Trust under the United States." It explicitly forbids the adoption of a state religion and the practice of religion in schools.

19. Qutb quoted in Judy, "Sayyid Qutb's *Fiqh al-waqi'i,* p. 119.

20. Mahmood Monshipouri, "Islamic Thinking and the Internationalization of Human Rights," *The Muslim World* 84 (1994): 217–239.

21. This is not to argue that a clear division can be made between the freedoms claimed by the individual and those claimed by the community. Indeed, Enlightenment thinkers were concerned with investigating questions of how the individual can be free within community. However, the liberal focus on the individual is widely accepted. See Jean-Jacques Rousseau, *The Social Contract,* trans. Maurice Cranston (Harmondsworth, UK: Penguin, 1983).

22. Judy, "Sayyid Qutb's *Fiqh al-waqi'i,*" pp.113–149.

23. Ankie Hoogvelt, *Globalization and the Postcolonial World: The New Political Economy of Development* (Basingstoke, UK: Palgrave, 2001) (emphasis in original).

24. M. Conley and D. Livermore, "Human Rights, Development, and Democracy," *Canadian Journal of Development Studies* 16, no. 1 (1996): 19–26.

25. Mary A. Tetrault, "Regimes and Liberal World Order," *Alternatives* 13, no. 1 (1988): 5–26.

26. Mustapha Kamel Pasha and David L. Blaney, "Elusive Paradise: The Promise and Perils of Global Civil Society," *Alternatives* 23, no. 4 (1998): 417–540.

27. Norani Othman, "Grounding Human Rights Arguments in Non-Western Culture: Shari'a and the Citizenship Rights of Women in a Modern Islamic State," in *The East Asian Challenge for Human Rights,* ed. Joanne R. Bauer and Daniel A. Bell (Cambridge: Cambridge University Press, 1999), pp. 169–192.

28. Ann Elizabeth Mayer, *Islam and Human Rights: Tradition and Politics* (London: Pinter, 1995).

29. Ernst cites the *Niche for Lamp* of al-Khatib alTabrizi (d. 1337) as another useful and widely drawn upon source that functions as a source of ethical behavior. See Carl W. Ernst, *Following Muhammad: Rethinking Islam in the Contemporary World* (London: University of Carolina Press, 2003).

30. The tenth-century *Ijtihad* saw an agreement that all important interpretations of the Quran and the hadith were settled and that no further argumentation would be countenanced. See Mahmoud Monshipouri, *Islam, Secularism, and Human Rights in the Middle East* (Boulder, Colo.: Lynne Rienner, 1998).

31. For a recent commentary on Khomeini's conception of freedom, see Susan Siavoshi, "Ayatollah Khomeini and the Contemporary Debate on Freedom," *Journal of Islamic Studies* 18, no. 1 (2007): 14–42.

32. Shaikh Salih Bin Abdullah Bin Humied. "Friday Sermon in the Holy Mosque—Human Rights." (Mecca, n.p., 2000).

33. Ibid.

34. Azzam Tamimi, "Islam and Human Rights," Institute of Islamic Political Thought, www.ii-pt.com/web/paper/islam&h.html, 2001.

35. Kees van der Pijl, "Transnational Class Formation and State Forms," in *Innovation and Transformation in International Studies*, ed. Stephen Gill and James Mittelman (Cambridge: Cambridge University Press, 1997), pp. 105–133.

36. Judy, "Sayyid Qutb's *Fiqh al-waqi'i*," pp. 113–149.

37. Suhrub Behdad, "Islamization of Economics in Iranian Universities," *International Journal of Middle East Studies* 27 (1995): 193–217.

38. Judy, "Sayyid Qutb's *Fiqh al-waqi'I*," pp. 113–149.

39. Abdolkarim Soroush, *Reason, Freedom, and Democracy in Islam,* ed. and trans. M. Sadri and A. Sadri (Oxford: Oxford University Press, 2002), p. 62.

40. For a recent exposition on individualism, see Tibor R. Machan (London: Routledge, 1998).

41. I. Khaldun, *The Muqaddimah,* vol. 2, trans. F. Rozenthal (London: Routledge & Kegan Paul, 1967).

42. Fatima Mernissi, *The Veil and the Male Elite: A Feminist Interpretation of Women's Rights in Islam* (New York: Basic Books, 1991).

43. Khaldun notes that slavery is a permitted commercial transaction, a tradition that, according to Lewis, was accepted until very recently. See Khaldun, *The Muqaddimah*; B. Lewis, *The Crisis of Islam: Holy War and Unholy Terror* (London: Phoenix, 2004).

44. Mohammadi, "Culture and Politics of Human Rights in the Context of Islam." This is not entirely true. The Universal Declaration was drafted at a time when Pakistan and Saudi Arabia were members of the United Nations. However, the Saudi representative on the Commission for Human Rights was a Lebanese Christian and the overwhelming majority of member-states were Christian. See also Mohamed Berween, "International Bills of Human Rights: An Islamic Critique," *International Journal of Human Rights* 7 (2003): 129–142; and Evans, *US Hegemony*.

45. Fred Halliday, *Islam and the Myth of Confrontation: Religion and Politics in the Middle East* (London: Tauris, 2003).

46. Ibid.

47. James Keeley, "Towards a Foucauldian Analysis of International Regimes," *International Organization* 44, no. 1 (1990): 83–105.

48. Barry Hindess, "Power and Rationality: The Western Conception of Political Community," *Alternatives* 17, no. 2 (1992): 149–163.

49. Fatima Mernissi, *Islam and Democracy: Fear of the Modern World* (Cambridge, Mass.: Persius Publishing, 1992).

50. Soroush, *Reason, Freedom, and Democracy in Islam*, p. 125.

51. Ibid.

52. Humied, "Friday Sermon ."

53. Khaldun, *The Muqaddimah*.

54. Maxime Rodinson, *Islam and Capitalism* (London: Alan Lane, 1974).

55. *Zakat* is usually calculated at a minimum of 2.5 percent of wealth, not income. While this may be achievable during times of growth and prosperity, in times of depression it may strain any economy. A general fall in profits makes zakat less sustainable at a time when there is growing unemployment.

56. Suhrub Behdad, "Islamization of Economics in Iranian Universities," *International Journal of Middle East Studies* 27 (1995): 193–217.

57. Nikhil Aziz, "Human Rights Debate in an Era of Globalization: Hegemony of Discourse," in *Debating Human Rights: Critical Essays from the United States and Asia*, ed. Peter Van Ness (London: Routledge, 1999), pp. 32–55.

58. For a brief outline of Ali Shariati's work, see Behdad, 1995. "Islamization of Economics."

59. Of course, the sacred texts of all religions have always been open to particular interpretations. The case of the Mujahedine is no different in this respect.

60. Karen Pfeifer, "Political Islam: Essays from the Middle East Report," Report by the Middle East Research and Information Project, 1997.

61. M. Umer Chapra, "Islamic Economics: What Is It and How It Developed," in *Economic History Net*, ed. Economic History Association, http://eh.net/encyclopedia/article/chapra.islam (Economic History Association, 2006).

62. The constitution of the Islamic Republic of Iran can be found at http://www.iran chamber.com/government/laws/constitution.php.

63. Pfeifer, "Political Islam: Essays."

64. Ahmed Vaezi, *Shia Political Thought* (London: Islamic Centre of England, 2004).

65. Ibid.

66. See the constitution of the Islamic Republic of Iran at http://www.servat.unibe.ch/icl/ir00000_.html

67. Vaezi, *Shia Political Thought*.

68. Diane K. Mauzy, "The Human Rights and 'Asian Values' Debate in Southeast Asia: Trying to Clarify the Key Issues," *Pacific Review* 10 (1997): 201–236.

69. Vaezi, *Shia Political Thought*.

70. Robert Cox, "Democracy in Hard Times: Economic Globalization and the Limits to Liberal Democracy," in *The Transformation of Democracy*, ed. Anthony McGrew (Cambridge, UK: Polity, 1997), pp. 49–75.

71. Soroush, *Reason, Freedom, and Democracy in Islam*, editors' introduction, p. xvi.

72. Ibid.

73. Hoogvelt, *Globalization and the Postcolonial World,* Chapter 9.

74. Soroush, *Reason, Freedom, and Democracy in Islam*, editors' introduction.

75. Bernard Lewis, *The Crisis of Islam: Holy War and Unholy Terror* (London: Phoenix, 2004).

76. Quoted in Mohammadi, "Culture and Politics of Human Rights in the Context of Islam."

77. Lewis, *Crisis of Islam.*

78. Mernissi, *Islam and Democracy: Fear of the Modern World.*

79. Ibid.

80. Vaezi, *Shia Political Thought.*

81. The literature on women's rights in Islam is extensive. See, for example, Abdulhamid A. Al-Hargan, "Saudi Arabia and the International Covenant on Civil and Political Rights, 1966: A Stalemate Situation," *International Journal of Human Rights* 9, no. 4 (1995); Berween, "International Bills of Human Rights"; Christopher Goodwin, "Woman at War with the Mullahs," *Sunday Times*, London, April 7, 2006; Mernissi, *The Veil and the Male Elite*; Monshipouri, "Islamic Thinking."

82. See United Nations Development Programme, *"Human Development Report, 2000—Human Rights and Human Development"* (Oxford, UK: UNDP, 2000).

83. Malcolm D. Brown, "An Ethnographic Reflection on Muslim-Christian Dialogue in the North of France: The Context of *Laicite*," *Islam and Christian-Muslim Relations* 13, no. 1 (2002); Mernissi, *Islam and Democracy: Fear of the Modern World*, p. 53.

84. Mernissi, *Islam and Democracy: Fear of the Modern World.*

85. Some Asian countries, Malaysia, for example, are both predominately Muslim and leading exponents of "Asian values." The similarity between Asian values founded upon ancient wisdom and those of Islam may explain why they share many social values.

86. William H. Meyer, *Human Rights and International Political Economy in Third World Nations* (Westport, Conn.: Praeger, 1998).

87. Mauzy, "The Human Rights and 'Asian Values' Debate," p. 229.

88. Christine A. Hemingway, "An Exploratory Analysis of Corporate Social Responsibility: Definitions, Motives, and Values," in *Centre for Management and Organisational Learning* (Hull, UK: University of Hull Business School, 2002).

89. Sachiko Takeda, "Individualism, Human Rights, and Modernization: The Case of Japan," Ph.D., diss., University of Southampton, 2005.

90. P. Alston, "The UN Human Rights Record: From San Francisco to Vienna and Beyond," *Human Rights Quarterly* 16, no. 2 (1994): 375–390; L. G. Arrigo, "A View from the United Nations Conference on Human Rights, Vienna, June 2003," *Bulletin of Concerned Asian Scholars* 25, no. 3 (1993): 69–72.

91. Michael C. Davies, "The Price of Rights: Constitution and East Asian Economic Development," *Human Rights Quarterly* 29, no. 2 (1998).

92. Kishore Mahbubani, "The West and the Rest," *The National Interest* (Summer 1992).

93. Anthony Woodiwiss, *Globalization, Human Rights, and Labour Law in Pacific Asia* (Cambridge: Cambridge University Press, 1998).

94. Mauzy, "The Human Rights and 'Asian Values' Debate."

95. Woodiwiss, *Globalization, Human Rights, and Labour Law.* Evidence for this claim might be seen in the UNDP Human Development report of 1998. In this report the authors note that although the wealth of people in the United States has more than doubled since the mid-1950s, the percentage of those claiming to be happy has been in continuous decline since 1957. See United Nations Development Programme, *Human Development Report, 1998—Consumption for Human Development* (Oxford, UK: UNDP, 1998).

96. Kenneth Christie and Denny Roy, *The Politics of Human Rights in East Asia* (London: Pluto Press, 2001), p. 46.

97. Ray Billington, *Understanding Eastern Philosophy* (London: Routledge, 1997).

98. Status is not necessarily a birthright. For much of Chinese history, for example, a system of public examinations, open to all, was designed to ensure that only the most able achieved high office.

99. Joseph Chan, "The Confucian Perspective on Human Rights for Contemporary China," in *East Asian Challenge for Human Rights*, ed. Joanne R. Bauer and Daniel A Bell (Cambridge: Cambridge University Press, 1999). Englehart notes that Singapore's People's Action Party resorted to publishing the school grades of its candidates as an indication of its superiority, creating a "hierarchical structure of unequals," an elitist group whose rationale for assuming power was one of natural superiority. See Neil A. Englehart, "Rights and Culture in the Asian Values Argument: The Rise and Fall of Confucian Ethics of Singapore," *Human Rights Quarterly* 22, no. 2 (2000).

100. Takeda, "Individualism, Human Rights, and Modernization: The Case of Japan."

101. Henry Rosemont, "Why Take Rights Seriously? A Confucian Critique," in *Human Rights and the World's Religions*, ed. Leroy S. Rouner (Notre Dame, Ind.: University of Notre Dame Press, 1988), p. 177.

102. Reported in the *New Straits Times,* July 2, 1991, p. 1.

103. Arif Dirlik, "Confucius in the Borderlands: Global Capitalism and the Reinvention of Confucianism," *boundary* 22, no. 3 (1995).

104. Mauzy, "The Human Rights and 'Asian Values' Debate." See also R. Whetherley (2002), "Harmony, Hierarchy, and Duty Based Morality: The Confucian Antipathy Towards Human Rights," *Journal of Asian Pacific Communications* 12, no. 2 (2002): 245–267. See V. T. Tamilmoran, *Human Rights in Third World Perspective* (Ithaca,

N.Y.: Cornell University Press, 1992), for arguments concerning the need to build a nation and achieve national independence in the postcolonial period.

105. Billington, *Understanding Eastern Philosophy.*

106. Chan, "Confucian Perspective."

107. Rosemont, "Human Rights: A Bill of Worries," p. 176.

108. Chan, "Confucian Perspective."

109. I. Jacobs, G. Guopei, and P. Herbig, "Confucian Roots in China: A Force for Today's Business," *Management Decision* 33, no. 10 (1995); Takeda, "Individualism, Human Rights, and Modernization: The Case of Japan."

110. Harriet T. Zurndofer, "Confusing Confucianism with Capitalism: Culture as Impediment and/or Stimulation to Chinese Economic Development," paper presented at the Third Global Economic History Network, Konstanz, Germany, 2004.

111. Dirlik, "Confucius in the Borderlands." Both Dirlik and Takeda note the growing levels of consumerism, job-hopping, and expressions of individualism in Asia, which seem to indicate a rejection of Confucianism.

112. Christie and Roy, *The Politics of Human Rights in East Asia.*

113. Takeda, "Individualism, Human Rights, and Modernization: The Case of Japan."

114. Clyde D. Stoltenbery, "Globalization, 'Asian Values,' and Economic Reform: The Impact of Tradition and Change on Ethical Values in Chinese Business," *Cornell International Law Journal* 33, no. 3 (2000): 715.

115. Dirlik, "Confucius in the Borderlands," p. 266. For an overview of Asian values associated with doing business, see Ngaire Woods, "Order, Globalization, and Inequality in World Politics," in *Inequality, Globalization, and World Politics*, ed. Andrew and Ngaire Woods Hurrell (Oxford: Oxford University Press, 1999), pp. 56–57.

116. Bauer and Bell, eds., introduction to *East Asian Challenge.*

117. Mark R. Thompson, "Pacific Asia After 'Asian Values': Authoritarianism, Democracy, and 'Good Governance,'" *Third World Quarterly* 25, no. 6 (2004).

118. "Asian Values Revisited: What Would Confucius Say Now?" *Economist,* July 24, 1989, pp. 25–27.

119. Van Ness, introduction to *Debating Human Rights.*

120. Thompson, "Pacific Asia After 'Asian Values.'"

121. Dirlik, "Confucius in the Borderlands."

122. K. Mahbubani, "The West and the Rest," *National Interest* 28 (Summer 1992): 3–12.

123. Mauzy, "The Human Rights and 'Asian Values' Debate," p. 229.

124. Stephen C. Angle, *Human Rights and Chinese Thought: A Cross-Cultural Inquiry* (Cambridge: Cambridge University Press, 2002), pp. 229–239.

125. Chan, "Confucian Perspective."

126. Bauer and Bell, *East Asian Challenge*; Takeda, "Individualism, Human Rights, and Modernization: The Case of Japan."

5

Human Rights
in Corporate and
Multilateral Organizations

This chapter moves on from the conceptual debate about human rights to examine the global political economy context in which rights are embedded. We have already looked at conceptual and theoretical critiques developed during recent decades. I have argued that while no single critique can claim to have fatally shaken the liberal foundations upon which the global human rights regime is built, collectively these critiques have eroded those foundations. The claim that the material interdependence characteristic of globalization would also bring moral interdependence assumed that the Western tradition of rights would outweigh all other cultures.[1] Instead, globalization has given greater voice to other cultural traditions, while also stimulating further critical reflection on Western political thought. At the very moment when the global human rights regime looks to extend its formal reach, to achieve objectives it set itself decades ago, the foundations upon which the regime is built seem less secure.

The institutions for promoting human rights assume that the state is the central actor on the global stage, and thus the appropriate actor for overseeing the implementation of regime rules and norms, even while the state is also considered to be the primary violator of human rights. A characteristic of globalization, however, is the rise of nonstate actors that are in possession of resources greater than many states.[2] For some, this phenomena offers an opportunity for transnational corporations, global financial institutions, and international organizations to act as a counterbalance to the excesses of governments implicated in gross violations of human rights, by spreading human rights expectations and practices to every corner of the world.[3] Hopkins, for instance, argues that if the "bottom line" is the only relevant consideration for business enterprises, then it is imperative that business seeks to reduce instances of social unrest, and consequent loss of profits by engaging with humanitarian issues.[4] To achieve this goal, Hopkins proposes the institutionalization of a "planetary bargain" that satisfies both the interests of capital and those of humanity. Accordingly, the success of a corporation should be judged not only as a measure of "doing well" in generating profits, but also on "doing good" by accepting moral responsibilities that include the promotion of human rights and environmental protection.[5]

Opponents of globalization, on the other hand, argue that the new global order offers ever greater opportunities for new kinds of exploitation and consequent violations of human rights. From this view, the so-called "planetary bargain" between business and human rights is little more than a public-relations exercise, which seeks to mask the singular profit maximization ethos of corporations by manufacturing the image of the vigilant, corporate, human rights campaigner. For critics, the "bargain" is more concerned with wielding power and influence on the institutions of global governance, not in the cause of human rights but in an attempt to gain control over regulation that defines the rights of capital. Part of this project includes restricting any attempt to promote rights that might challenge the global free market and the continued expansion of economic globalization.[6] In particular, capital seeks to expand the freedoms associated with property, including intellectual and investment rights. Moreover, critics argue that recent high-profile corporate activity designed to demonstrate concern for social issues (e.g., the Global Compact, measures to monitor supply-chain producers' human rights records, and acts of philanthropy) are merely an attempt to placate public outrage following well-publicized human rights failures: Union Carbide in India (Bhopal), Shell in Nigeria (Ogoniland), Unocal (Burma), and the Nestlé infant-formula marketing campaigns in less-developed states. The multilateral trade and financial organizations have also drawn the attention of critics, who argue that current policy and practice show a complete disregard for human rights.[7]

Hierarchy, Power, and Influence

The transformation of the global order from an international to a global economy brought calls for a reassessment of methods for promoting and protecting human rights. Critics of globalization painted a world order where the imperative of sustained economic expansion took priority over all other considerations. It was argued that human beings were seen increasingly as workers—as a means to achieving some higher economic end, rather than as individuals with human wants, needs, and rights.[8] Continued talk of rights, so the criticism continued, was becoming more concerned with legitimating and maintaining the rights of capitalist, free market relations and less with fulfilling the promise of universal human rights.[9] Those who sought to claim rights beyond this narrow view were increasingly disparaged as conservative traditionalists standing in the way of progress toward prosperity for future generations.[10] At the heart of these criticisms was the view that the post–Cold War era was characterized by a new complex of socioeconomic actors who did not sit comfortably within existing policies and practices for promoting and protecting human rights. In particular, critics began to voice concern about transnational corporate and international economic institutional complicity with human rights violations, which, they argued, could not be addressed through international law.

Against this, according to many world leaders, economic globalization is a "fact" rather than a "political choice,"[11] an "irresistible and irreversible" historic event,[12] and a "force of nature" that "seemed to lead inexorably in one direction."[13] Keeping in mind the postmodernist argument that we first encountered in Chapter 3—that language signifies complex categories of thought and meaning beyond the external reality it seeks to describe[14]—this use of language asserts a "naturalist" account of globalization, which also resonates with the natural rights foundations that support the dominant liberal view of human rights. In this account, globalization is a new phase of history, preordained and impervious to all resistance. Global capitalism and its associated liberal rights should therefore be accepted for what they are: an inherent characteristic of humankind, not a self-consciously made choice about our preferred pathway to the good life.[15]

Accordingly, the global order is characterized as a "natural" hierarchical structure that places economic interests at the top. Despite the rhetoric, which often suggests that the new order represents a new moral turn in the events of humankind, trade issues and financial flows continue to take priority over all other considerations. And since the new order is "natural," resistance is futile. Acquiescence, on the other hand, brings the promise of a better life for all, at some unspecified time. The former UN Secretary-General, Kofi Annan, seemed to accept this account when he argued that, in "many cases, governments only find the courage and resources to do the right thing when business takes the lead."[16] In this view, within the current stage of the evolutionary "natural" global order, "society's needs have exceeded the capabilities of governments."[17] Thus, governments, including democratically elected governments, no longer have the capacity to fulfill their obligations to protect and promote human rights. Where in the past it was assumed that governments played the lead role in securing the human rights of citizens, today it is necessary to involve powerful transnational corporations in any future planning for human rights. In defending this important shift in focus, proponents of the naturalist account deny that it represents a move toward nondemocratic forms of governance. Instead, proponents argue that it merely reflects the new realities of the global market, where consumer, investor, and worker "stakeholders" demand higher standards of ethical behavior for production and exchange. In short, market-driven ethical behavior is commensurate with democracy. We return to this issue later.

The new complexities confronting the implementation of human rights within the emerging hierarchical global order is seen in several arguments found in recent human rights talk. Critics claim to have detected that the interests of the global political economy are consistently privileged over those of human rights. In a report for the Sub-Commission on Promotion and Protection of Human Rights, Oloka-Onyango and Deepika Udagana observe that there exists a "new orthodoxy or ethos about the economic dimensions of globalization that exalts it above all other human values or phenomena [even] above the basic conditions of human beings themselves."[18] This is seen most clearly in programs for economic restructuring, where the "measures being pursued actually undermine the progressive realization of [human rights]."[19] While the major multilateral economic institutions have recently voiced an interest in the human rights consequences of their own policies, the development of new measures is conducted in "splendid isolation" from the human rights machinery, raising many unanswered questions.[20] Crucially, should human rights or economic interests take priority when there is a clear conflict of interest?[21] Although Article 103 of the UN Charter makes provision for member-states to prioritize the aims and objectives of the Organization (security and human rights), where these obligations conflict with other obligations made under other international agreements, the subcommission concludes that economic interests continue to take precedence.[22]

A second argument concerns the emergence of influential economic non-state actors as major players within the global political economy, raising questions about where power is located under conditions of globalization. As we shall see in Chapter 6, while in the past it was assumed that state power eclipsed the power of all other global actors, today many argue that this is no longer clear.[23] Within the context of economic globalization, the central policy objectives of economic growth and development cannot be achieved without the state cooperating with the private interests of nonstate actors, including large transnational corporations and international trade and financial institutions.[24] Given the focus of economic development that these new relationships are supposed to foster, and the potential for a state's human rights obligations to be compromised, it remains unclear whether humanitarian interests can be secured within this context. As the UN subcommission's report notes, we need only recall how developing states are compelled by trade rules and the conditionalities imposed for aid to recognize the negative impact such relationships bring for human rights.[25] Moreover, the common practice of using the terms *economic growth* and *economic development* synonymously confuses the generation of wealth with improvements in the quality of life for some with that of improvements for all.[26] For critics of the globalization/human rights nexus, development implies something more than wealth creation; it must include the provision of public goods, access to healthcare, education, housing, fresh water, nutrition, and the protection of human rights, no matter the individual's position in relation to the global political economy.

A further argument suggests that economic globalization has seen a shift of emphasis from ideas of a national economy to that of the global economy. The welfare state that dominated liberal thinking during the second half of the twentieth century, which presupposed the existence of an international system of states and national economies, each engaged in external trade across borders, has given way to a new borderless order. As Ruggie has argued, "markets have gone global, diminishing the effectiveness of border measures and putting enormous pressure on merely national grand social bargains."[27] Whereas in the previous period states could apply tariffs and manipulate exchange rates, today such measures cannot be implemented. Rather than managing the national economy, states are now engaged in responding to the needs of the global economy. As we shall see in Chapter 7, it is the separation of the economy from democratic decision-making processes that inspires criticism of, and resistance to, economic globalization.

Perhaps most crucially, from the perspective of developing human rights machinery, agency is given priority over structure when considering violations of human rights. The creation of the International Criminal Court, the tribunals for Rwanda and Former Yugoslavia, and many of the campaigns conducted by nongovernmental organizations are all concerned with identifying those individuals who are responsible for violations. While it should not be denied that many violations of human rights are perpetrated purposefully and intentionally by individual agents, to narrow our understanding of violations to the level of personal responsibility alone overlooks the far greater number of violations that are a consequence of the structures of the current world order. As Johan Galtung has noted, structures are not amenable to arrest, legal proceedings, and punishment, even though structure is often at the root of many violations of human rights.[28] Who, critics ask, is personally responsible for the 750 million who do not have enough food to eat each day to lead a dignified life? Or the one-third of the global populations who lack access to clean water, the one-half who do not have adequate sanitation, and the thirty-five thousand children who die each day from malnutrition and diseases related to malnutrition?[29]

A final argument that confronts the full implementation of all human rights under conditions of economic globalization concerns a reluctance to act upon the accepted principle of the unity of rights: economic, social, cultural, civil, and political. While it is common practice for states to assert the unity of rights during UN debates and summits, civil and political rights are often seen as taking priority over economic, social, and cultural rights. This is not a new phenomenon. Even before the first draft of the Universal Declaration, Western powers were determined to promote a definition of human rights that valorized liberal freedoms over those associated with social welfare.[30] Although the formal human rights regime is said to embrace the unity of all rights, the image of rights as negative freedoms that sustain free market capitalism has achieved the status that is widely accepted. Economic, social, and cultural rights may be aspirations, but, as we saw in Chapter 2, they are not fully acknowledged in the policies and practices found in the global economic order.

The defense of the "natural" hierarchical order claimed for the political economy of human rights has been twofold. First, proponents of globalization reject any attempt to implement new measures designed to regulate the emerging hierarchy, reaffirming the liberal principles of minimum government and noninterference in the realm of economic activity. Policies for redistribution, for example, are seen as counterproductive and wasteful of scarce resources that should be channelled into building the conditions for wealth creation. In other words, policies for redistribution would place too big a burden on wealth creators, causing a chaotic collapse of the order and a precipitous decline in everyone's quality of life.[31] The counter to this—that the current order places too much of a burden on the poor—is not widely accepted. Furthermore, this defense did not seem to apply during the 2008–2009 global financial crises, which saw states redistributing billions of public funds in support of wealth creators.

Second, to ensure against the introduction of further regulation, which is anathema to the values that support global free market principles, transnational business and finance has sought to engage with the institutions of global governance in an effort to demonstrate concern for human rights. Such an engagement, it is thought, will offer opportunities to associate capital with the attempt to "give a human face to the global market."[32] What was proposed was a "third way," which, it was argued, avoided both the restrictive regulation of business and the escalation of public criticism, social unrest, chaos, and market collapse. Whether this concern was a "fig leaf to avoid awkward questions at [shareholder] meetings" provides a central focus for much human rights talk.[33]

Responses to Violations: Multilateral Organizations

As followers of the "naturalist" account, the World Bank, the International Monetary Fund, and the World Trade Organization have all sought to assert that their policies are neutral, value-free, and apolitical. In recent times, this approach has attracted a number of critical voices from international nongovernmental organizations, aimed at encouraging greater reflection on human rights aspects of these organizations' operations. In response, the multilateral trade and finance organizations have signaled some interest in engaging with humanitarian issues. For critics, this should not, however, be understood as a "Damascene moment," where the light of human rights exposes economic efficiency as a tool rather than a goal of human endeavor. As Susan George notes, a system built upon "individual freedom, self-regulation and 'Darwinian' competition and survival of the fittest" will not spontaneously transform itself into a compassionate and caring mechanism for the promotion and protection of human rights.[34] Whether the response of the multilateral organizations does, in fact, demonstrate a real concern for human rights or is merely a superficial reaction to public opinion continues to attract critical attention.[35]

Much of the debate on human rights is concerned with the role of organizations established to promote development, trade, and economic efficiency. One of three approaches may be adopted. First, the "means-to-ends" approach assumes that the purpose of all economic development is to secure human rights and dignity for those otherwise denied these virtues. For this approach, which is adopted by some INGOs, all the policies and actions of multilateral organizations should be oriented toward achieving this goal: economic development serves the higher purpose of human rights and dignity. Proponents of this approach typically point to the social dangers brought by further economic globalization—ecological breakdown, loss of cultural identity, and widespread immiseration—which threatens great numbers across the world. Capital's increasing awareness of these threats, particularly the threat of resistance, social unrest, and political movements aimed at challenging the value system that supports dominant interests, demands a positive response. Although the machinery for coercion remains available should unrest and resistance reach unacceptable heights, the economic and political costs associated with police and military intervention are often unacceptably high. The less-costly alternative is to provide humanitarian assistance as the central means of pacification. This path has become the top priority for the United Nations and many nongovernmental organizations. Together, pacification and the threat of coercion "help to sustain the emerging social structure of the world by minimizing the risk of chaos in the bottom layer."[36]

Second, and in direct opposition to the "means-to-ends" approach, is the "end-in-itself" approach, which valorizes economic efficiency as the only rationale for economic planning. This is the view often expressed by those who seek to adhere to the founding principles of the multilateral trade and finance organizations. It is a view iterated by proponents when seeking to proselytize an understanding of economics as separated from all other aspects of society. However, this approach acknowledges the necessity of creating and maintaining a set of values that stress individual freedoms, minimum government, free trade, financial liberalism, and the right to private property if the capitalist project is to continue along the path of further expansion and intensification. As Danino argues, in this sense "there is no stark distinction between economic and political considerations."[37] Thus, although the World Bank's rules call for economic efficiency as the only criterion for making decisions on development loans, the link between civil and political freedoms and economic growth makes human rights an economic efficiency issue also. Although this does permit proponents of this approach to argue that they do, in fact, have an interest in human rights, it offers a set of rights limited to those necessary for legitimating and reproducing capitalist exchange relations.

Third, and somewhere between the first two approaches, is the "ends-as-variable" approach, which sees human rights as just one among many goals to be factored in whenever difficult decisions about trade and economic development permit. It is this approach that has received considerable attention by the multilateral trade and finance organizations in recent years. For example, in a World Bank policy review paper titled *Legal Opinion on Human Rights and the Work of the World Bank*,[38] the authors conclude that while "Articles of Agreement permit, and in some cases require, the Bank to recognize the human rights dimensions of its development policies and activities," it is not clear that the Bank is mandated to do so. The paper continues by arguing that whether human rights are included as a prominent variable in decision-making processes depends upon a purposeful and contextual interpretation of the "demands and values of the times."[39] This somewhat ambiguous position, which does not offer a detailed explanation of the terms *purposeful* and *contextual* or how they can be operationalized in any decision-making process, remains unclear.

The recent shift to "end-as-variable" approach is sometimes claimed as the beginning of a radical shift to a human-rights-centered culture within the multilateral organization. This view should, however, be tempered with several cautionary observations. The distinction between the "end-in-itself" and the "end-as-variable" approaches is not always clear, since both are ultimately concerned with achieving the expansion of global markets and greater economic efficiency. These goals are achieved by increasing neoliberal economic competition within a framework of social stability, maintained through a system of rights. Normative and moral issues play an important role in this endeavor, but must take second place to creating the conditions for achieving the greatest possible economic returns. From this perspective, Kaufmann's argument that the "causality direction is from improved governance (including civil and political liberties) to economic development, not vice versa"[40] is a functional rather than a normative statement. There may be a need to guarantee certain civil and political rights as an essential prerequisite for achieving successful capitalist growth, but this does not imply that human rights must always, and in all contexts and circumstances, assume a central role in economic decision-making. Nor does it assume the necessity to embrace the full range of rights found in the global human rights regime.[41] In short, the approach is "if a capitalist political economy, then capitalist rights."

A second argument that doubts the "ends-as-variable" approach concerns capabilities. The tools available to the multilateral economic organizations, cited as evidence that they take rights seriously, are far from adequate. Under the rules of the WTO, a member cannot be expelled on grounds of its human rights record. Nor has the dispute settlement procedure been used to challenge the human rights of a member, not even on grounds of, say, the economic advantages of not outlawing child or forced labor. However, the WTO might point to provisions made under the waiver system, which allow a member state to suspend the rules of trade in cases where human dignity might be endangered. The 2003 waiver that permits poor countries to import cheap generic drugs is an example here.[42] The special Kimberley waiver was introduced in response to a Security Council resolution concerning civil war funded by the diamond trade in Sierra Leone, but this also has limitations.[43] In approving the waiver, the Ministerial Conference permitted member states to apply separately and individually to waive the rules of trade where there is evidence that a country is violating human rights and where to continue the trade in diamonds might prolong or worsen the situation. However, there is no obligation to discontinue trade with violators.

Furthermore, although the WTO might claim that it does scrutinize a state's human rights record when applications for membership are received, and during the trade policy review process, the focus remains on trade-related, comparative advantage issues. These are mostly concerned with labor rights, where a comparative advantage might be gained by denying the rights of organized labor, collective bargaining, discrimination in the workplace, child labor, and forced labor.[44] Supporting this criticism, the WTO trade court has consistently ruled that actions based upon human rights, environmental, and humanitarian arguments are inadmissible if the inclusion of such arguments is likely to impede the free market.[45] Thus, any claims that the WTO might make about human rights should be seen as tautological: free market capitalism includes only rights associated with free market capitalism.

Doubts have also been raised about the competence of multilateral trade and financial organizations to make incisive judgments about human rights. The language of rights and that of economics are not the same. Without procedures for the scrutiny of economic measures by qualified human rights specialists, independent of the economic purposes pursued by these organizations, the prospect for building public confidence seems unlikely. Although there is a plethora of UN agencies with responsibility for almost every aspect of economic development and the promotion of human rights, little has so far been done to set up cooperative procedures for analyzing and scrutinizing the human rights implications of trade, business and financial procedures, and agreements. The report by Oloka-Onyango for the UN subcommission offers a rare example of reflection on the human rights consequences of a globalized economy.[46]

The constitutional position of the multilateral organizations is often seen as presenting further difficulties when considering human rights. Although the World Bank, for example, argues that its Articles of Agreement forbid it to interfere in the domestic affairs of any country, or to take account of any ideological issues in its decision-making processes, this claim is challenged by many in the critical literature. According to critics, the Bank's claim of neutrality can be sustained only if we accept that questions of poverty, social welfare, health, education, and many other social issues have no correspondence with the conditions imposed to secure the Bank's economic assistance.[47] Nor can it be sustained unless we accept that the capitalist global political economy is itself an ideologically neutral order.[48]

During the last few years, and particularly since the events in Seattle during 1999,[49] the WTO, International Monetary Fund (IMF), and World Bank have engaged in the debate over the role of multilateral organizations in the promotion and protection of human rights. For most of their history, these organizations have repeated the convention that human rights remains beyond their remit. Rational economic decisionmaking should guide policy, not moral and normative issues like human rights. There is no mention of human rights in the Articles of Agreement for either the World Bank or the WTO. Brief references to "higher levels of employment" (IMF) and assisting in raising "the standard of living" (World Bank) are mentioned, but these references fall far short of accepting any obligations to promote and protect human rights.[50]

The WTO, which has suffered the greatest criticism for its failure to consider human rights, remains an "organization dealing with trade negotiations and the resulting agreements." Other than a few minor exceptions "[i]t does not have statements on human rights as such." Furthermore, "[e]ssentially the WTO defers to other international organizations and international law on the subject."[51] The WTO defends this approach by reference to its formal constitution as a body representing the collective wishes of its members, rather than a body invested with the capability to develop independent policies. It is therefore an institution whose primary function is to provide a forum for its members to negotiate a consensus on policies for creating and maintaining open markets on a global scale. Internal social and political arrangements for the protection of human rights remain a matter for each member state and cannot, therefore, become a consideration within international trade negotiation. The current Doha Round of trade negotiations, for example, makes no reference to human rights even though many of the issues under negotiation have human rights implications, particularly those concerned with agriculture and services.[52]

Although the formal, constitutional argument appears to proscribe WTO involvement with human rights issues, the Organization argues that many of its existing agreements "imply" that human rights are, in fact, an important consideration when making trade-related decisions.[53] In defense of this approach, the WTO points to Article 20 of the GATT. This article provides for member states to take action "necessary to protect public morals" and "to protect human, animal or plant life or health."[54] Article 21 (security exceptions), which refers to peace and the UN Charter, is also interpreted by the WTO as indicative of its human rights responsibilities, although there is no jurisprudence on this so far. Several other agreements are also said to provide potential avenues for including human rights, for instance, the General Agreement on Trade in Services (GATS) permits some exclusions from the imposition of liberal conditionalities (health and education in particular), where rights to access and provision are better served by state intervention.[55] Thus, the WTO adopts a guarded and often ambiguous approach to human rights that continues to attract critical attention.[56]

Other international financial organizations have also begun to engage in a cautious debate that shifts attention from constitutional responsibilities toward one that accepts some limited obligations for human rights. The World Bank, for example, accepts that there are linkages between human rights and development, to which the Bank should respond, but accepts that its "policies, programs and projects have never been explicitly or deliberately aimed towards the realization of human rights."[57] Similarly, a prominent member of the IMF argues that, "in light of the evolving connections between human rights and development, human rights are now "an issue ripe for analysis."[58] For the IMF, although the organization is primarily concerned with international monetary cooperation, exchange rate mechanisms, balanced growth, and helping members to resolve balance of payment issues, it has responded to criticism by claiming to be dedicated to contributing to the promotion of human rights, and is already doing so "if one looks below the surface" of its work.[59] However, the approach to human rights remains cautious, pointing to the need for further "analysis" and hidden agendas aimed at promoting and protecting human rights, rather than presenting human rights as a goal for strategic planning and a necessary condition for legitimate and continuing economic relations.

In response to some of the these criticisms, the Office of the UN High Commissioner for Human Rights (UNHCHR) prepared a statement for the 2003 Fifth WTO Ministerial Conference held in Cancún, Mexico. This statement called for a "normative" framework for achieving consensus upon "how trade affects the enjoyment of human rights" by placing the "promotion and protection of human rights among the objectives of trade reform."[60] The UNHCHR proposed the introduction of transparent and independent monitoring procedures to assess the impact of trade liberalization, which should be applied to all existing and future agreements. Supporting this call, Amnesty International, which itself focuses largely upon civil and political rights associated with the current order,[61] is troubled by the failure to move the debate forward on the global economy and development. In a statement that urges WTO members to take account of human rights in trade negotiations, Amnesty notes how little attention has been given to assessing the potential human rights impact of trade liberalization or to investigating the necessary measures to ensure all sectors of society benefit from future trade agreements. To fulfill this demand, Amnesty calls for all states to undertake "human rights impact assessments" before adopting any new agreement. Amnesty also calls for states to monitor the impact of existing trade agreements, with a view to ensuring that trade-related human rights violations are eradicated.[62]

Critics of multinational trade and financial organizations would be unlikely to share Amnesty's optimism for such a change in approach. The narrow view of rights and freedoms adopted by these organizations remains part of a framework of rules that limit the actions of governments to intervene in processes of economic globalization. Gill, for example, argues that the rules defining the global economy are no longer created, administered, and managed by the state but by multilateral organizations, which have displaced the state as the legitimate decision-making agent. Today, he argues, there is a "new constitutionalism," which is no longer "concerned with overarching frameworks of 'quasi-permanent' rules to define the parameters of 'ordinary politics,'" involving struggle and debate *within* these rules.[63] Instead, the new constitutional framework is directed at promoting the rights of capital by legitimating particular freedoms associated with the free market. Justice in the new order, and the claim to create a rights-based global society, is defined by the equal application of the rules, not by reference to normative and moral principles. Consequently, the dynamics of economic globalization impact on the enjoyment of human rights by limiting state actions designed to fulfill obligations undertaken within the legal human rights regime. As Howse argues, the trade-off offered to many states is either to engage fully with international economic organizations, in an effort to satisfy the economic aspirations of some citizens but at a cost of economic and social rights to others, or to fulfill the full range of human rights obligations, including economic and social rights, but fail to satisfy the conditions for attracting aid and investment that promises national economic development within the global economic order: an irresolvable catch-22.[64]

Emerging from this examination of the institutional and organizational structures that describe economic globalization is the conclusion that human rights are embraced only insofar as they support the economic objectives of capital. The structures of global capitalism were not created as a means for fostering the full range of human rights, including economic and social rights, but to give legitimacy to a particular form of global political economy. In their highly critical report for the Sub-Commission on the Promotion and Protection of Human Rights, Oloka-Onyango and Udagana argue that "the institutional mechanisms of globalization have yet to seriously address the issue of human rights in a fundamental and democratic fashion—both with respect to their operations within countries and also to the internal make-up and functioning of their institutions."[65] In answer to the question why the multilateral economic organizations are so dilatory in making the linkage between trade liberalization and the promotion and protection of human rights, the report is equally forthright: it is because many of the policies of these organizations undermine the progressive realization of economic and social rights. Furthermore, in the case of civil and political rights, were the linkages to be investigated, it would expose the inconsistencies and interests associated with the dominant global political economy.

From this critical perspective, the structures of the global political economy prejudice the move to a rights-based global order. The global order serves "dominant corporate interests that already monopolize the arena of international trade," rather than the interests of the poor, women, and labor.[66] Although the multilateral economic organizations have learned the techniques for courteous dialogue with partner INGOs, who call for reform of the global political economy, the greatest reform movement is managed and orchestrated by corporations in their own interests. Indeed, the assumption that negotiating rule changes, and arriving at new agreements in favor of a human-rights-based political economy, is a form of methodological individualism that confuses changes *within* a particular socioeconomic order with change *of* the order. For critics, the still-developing structures of the means of production on a global scale are the cause of the majority of violations of human rights, not the actions of particular individuals or the development of new technologies.[67] The reconfiguration of global institutions, oriented toward building and sustaining a global free market, has brought a decline in the capacity of the state to deliver socioeconomic rights. While calls for redistributive measures are rejected by those closest to the center of economic globalization, on grounds that it would be too demanding on wealth creators, critics argue that the current order is too demanding on the poor.[68]

For many critics, the response of the multilateral trade and financial organizations is therefore little more than window dressing. Chossudovsky, for instance, asserts that many INGOs are courted by the WTO for the role they play in increasing public awareness and respect for the WTO. This relationship, he argues, nurtures a politically correct counterdiscourse backed by token environmental and human rights clauses in agreements but does not hinder the central purpose of the WTO, which is to ensure that free market economics prevails.[69] The complicity of state leaders in this process is seen in techniques for managing and sustaining the structures of economic globalization while simultaneously offering sufficient concessions to the world's peoples to keep social unrest at bay. While democracy may deliver different leaders, the task of administering the global economy in the interests of global capital goes on.[70]

Responses to Violations: Corporations

At the World Economic Forum in Davos in 1999, the UN Secretary-General, Kofi Annan, called upon business to "give a human face to the global market."[71] Annan feared the consequences of the rapid shift to global markets, particularly the loss of identity, community, and security as national markets declined. The failure to respond to this loss of shared values would, he argued, encourage a countermove to protectionism, nationalism, ethnic chauvinism, fanaticism, and terrorism, which would challenge the cause of further economic globalization, bringing the danger of social unrest and market collapse. What was required, he argued, was some kind of "third way" that transcended the alternatives—the stultifying effects of market regulation or the chaos of doing nothing—that marked the Great Depression of the interwar years. To achieve this, and in response to business's abhorrence of regulation, he urged corporate leaders to preempt the introduction of international law by developing voluntary procedures for ensuring that their global business dealings brought no consequence for human rights and the environment. At worst, he argued, "you can at least make sure that your own employees and those of your subcontractors" enjoy human rights.[72]

Following Annan's 1999 speech, the UN established the Office for the Global Compact. During the decade of its existence, membership in the compact has become an important symbol whereby corporations can demonstrate their ethical and moral credentials in a public forum. Its creation was also intended to signal that the institutions of global governance now fully accept the necessity of enlisting corporate cooperation on issues like human rights and the environment. The aim of the Global Compact is to promote "responsible global corporate citizenship" based upon ten "universal" principles divided between human rights, labor issues, the environment, and anticorruption.[73] The conditions for membership are straightforward. A corporation simply registers its membership with the Global Compact Office, undertaking to file an annual report that sets out the progressive actions that the corporation has taken to satisfy the ten principles during the preceding twelve months. The quid pro quo for voluntarily engaging with the Global Compact is the UN's undertaking to permit corporate access to all its major agencies, including the International Labour Organization, the United Nations Environmental Programme, and the Office of the UN High Commissioner for Human Rights.

The changing configuration of power relations characteristic of economic globalization offers the rationale for creating a Global Compact. According to Ruggie, in an order where the capability of the state to deal with new global problems is in doubt but where alternative institutions are not yet established, "the corporate world has demonstrable global reach and capacity."[74] Although in the past the speed of socioeconomic change often matched the capacity of the state to respond to global issues, this is not so today. The advent of new technology, particularly information technology, has introduced a global dynamic that circumvents or evades many institutional arrangements developed in another era. Consequently, for some the rise of global corporations, with resources that far outstrip those of many states, has emerged as the only alternative for establishing new structures of global governance. Accordingly, since order is a necessary element for market maintenance, corporate actors must undertake new social and environmental obligations that promise to deliver the benefits of globalization to all, including marginalized and excluded groups.[75]

As an alternative to the threat of regulation on moral and ethical issues, the Global Compact provides corporations with an opportunity, sanctioned by the United Nations, to demonstrate concern for human rights publicly. Regulation is rejected by business on two general grounds; first, that corporations do not, in fact, have the power and influence often attributed to them by critics, and may not, therefore, be able to comply; second, that the costs to business of fulfilling statutory obligations are too high. Indeed, corporations often argue that existing levels of surveillance and monitoring, which have been facilitated by the introduction of new communications technology, already hold corporations to account for every aspect of their behavior, and at great cost. For these reasons former High Commissioner for Human Rights Mary Robinson has argued that the rapid changes brought by globalization offer clear evidence that corporations should develop voluntary procedures for factoring human rights values in their business strategies.[76] Rather than time being wasted awaiting new regulations, corporations should act immediately to protect and promote human rights within their own sphere of influence, ensuring that their own actions and policies do not make them complicit in violations. Following this advice, she argued, would help ensure that regulation was unnecessary, thus relieving corporations of the costs associated with compliance while simultaneously ensuring that compliance would not be beyond their capabilities. Consequently, by seeking to develop a self-regulatory regime for the protection of human rights, "new rules or laws in this area may well be unnecessary, because corporations will see for themselves—and many have seen this already—the need to behave responsibly in the social area."[77]

Proponents of the Global Compact suggest that many social and ethical problems could be alleviated by bringing together the different skills, capacities, and resources of the UN and global corporations. For instance, the UN brings its considerable experience as an "honest broker" for reaching consensus between competing interests. The UN also offers considerable experience and knowledge on issues of peace and security, which is applied to creating a stable global order, a necessary condition for corporate long-term planning and investment. On the business side, the promotion and protection of human rights is understood as a particular set of civil and political rights that support the conduct of the global free market. Corporations therefore have a clear responsibility to contribute to the human rights agenda by acting voluntarily to factor human rights issues into strategic planning and operational processes. Through the Global Compact, it is argued, the separate skills of business and the UN are brought together in pursuit of common interests; for example, investment and innovation to achieve economic growth and development, bringing the prospect of prosperity, economic security, and human rights to many more people. Finally, proponents of the Global Compact noted that all parties—the UN and its agencies, business, and civil society groups—are becoming increasingly conscious of the new responsibilities and obligations that globalization engenders. The Global Compact offers an opportunity to channel the increasing power and influence of corporations toward achieving their own economic goals, while simultaneously permitting the claim that they are serving the world's peoples by implementing moral and responsible policies.[78]

Linked to the creation of the Global Compact is the idea of Corporate Social Responsibility (CSR), which many would claim has now become part of normal business practice. The idea of CSR was developed as a means for corporations to build an ethical dimension to existing business models. It continues with the theme of self-regulation found in the Global Compact, including processes intended to enable self-reflection on compliance with international law, human rights, and environmental obligations. Through exercising CSR, business hopes to create images of responsible global actors contributing toward the protection of human rights enthusiastically. The CSR movement is thus an attempt to answer critics who see the public interest violated by the private decision-making practices of corporations.[79]

The spectrum of definitions found in the literature is so wide and varied that the arguments in favor of CSR are often difficult to assess. At one end of the spectrum are those who view CSR as little more than the exercise of philanthropy, discharged in the image of eighteenth- and nineteenth-century industrialists and merchants. Critics remind us that many of these philanthropists were cruel employers and the beneficiaries of the slave trade and slave labor.[80] At the other end are those who understand CSR as a moral obligation requiring corporations to question the socioeconomic structures in which profits are generated. Further definitions focus on fulfilling legal obligations, responsibilities to stakeholders, and the need to avoid any form of public disapprobation that might affect the so-called bottom line.[81] Whatever definition is adopted, all share the belief that CSR must remain market driven, that it should not be mandatory, and that any effort to exercise CSR will fluctuate, depending upon the market position of each corporation within the existing global economy.

The link between human rights and corporate action did not arouse much interest until recent times. In the early years following the period of decolonization of the 1960s and 1970s, host governments sought to exercise control over foreign investors through legal means, including the creation of special laws aimed at regulating corporate behavior, codes of conduct, and contractual conditionalities. The spectre of expropriation was always present for those who failed to fulfill their obligations. The drive for economic globalization has, however, increased interstate competition to attract foreign investment. Many states now offer concessions on social and welfare rights, taxation, labor standards, and health and safety laws as incentives for attracting investment. In some cases, publicly owned land or land claimed under traditional tribal and ethnic laws has been handed over to corporations for their exclusive use.[82] Critics argue that this reverses the past agenda where the state called the tune. While in the past the conditions imposed by host states on foreign investors was that they comply with existing laws, today the conditions imposed by foreign investors on states is that their investment needs are accommodated. For corporations, the relationship with the state remains oriented toward gaining the most profitable terms.[83]

Earnest Proponents of Human Rights?

Critical voices have not been slow in pointing to the shortcomings of both the Global Compact and the CSR movement. In his 1999 speech, Annan accepted that the UN's attempt to promote human rights within the context of economic globalization, particularly the rise of powerful corporate actors, was failing. The moral power of human rights, which was at the center of all UN activity, proved insufficient to shift corporations from the view that the duties of business stopped with their shareholders. In recognizing shifting power relations within the global order, Annan also recognized that previously held assumptions about the state's capacities and capabilities to promote and protect human rights were no longer secure. The creation of the Global Compact and the CSR movement marked the conclusion that moral argument alone was insufficient to convince corporations to implement human rights policies. The new approach to human rights sought to gain the cooperation of business not by appeal to moral values but to self-interest—a market-led business transaction that supported the goals of economic stability, order, and profit maximization. Although this shift went largely unnoticed at the time, it signaled a move away from the goals of justice and fairness expressed in the UN Charter to a position where economic expansion is placed at the top of the global agenda. Provided corporations demonstrated a willingness to cooperate on human rights issues, tolerance would be exercised when cases of inequality, injustice, and exclusion were found. Annan himself acknowledged the dangers of embarking on such a course when he accepted that many would see it as a "pact with the Devil."[84]

This view appears to be supported by the Global Compact Office itself, which sees the motivation for joining the compact as "self-interest," rather than concern for ethical and moral issues.[85] As corporations come to realize the dangers of social and political unrest, which often identifies their business activities as the cause of human rights violations, poverty, and environmental decay, the possibility of engaging in "multistakeholder" cooperative ventures offers an attractive option for addressing present and future problems. However, critics argue that the Global Compact has been "hijacked" by companies keen to maintain a carefully manufactured public image, rather than to make a contribution to creating the conditions for human rights.[86] Indeed, for many critics both the Global Compact and the CSR movement are little more than a public-relations exercise to assuage public concerns over the human rights consequences of corporate activities and thus avoid consumer reaction that could escalate, for example, into consumer boycotts that hit a corporation's bottom line.

Criticism is also aimed at the much-vaunted achievements of the Global Compact. At best, critics argue, the Global Compact and CSR movement has motivated big corporations to produce annual glossy reports in response to public and investor demand. In particular, the requirement to submit an annual report to the Global Compact Office, which remains the only significant requirement for a corporation to maintain its membership, has proved disappointing. The reporting system is supposed to describe corporate action in fulfillment of obligations regarding human rights, the environment, and labor relations undertaken in the previous twelve months. However, although the reports are often full of grand phrases and statements, the quality remains mixed, with some running to several hundred pages and others to fewer than six.[87] Although it may be possible to describe the operations of some corporations in a few pages, Andy Favell concludes that many provide little detail upon which to judge progress toward socially responsible behavior.[88] In addition, the reports are often poorly constructed, lack careful analysis of current policy and outcome, provide little sense of disclosure, and rarely provide well-defined targets. Even when a corporation does attempt to define the impact of its activities on human rights and the environment, "qualified performance indicators that illustrate how they are managed are mostly absent."[89] Whether the attempt to increase the standard through the introduction of a new "Communications on Progress" format succeeds remains to be seen.

In proposing the creation of the Global Compact, Annan was motivated to promote the image of "multistakeholder" cooperation, negotiating and sharing economic, social, and political interests as a means for making progress on the ten principles.[90] In the face of the realities of globalization, proponents of the Global Compact and the CSR movement argue that corporate power must be placed at the forefront of the global political economy, if solutions for social and economic ills are to be found. This is because in any list that compares GDP of states with corporate annual turnover, more than one-half of the top one hundred on the list are well-known transnational corporations.[91] Through acknowledging the link between economic and political power, the UN thus accepts that corporate power cannot be left outside debates on pressing issues, like human rights and the protection of the environment. Arguments for establishing closer relations between business and UN agencies—explicit in the Global Compact—may therefore offer an opportunity for business to challenge national economic planning, to subvert patterns of consumption and production, and to displace local products and services,[92] further impeding the capacities of democratic governments to promote and protect human rights.

In this way, the Global Compact and CSR represent a move toward corporate parity with the UN and members of international society. Democratic legitimacy for this is justified by pointing to consumer demand, which, it is claimed, enables the voice of the majority to participate when exercising their right to property. However, the claims of the stakeholder-as-consumer approach do not introduce a new dimension to democracy and the democratization of the global political economy, as some claim, because those who are unable to consume have no voice. By definition, the excluded cannot be stakeholders, because they cannot enter the market. Consequently, the market cannot deliver democratic outcomes, including moral goods, in the way that proponents of CSR and the Global Compact suggest.[93] Rather than reflecting new forms of democracy, critics of the Global Compact argue that it should be seen as a forum for what it is: self-interest, double standards, and hypocrisy.[94]

Crucially, many corporations that are members of the Global Compact and that may also boast of their CSR credentials are implicated in human rights violations. The association with the UN and its agencies can therefore become a "bluewash" to cover well-documented corporate complicity with violations of human rights.[95] As the managing director of Kestral OPS has argued with forthright honesty, "the emperor has no clothes. . . . Corporate Social Responsibility is a nonsense."[96] Given this reaction to CSR and the Global Compact, critics argue that the image of transnational corporations working hard in support of human rights remains just that: an image, with no substance.

Finally, the voluntary nature of the Global Compact was questioned by Irene Khan at the July 2007 Leaders' Summit on the Global Compact. She argued that the reporting system was more procedural than substantive—an obligation that was easily fulfilled without too heavy a cost to members. For her, it was a puzzle that business/finance was content to seek security in the creation of international law when trade and investment was an issue, but rejected it as a solution for violations of human rights and the environment. Supporting the call for compulsory measures, Guy Ryder of the International Trade Union Confederation has noted that corporations did not protest when governments brought in laws to outlaw collective bargaining, and in some cases actively supported legal controls over trade union rights, but were reluctant to agree to any regulation that would impose legal duties within the Global Compact. Both Khan and Ryder suggested that the achievements of the Global Compact remained limited and could not be further improved without regulation.[97]

John Ruggie, the special representative of the UN Secretary-General (SRSG) on the issue of human rights and transnational corporations, sought to engage some of this criticism in his 2007 report to the UN Human Rights Council.[98] The report was based upon an extensive survey of state and corporate policies and practices for the protection of human rights, although Ruggie accepts that the low response rate did not permit any robust conclusions to be drawn. Of those who did respond, Ruggie noted "very few report having policies, programs or tools designed specifically to deal with corporate human rights challenges."[99] The central conclusion of the report was that a "fundamental institutional misalignment is present: between the scope and impact of economic forces and actors, on the one hand, and the capacity of societies to manage their adverse consequences, on the other."[100] This misalignment has emerged because conditions that describe the contemporary global political economy offer a "permissive environment within which blameworthy acts by corporations may occur without adequate sanctioning or reparation."[101] Given this environment, the prospect for developing a global human rights culture within the corporate sphere, while retaining the clear material advantages brought by globalization, will remain beyond reach because the exercise of economic freedoms associated with globalization continue to outstrip the capacities of governance.

Furthermore, Ruggie reported that very few states appeared to have developed specific policies, tools, or programs designed to deal with the challenges to human rights brought by corporate activities, preferring instead to reiterate the principles set out in the Global Compact or to emphasize their engagement with the discourse of Corporate Social Responsibility. From the survey evidence, most states did not factor in human rights when developing export credit and investment-promotion policies or policies to do with bilateral trade. Specifically, the report noted that there was little evidence that corporations undertook human rights impact assessments before undertaking new investments.[102] Of those who have included at least some assessment of human rights impact in their planning, only one had made this public. If the central tool for promoting human rights within the corporate world is accountability, this strategy seems to have failed so far.

Further evidence from Ruggie's survey suggests that while the number of corporations reporting on measures to prevent violations of human rights as a consequence of their own actions may have increased, transparency remains poor. Few corporations have initiated systematic procedures for reporting on the human rights impact of their current activities beyond "anecdotal descriptions of isolated projects and philanthropic activity."[103] Few combine social and financial reporting, "despite the fact that the former has 'sustainability' implications for the latter."[104] An assurance to the public that the information provided is accurate and full is therefore lacking, making any assessment of the future for a human rights business culture difficult. Moreover, there remains a conflict of interests if the state is required to act as both poacher and gamekeeper, on the one hand acting to support greater freedoms for access to markets, while on the other acting in support of collective goals like universal human rights or the protection of the environment. Ruggie's 2008 report continues to express his exasperation that so little has so far been achieved.

> Without in any manner disparaging these steps, our fundamental problem is that there are too few of them, none has reached a scale commensurate with the challenges at hand, there is little cross-learning, and they do not cohere as parts of a more systemic response with cumulative effects. That is what needs fixing. And that is what the framework of "protect, respect and remedy" is intended to help achieve.[105]

For proponents of the Global Compact and the CSR movement, these developments provide an imaginative and radical way of bringing governments and business together in a joint project to create new ways for protecting and promoting human rights. For critics, on the other hand, the Global Compact devalues the work of the United Nations, leaving the Organization open to the charge of being an apologist for behavior contrary to the values of human rights, for which the United Nations has worked for more than six decades. While many critics would agree with Ruggie that the Battle in Seattle and the court proceedings over the price of drugs to treat HIV patients in Africa are a reaction to "imbalances in global rule making,"[106] the beneficiaries of those imbalances will not voluntarily renounce their privileged position. Corporations cannot be both the savage and the savior on human rights issues. The Global Compact may therefore be a "Trojan horse"[107]—a means for corporations to conceal their poor record of complicity in human rights violations by legitimating their actions through the offices of the United Nations.

*   *   *

For those engaged in promoting human rights as a necessary element in current and future economic planning, the achievements made through the Global Compact and the discourse on Corporate Social Responsibility provide a limited but encouraging indication of what can be achieved. Against this are those who argue that the force of global free market ideology has diminished all prospects for promoting human rights. In a world where "the great beauty of globalization is that nobody is in control,"[108] any improvements in human rights are likely to be incidental, fragmentary, and ephemeral.[109] Indeed, for some commentators, the creation of the Global Compact, which is not a code of conduct and has no enforcement capabilities backed by law, is a sign that the authority of the state is in decline. The Global Compact and the CSR movement thus provide a "forum for hypocrisy," which affords corporations culpable of human rights violations a measure of protection from public criticism.[110] Ruggie's observation that there is a misalignment between world order, forms of state, and global institutions suggests that the state is understood today more as a catalyst, facilitator, and administrator for economic growth, rather than as the guardian of human rights and welfare.[111] This is further examined in the next chapter.

Notes

1. Jack Donnelly, "International Human Rights: A Regime Analysis," *International Organization* 40, no. 3 (1986).

2. Monshipouri notes that Walmart has profits greater than the Canadian tax revenue. See Mahmood Monshipouri Jr., Claude E. Welch, and T. Evan Kennedy, "Multinational Corporations and the Ethics of Global Responsibility: Problems and Possibilities," *Human Rights Quarterly* 25, no. 4 (2003).

3. Clair Apodaca, "The Globalization of Capital in East and Southeast Asia: Measuring the Impact on Human Rights Standards," *Asian Survey* 42, no. 6 (2002): 887.

4. Michael Hopkins, *The Planetary Bargain* (London: Earthscan, 2003).

5. Gary Duncan, "World Leaders Are Stuck in Moral Maze," *Times*, London, January 31, 2005. Duncan notes the high moral tone adopted in discussions on social responsibility conducted at Davos. The phrase "do well and do good" comes from a presentation at Davos by Carly Fiorina of Hewlett-Packard.

6. Joyce V. Millen, Evan Lyon, and Alec Irwin, "Dying for Growth: The Political Influence of National and Transnational Corporations," in *Dying for Growth: Global Inequality and the Health of the Poor*, ed. Jim Young Kim et al. (Monroe, Maine: Common Courage Press, 2000).

7. Caroline Thomas, "International Financial Institutions and Social and Economic Rights: An Exploration," in *Human Rights Fifty Years On: A Reappraisal*, ed. Tony Evans (Manchester: Manchester University Press, 1998).

8. Noam Chomsky, "The United States and the Challenge of Relativity," in Evans, ed., *Human Rights Fifty Years On*.

9. See, for example, Noam Chomsky, *World Orders, Old and New* (London: Pluto, 1994).

10. V. T. Tamilmoran, *Human Rights in Third World Perspective* (Ithica, N.Y.: Cornell University Press, 1992).

11. President Bill Clinton, WTO, May 18, 1998.

12. Prime Minister Tony Blair, WTO, May 19, 1998.

13. Kofi Annan, "Secretary-General's Address to the World Economic Forum," January 23, 2004.

14. Michel Foucault, "What Is Critique?" in *Twentieth-Century Questions*, ed. James Schmidt (Berkeley: University of California Press, 1996); Duncan Ivison, "The Disciplinary Moment: Foucault, Law, and the Reinscription of Rights," in *The Later Foucault: Politics and Philosophy*, ed. Jeremy Moss (London: Sage, 1998); Richard Rorty, "Universality and Truth," in *Rorty and His Critics*, ed. Roper R. Brandon (Oxford, UK: Blackwell, 2000); Joseph Rouse, "Power/Knowledge," in *The Cambridge Companion to Foucault*, ed. Gary Cutting (Cambridge: Cambridge University Press, 1994).

15. Charles Jones, *Global Justice: Defending Cosmopolitanism* (Oxford: Oxford University Press, 2000).

16. Kofi Annan, "The Secretary-General Addresses the World Economic Forum" (World Economic Forum, 2002).

17. Dima Jamali and Ramez Mirshak, "Corporate Social Responsibility (CSR):

Theory and Practice in a Developing Country Context," *Journal of Business Ethics*, no. 72 (2007): 243.

18. J. Oloka-Onyango and Deepika Udagana, "The Realization of Economic, Social, and Cultural Rights: Globalization and Its Impact on the Full Enjoyment of Human Rights" (Sub-Commission on the Promotion and Protection of Human Rights, 2000), pp. 3–4.

19. Ibid., p. 6.

20. Robert Howse and Makau Mutua, "Protecting Human Rights in a Global Economy: Challenges for the World Trade Organization" www.dd-rd.ca/english/commdoc/publications/gobalizaiton/wtoRightsGlob.htm (Rights and Democracy, 2000).

21. John Gershman and Alec Irwin, "Getting a Grip on the Global Economy," in *Dying for Growth: Global Inequality and the Health of the Poor*, ed. Jim Young Kim et al. (Monroe, Maine: Common Courage Press, 2000).

22. Human Rights Watch (HRW), *"No Guarantee: Sex Discrimination in Mexico's Maquiladora Sector"* (HRW, Women's Rights Project, 1996).

23. See, for example, Joseph A. Camilleri and Jim Falk, *The End of Sovereignty? The Politics of a Shrinking and Fragmenting World* (Aldershot, UK: Edward Elgar, 1992); Ankie Hoogvelt, *Globalization and the Postcolonial World: The New Political Economy of Development* (Basingstoke, UK: Palgrave, 2001); John H. Jackson, "Sovereignty-Modern: A New Approach to an Outdated Concept," *American Journal of International Law* 97, no. 4 (2003); Jan Aart Scholte, "Globalization and the State," *International Affairs* 73, no. 3 (1997).

24. The 2008 global banking crisis exemplifies relations between business, finance, and the state. States provided billions of US dollars in the effort to sustain a banking system and industry that has come to rely on the ready availability of loans.

25. Oloka-Onyango and Udagana, "The Realization of Economic, Social, and Cultural Rights: Globalization and Its Impact on the Full Enjoyment of Human Rights."

26. Gershman and Irwin, "Getting a Grip."

27. John Ruggie, "The Global Compact and the Challenges of Global Governance—Berlin" (UN Global Compact Learning Forum, 2002).

28. Johan Galtung, *Human Rights in Another Key* (Cambridge, UK: Polity, 1994).

29. United Nations Development Programme, *Human Development Report, 2000—Human Rights and Human Development* (Oxford, UK: UNDP, 2000); UNICEF, *The State of the World's Children—1998* (Oxford: Oxford University Press, 1998).

30. Tony Evans, *US Hegemony and the Project of Universal Human Rights* (Basingstoke, UK: Macmillan, 1996); Alex Kirkup and Tony Evans, "The Myth of Western Opposition to Economic, Social, and Cultural Rights? A Reply to Whelan and Donnelly," *Human Rights Quarterly* 31, no. 1 (2009).

31. Duncan, "World Leaders Are Stuck."

32. Kofi Annan, "Address to the World Economic Forum in Davos," ed. UN Secretary-General, press release, 1999.

33. Christine A. Hemingway, "An Exploratory Analysis of Corporate Social Responsibility: Definitions, Motives, and Values," in *Centre for Management and Organisational Learning* (Hull, UK: University of Hull Business School, 2002), p. 10.

34. Susan George, *The Lucano Report* (London: Pluto, 1999), p. 29.

35. Hemingway, "Exploratory Analysis."

36. Robert Cox, "Democracy in Hard Times: Economic Globalization and the Limits to Liberal Democracy," in *The Transformation of Democracy*, ed. Anthony McGrew (Cambridge, UK: Polity, 1997), p. 58.

37. Robert Danino et al., "Human Rights and Development" (World Bank Institute, 2006).

38. At http://www.ifiwatchnet.org/sites/ifiwatchnet.org/files/DaninoLegalOpinion0106.pdf.

39. Danino et al., "Human Rights and Development."

40. Daniel Kaufmann, "Human Rights and Development: Towards Mutual Reinforcement," paper presented at the conference "Human Rights and Global Justice," New York University Law School, March 1, 2004.

41. Mark Rupert, "Globalising Common Sense: A Marxian-Gramscian (Re)-Vision of the Politics of Governance and Resistance," *Review of International Studies* 29, special issue (2003).

42. See Mark A. Wainberg, "Generic HIV Drugs: Enlightened Policy for Global Health," *New England Journal of Medicine,* no.8 (2005), at http://content.nejm.org/cgi/content/full/352/8/747.

43. For a review of the legal responsibilities of the WTO, including the Kimberley Waiver system, see Peter van den Bossche, *Law and Policy of the World Trade Organization: Text, Cases, and Materials* (Cambridge: Cambridge University Press, 2005).

44. Susan Ariel Aaronson and Jamie M. Zimmerman, "The World Trade Organization and Human Rights: Providing Some Power to the People Some of the Time," in *International Studies Association Annual Conference* (San Diego, Calif.: 2006).

45. Global Exchange, "The WTO Erodes Human Rights Protection: Three Case Studies," (Global Exchange, 1999).

46. Oloka-Onyango and Udagana, "Realization of Economic, Social, and Cultural Rights."

47. For example, see Thomas, "An Exploration."

48. Gary Teeple, *The Riddle of Human Rights* (Aurora, Canada: Garamond Press, 2005).

49. For a view of resistance to globalization, see Louise Amoore, introduction, "Global Resistance—Global Politics," in *The Global Resistance Reader*, ed. Louise Amoore (Abingdon, UK: Routledge, 2005).

50. For the World Bank Articles of Agreement, see web.worldbank.org/WBSITE/EXTERNAL/EXTABOUTUS/0,,contentMDK:20; for the IMF see www.imf.org/external/pubs/ft/aa/aa01.html.

51. Peter Ungphakorn, e-mail, June 14, 2007.

52. Andreas Bluthner, "Trade and Human Rights at Work: Next Round Please . . . ?" in *Agreeing and Implementing the Doha Round of the WTO,* ed. Harold Hohmann (Cambridge, UK: Cambridge University Press, 2004), pp. 335–373.

53. Ungphakorn, e-mail, June 14, 2007.

54. www.wto.org/english/docs_e/legal_e/gatt47_02_e.htm#articleXX. No state has ever sought to use this article on human rights grounds.

55. For the WTO's overview of GATS, see http://www.wto.org/english/tratop_e/serv_e/serv_e.htm.

56. See, for example, Caroline Thomas, *Global Governance, Development, and Human Security*, ed. Caroline Thomas, Human Security and the Global Economy (London: Pluto Press, 2001); and Thomas, "An Exploration."

57. See World Bank website at http://web.worldbank.org/WBSITE/EXTERNAL/EXTSITETOOLS/0,,contentMDK:20749693~pagePK:98400~piPK:98424~theSitePK:95474,00.html.

58. Ana Palacio, "Human Rights Day, 2006" (World Bank, 2006).

59. Sergio Pereira Leite, "Human Rights and the IMF," *Finance and Development* [an IMF quarterly] 38, no. 4 (2001).

60. OHCHR, "Human Rights and Trade," OHCHR website, 2003.

61. Amnesty has attempted to give economic and social rights a higher profile in its operations in recent times. This is discussed in Chapter 7. See http://thereport.amnesty.org/en/introduction

62. Amnesty International, *Amnesty International Urges WTO Members to Respect*

Human Rights Obligations in Trade Negotiations in Hong Kong; available at http://web.amnesty.org/library/engindex (cited 2005).

63. Stephen Gill, "Constitutionalizing Inequality and the Clash of Civilizations," *International Studies Review* 4, no. 2 (2002): 49.

64. HRW, "*No Guarantee: Sex Discrimination in Mexico's Maquiladora Sector.*"

65. Oloka-Onyango and Udagana, "The Realization of Economic, Social, and Cultural Rights," p. 11.

66. Ibid. The report argues that globalization is as much female led as it is export led. That is, without the availability of women workers, increased trade would not be possible. Furthermore, the report notes that Export Processing Zones spawn a class of worker, often female, that is nonunionized, denied an opportunity for collective bargaining, and working under conditions where health and safety laws are suspended.

67. Jones, *Global Justice: Defending Cosmopolitanism;* William H. Meyer, *Human Rights and International Political Economy in Third World Nations* (Westport, Conn.: Praeger, 1998). Meyer uses the expression "fallacy of methodological individualism" to indicate the distinction between corporate responsibility and the actions of individuals within corporations.

68. Jones, *Global Justice.*

69. Michel Chossudovsky, "World Trade Organisation (WTO): An Illegal Organisation That Violates the Universal Declaration of Human Rights," www.derechos.org/nizker/doc/articles/eng.html (1999).

70. Teeple, *Riddle of Human Rights.*

71. Annan, "Address to the World Economic Forum in Davos."

72. Ibid. This was not the first venture by the United Nations to engage with business. The idea arose in the UNDP, with the move to create a Global Sustainable Development Facility—a proposal eventually withdrawn following sustained criticism. Other UN-business partnerships include UNESCO's educational project to engage with Disney and McDonald's in the "Millennium Dreamer" youth awards. This scheme, too, was heavily criticized for its failure to distinguish between commercial motivation and educational values. Secondment of corporation personnel to UN agencies is also practiced. See Kenny Bruno, *Perilous Partners*, www.multinationalmonitor.org (Multinational Monitor, 2000 [cited April 17, 2007]). There was also a meeting in 1997 to consider the terms of corporate involvement in the setting of UN policy, attended by Kofi Annan, ten CEOs, the International Chamber of Commerce, and fifteen high-ranking government officials.

73. See Global Compact, *What Is the Global Compact?* UN Global Compact www pages, cited March 13, 2007, for an overview of the ten principles.

74. Ruggie, "The Global Compact ." John Ruggie was an adviser to Kofi Annan on the Global Compact.

75. Gavin Power, "Who Cares Wins—the Convergence of Global Corporate Citizenship and Financial Markets," at the Investment Management Institute Conference, New York, 2006.

76. Mary Robinson, "Beyond Good Intentions: Corporate Citizenship for a New Century," RSA (Rivest, Shamir, and Adleman) World Leaders' Lecture, 2002.

77. Hopkins, *Planetary Bargain, p.* xii.

78. Bluthner, "Trade and Human Rights at Work."

79. There is a large and growing literature on CSR. See, for example, Hemingway, "Exploratory Analysis"; Power, "Who Cares Wins"; Source Watch, *Corporate Social Responsibility*, Centre for Media and Democracy website (cited May 17, 2007).

80. J. Stobart, "Culture Versus Commerce: Societies and Spaces for Elites in Eighteenth-century Liverpool," *Journal of Historical Geography* 28, no. 4 (2002): 471–485.

81. Hemingway, "Exploratory Analysis"; Hopkins, *Planetary Bargain;* Jamali and Mirshak, "Corporate Social Responsibility."

82. See the examples set out in Jeremy Seabrook, *Victims of Development* (London: Verso, 1993). See also Thomas, *Global Governance.*

83. Steven R. Ratner, "Corporations and Human Rights: A Theory of Legal Responsibility," *Yale Law Journal* 111 (2001).

84. Kofi Annan, "The United Nations Cannot Stand Still, Because the Threats to Humanity Do Not Stand Still" (Davos: World Economic Forum, 2006).

85. Global Compact Office, "The United Nations Global Compact: Advancing Corporate Citizenship" (UN Global Compact Office, 2005).

86. Alexandra Frean, "Corporate Aid or Plain Hypocrisy?" *Times,* London, February 2, 2004.

87. Sorcha MacLeod and Douglas Lewis, "Transnational Corporations: Power, Influence, and Responsibility," in *Global Ethics and Civil Society,* ed. John Eade and Darren O'Byrne (Aldershot, UK: Ashgate, 2005).

88. Andy Favell, "Do Blue Chips' Green Reports Show Their Blue Colours?" *Independent,* London, February 19, 2006.

89. Tessa Younger, "CSR a Heavy Responsibility," *Times,* London, April 5, 2004.

90. Global Exchange, "WTO Erodes Human Rights Protection."

91. This is often recognized in the UNDP Human Development Index Report. See, for example, 1996, *Economic Growth and Human Development* (Oxford: UNDP, 1996); 1997, *Human Development to Eradicate Poverty* (Oxford: UNDP, 1997); 1999, *Globalization with a Human Face* (Oxford: UNDP, 1999).

92. Peter Utting, "The Global Compact: Why All the Fuss?" in *UN Chronicle* (New York: 2003).

93. NGO Coalition, *Coalition Says Global Compact Threatens UN Mission and Integrity,* Corporate Watch, 2000, available at www.commandreams.org/news2000/0725-08.htm (cited April 17, 2007); Utting, "Why All the Fuss?"; Source Watch, *Corporate Social Responsibility.*

94. Monshipouri, Welch, and Kennedy, "Multinational Corporations and the Ethics of Global Responsibility: Problems and Possibilities."

95. For the Global Compact reaction to the charge of "bluewash," see http://www.unglobalcompact.org/AbouttheGC/faq.html.

96. Bill Young, "Forget Social Responsibility, Supply Management," *Times,* London, April 5, 2005.

97. Speeches by Irene Khan and Guy Ryder, Leaders' Summit on the Global Compact, Geneva, July 7, 2007. In 2006 the Global Compact Office lists as its achievements a series of seminars on implementation in Egypt and a meeting of two hundred participants at a Global Compact gathering in India. See Global Compact Office, "The United Nations Global Compact: Advancing Corporate Citizenship." See also Favell, "Do Blue Chips' Green Reports Show Their Blue Colours?"; Andy Favell, "Green Grocers? The Big Chains Talk a Good Game but Their True Ethical Colours Are Hard to Determine," *Independent,* London, 2006, for a critical review of the reporting system.

98. John Ruggie, "Report of the Special Representative of the Secretary-General (SRSG) on the Issue of Human Rights and Transnational Corporations and Other Business Enterprises" (Geneva: Human Rights Council, 4th session, 2007).

99. Ibid., Paragraph 13.

100. Ibid., Paragraph 3.

101. Ibid.

102. Ibid., Paragraph 77.

103. Ibid., Parapraph 78.

104. Ibid. In 2006, the United Kingdom did introduce new company law that required big companies to report annually on environmental, employee, social, and community matters, including the role played by business partners in these issues. The Global Reporting Initiative (GRI) provides standardized protocols to improve the quality and

comparability of company reporting, but few companies take the opportunity to receive their advice.

105. John Ruggie, "Protect, Respect, and Remedy: A Framework for Business and Human Rights" (Geneva: Human Rights Council, 2008).

106. John G. Ruggie, "Creating Public Value: Everybody's Business" (Berlin: Herrhausen Society, 2004).

107. Bruno, "Perilous Partners."

108. Robert Hormats, "Globalization and Human Rights" (Washington, D.C.: Public Broadcasting Service, 1998).

109. Robert McCorquodale and Richard Fairbrother, "Globalization and Human Rights," *Human Rights Quarterly* 21, no. 3 (1999).

110. Monshipouri, Welch, and Kennedy, "Multinational Corporations and the Ethics of Global Responsiblity," p. 980

111. World Bank, *World Development Report, 1997: The State of a Changing World* (Oxford, UK: World Bank/Oxford University Press, 1997).

6

States, Sovereignty, and Human Rights

The language of the universal human rights regime assumes that the sovereign state is the central actor. However, while no general agreement has been achieved as to the exact nature of the current global order, the number of commentators arguing that little has altered since the end of World War II is in decline. The literature on the dynamics of globalization has shown that the global order is constructed and conditioned by the interactions of many actors, including international organizations, nongovernmental organizations, and business and financial interests.[1] While the potential to increase the quantity of these interactions has been facilitated by new communications technologies, the creation of complex social networks has also brought qualitative changes. As many scholars have noted, these quantitative and qualitative changes have transformed the nature, capacities, and capabilities of the sovereign state and its role within the global order.[2] This body of work notwithstanding, faith in the sovereign state as the facilitator for change—for solving the problems that the present and future hold—continues to flourish in many academic and political practitioner circles. The lingua franca of state sovereignty continues in discussions and decisions concerning, for example, HIV/AIDS, the environment, population movements, poverty, and many other issues that are consequential to the globalizing world order.

Universal human rights are no exception in this respect. The human rights regime, which is largely an international legal construct, reinforces the view that the sovereign state remains the appropriate actor for guaranteeing the rights and freedoms agreed by states. Although it has often been argued that the Universal Declaration "subverted the rules of the Westphalian system of international relations, in which sovereign states were the only actors, by conferring upon the human person the status of a subject of law beyond domestic jurisdiction,"[3] human rights talk clings tenaciously to the state as the primary, if not the only, actor for protecting human rights.

Two broad points militate against sustaining such a view. Firstly, sovereign states are increasingly "enmeshed in and functionally part of a larger pattern of global transformations and global flows,"[4] creating transnational networks and relations that touch almost all human activities. Although the state may continue to play a leading role within this complex order, it is no longer clear that the state is sovereign, at least not in the sense imagined in the post–World War II settlement. While the state has been assigned primary responsibility for the protection of human rights under international law, new socioeconomic networks and relations limit the power of the state, whether acting singly or in cooperation with others, to carry out this task. Secondly, the emerging structures of globalization, particularly the globalization of markets, finance, and production, create conditions under which the integrity of human rights cannot be sustained. While the sovereign state continues to play a role within global politics, the newly emerging socioeconomic structures have created conditions under which violations occur beyond the reach of the state.[5]

In Chapters 3 and 4 we encountered arguments suggesting that the practice of rights in any particular historic period should be viewed as a reflection of sociopolitical struggles characteristic of that period. In the period in which the human rights regime was created, it seemed natural to frame all global issues in terms of a Westphalian order of sovereign states engaged in interstate relations. Within this model, the sovereign state was portrayed as a potential realm of peace, order, security, justice, and identity; a sociopolitical sphere where rights and freedoms could flourish. However, the new conditions of economic globalization suggest that the transformation of state sovereignty makes the state an unreliable agent for fulfilling these expectations internally, and less able than was anticipated to fulfill obligations under international law externally.[6] In short, while the socioeconomic context has undergone significant changes during the past six decades, the language of state sovereignty retains its appeal in human rights talk.

The Sovereign State in the Tradition of International Relations

The standard treatment of the sovereign state is well known within the discipline of international relations. Since the creation of the Westphalian order and its evolution into the modern state system, the sovereign state has been recognized as an independent, autonomous actor. Sovereignty assumes that the state takes responsibility for all central political tasks, both internally and externally. Internally, the state is said to exercise supreme political authority over its territory, controlling movements across borders and exercising a monopoly over the means of violence. Externally, given the Westphalian anarchical order, the state must prepare to defend its sovereignty at all times, reacting to all attempts by others to interfere with any aspect of its internal social, economic, or political life. Social cohesion is maintained through institutional arrangements that define and protect the internal order. The sovereign state may therefore be seen as "a constitutive political practice, one which has the effect of defining the social bonds in terms of unity, exclusivity, territory, and boundedness and by the state's monopoly of authority, territory, and community."[7]

In contrast to an order that springs from shared values found within the state, anarchy is said to prevail within the international order. Since no other authority is higher than the state, and no effective government exists beyond the state, self-help characterizes relations in the external world. Conflicts of interest must therefore be settled between interested parties who mobilize their own diplomatic, military, and economic resources as they seek to prevail. Within this model, "the logic of the principle of effectiveness [determines that] might eventually makes right."[8] The state is sovereign, its borders cannot be breached legitimately, nor can any interference with its internal institutional arrangements be tolerated. The sovereign state in traditional thinking can therefore be characterized through a series of contrasts between the internal and external: community and anarchy, justice and inequality, and effective institutions and shifting alliances. In this way, international politics is presented as the negation of "normal" domestic politics.[9]

While this model suggests that sovereignty and the state are conterminous, this cannot be said of sovereignty and government. According to John Locke, security and property could not be guaranteed if the ruler assumed absolute, sovereign power. As a reaction to Hobbes's *Leviathan*,[10] which sought to establish that to avoid a "war of all against all" government should assume absolute power, Locke's *Second Treatise of Civil Government* reasoned that since natural law determined that the individual's right to life, liberty, and property were at the center of social existence, the powers of the ruler should be limited to enacting laws that protected these rights.[11] In exchange for obedience to the ruler, the sovereign individual was offered the conditions for protection of the individual's natural rights, rights that provide the conditions to pursue private interests unhindered within civil society. The role of government is therefore to act as the guardian of liberal rights, to protect the citizen from threats that impede the exercise of freedom in the private sphere, and to secure the operation of the free market.[12] Later, Rousseau asserted that the "general will" represented the moral authority of the people over government, further strengthening the principle of nonintervention. The only permissible exception to this principle concerned sanctions against states that transgressed the rules of coexistence, which provide the foundation for the conduct of international relations and the conditions for peace.[13]

The emphasis placed on the sovereign state within the tradition of Westphalia suggests that it would be problematic to say anything about international relations without including a clear understanding of sovereignty and the state. However, the literature on international relations displays little interest in engaging in an appropriate analytical research program that seeks to explain manifestations of sovereignty historically.[14] Instead, the discipline of international relations proceeds either through the realist tradition, which simply asserts the sovereign state as the starting point of analysis without explanation, or through an idealist tradition, which assumes some kind of a society of states as a given. In this way "sovereignty serves as a fundamental point of reference in international relations, a ground or essential modifier for the state" without explanation or justification.[15] This permits analysis to proceed on the assumption that the state exercises absolute authority over territory and peoples, independent of other states and actors. In rare cases where sovereignty is discussed in the literature it is usual to limit the discussion to the state as it is assumed to function within the Westphalian order, rather than as a foundational claim for international relations located within historic context.

In summary, the traditional understanding of the sovereign state within international relations might be characterized as the "container" theory of society.[16] Within this framework, society and the state are contiguous. As a container, the state exercises both internal and external authority in the struggle to achieve the conditions for the "good life." Territorial integrity, security, and a monopoly on the use of force are presented as the defining principles of the sovereign state. The language of liberalism and representation has added further to the notion that the legitimate sovereign state continues to hold center stage in the theory and practice of international relations. Despite the increasing evidence pointing to recent changes in the structures of the global socioeconomic order, the language, concepts, and ideas that inform international relations, particularly foundational ideas associated with statehood, sovereignty, and nonintervention, remain "steadfastly unaffected."[17] As John Vincent observed, even though it remains common to see the cosmopolitan notion of universal human rights presented as a challenge to the particularist claims of the sovereign state, and therefore a challenge to the international order itself, the language of "normal" international relations persists as the dominant voice.[18]

Within this tradition of international relations, the dominant language of state sovereignty presents significant problems for the implementation of universal human rights. By defining state sovereignty as the exercise of absolute internal authority, the Westphalian order has created a "Maginot line against the invasion of new ideas in the international world," a rampart behind which "the demagogue and the reactionary are enthroned."[19] No matter that the idea of universal human rights has achieved widespread acceptance during the post–World War II period, the claim of state sovereignty remains the last bastion for those who seek immunity from international law following ruthless, inhuman, and brutal acts perpetrated against their own people. The principles of the international system of sovereign states therefore act as a barrier to holding repressive governments to account. Succinctly expressed by former US Secretary of State Robert Lansing, the "essence of sovereignty is the absence of responsibility."[20] For these reasons, some scholars have called for a separation of sovereignty from the state to avoid further analytical confusion. Others have gone further, arguing that the concept of sovereignty be abandoned altogether because of its multiple uses in the literature and lack of conceptual development.[21]

State, Sovereignty, and Globalization

In the current period, where globalization has brought changes to almost all aspects of social, economic, and political life, "the essential character of sovereignty becomes more and more elusive and subject to renegotiation by the play of political forces, moral attitudes, and prevailing perceptions."[22] Claims that the state and community coincide and that the state therefore represents the community at the international level overlook the historic record of refugees, illegal aliens, and excluded groups, who occupy a place within the territorial state but may not be thought of as occupying a place within the community represented by the state. Weber, for instance, argues that domestic community is always in flux, the range of authority that the community exercises is always unsettled, and the membership that the state is said to represent is never easily defined.[23] Moreover, under conditions of globalization, new social networks encourage forms of loyalty that do not focus on the state or nation.[24] Having noted this, however, questions about representation and community often remain unasked because such questions threaten the foundational authority of international relations, both as an academic project and a practical guide for action.

The persistence of the traditional approach to international relations in the face of a growing body of evidence that points to a more complex view of sovereignty needs some explanation. For Camilleri and Falk, the explanation is found in the language of politics itself, which is central to power relations that seek to "naturalize" the existing order. Interests associated with notions of the sovereign state as the central actor on the global stage, particularly "the notion of strength understood as the state's capacity to impose its will whether on its own people or other states,"[25] continues to use traditional thinking in support of the existing hierarchical order. In this sense, sovereignty is not a "fact" but an attempt to promote a concept that supports existing relations of political power and to sustain the notion that what has been should continue to be. In this way, although the material conditions that brought the sovereign state into existence are no longer intact, the language endures. The sovereign state is thus a fiction, an exercise in "organized hypocrisy,"[26] that seeks to reaffirm the legitimacy of a past order, ignoring the new conditions of globalization, and attempting to "naturalize" international relations.

The tradition of international relations overlooks critics who argue that, historically, manifestations of the state are the outcome of social formations derived and ordered by interests associated with the global political economy. According to this argument, notions of the "state" are socially constructed in ways that reflect socioeconomic relations and the dominant values prevailing in any given period. In the current global order, where the individual is free in the sense of assumed equality within exchange relations, human rights theory and practice are organized in ways that support capitalist social relations. These are the arguments first encountered in Chapter 3, which suggested that the primary task of the state is to secure and promote those rights that legitimate freedoms associated with property and personal wealth while denying any other claims, either by extending rights beyond those associated with exchange relations or to those who claim rights outside exchange relations. Rosenberg, for example, argues that social reproduction "does not simply accord greater recognition to individual rights" but "actually constitutes the individual as a novel social form" peculiar to the period.[27]

Today, the familiar and comfortable language of state sovereignty—which draws clear distinctions between the particular and the global—often seems at odds with the issues that confront humankind: environmental degradation, global terrorism, diseases like HIV/AIDS, threats to agricultural production from animal infections, and poverty. These and other issues are intimately related to the imperative for economic growth and development, organized on a global scale—an imperative that enjoins all peoples to abandon their old ways and to embrace the principles of free market capitalism.[28] The tension between claims of state sovereignty and individual freedoms, which in the past provided an important theme in political theory generally, and human rights talk in particular has now been superseded by the tension between the economic imperatives of globalization and individual rights. For example, the destruction of cultural traditions, family relations, and ties to tribal homeland are often justified in the name of economic "progress" and modernization as states move to achieve ever-greater levels of integration in the global political economy.[29] A further example is seen in the willingness to maintain profitable trading relations with known human rights violators, including the supply of military equipment that could be used to repress and subjugate peoples.[30]

Confusion over the nature and current status of state sovereignty is articulated vividly in UN Secretary-General Boutros Boutros-Ghali's 1992 report *Agenda for Peace*.[31] Paragraph 17 notes that although the foundation stone for building a peaceful world order remains the state, and that respect for its "fundamental sovereignty and integrity are crucial to any international common progress . . . the time for absolute and exclusive sovereignty has, however, passed, its theory never matched by reality." Furthermore, Boutros-Ghali continues:

> It is the task of leaders of States today to understand this and to find a balance between the needs of good internal government and the requirements of an ever more interdependent world. Commerce, communications and environmental matters transcend administrative borders, but inside these borders is where individuals carry out the first order of their economic, political and social lives. The United Nations has not shut its door. Yet if every ethnic, religious or linguistic group claimed statehood, there would be no limit to fragmentation, and peace, security and economic well-being for all would become ever more difficult to achieve.[32]

What this passage expresses is the paradox of state sovereignty in the current global order. The World Bank confirmed this view in its 1997 report, which asserted that "the state is central to economic and social development, not as a direct provider of growth but as a partner, a catalyst, and facilitator," and thus a unit of administration rather than a political decisionmaker.[33] While on the one hand the authority of the state remains a foundational component for tackling the major problems that face humankind today, and therefore state sovereignty must be strengthened and sustained, on the other hand state borders are becoming increasingly permeable, weakening state sovereignty and the state's potential to manage the political economy in the interests of its population.

Boutros-Ghali's solution to this paradox is to embrace the state's new role as facilitator for expanding global economic, political, and social agendas that satisfy the needs of the people—needs that are no longer defined by the sovereign state but by the "hidden hand" of economic necessity.[34] The modern state should be characterized by the attenuation of sovereignty derived from boundary transgressions associated with the globalization of markets, which in turn give rise to problems of global governance and expressions of sovereignty.[35] Where sovereignty resides within this new order remains unclear. However, if the underlying suggestion is that the global populations assume sovereignty, then questions must be asked about how the global order assesses those wishes, for at present no such mechanism exists.[36]

This is not to suggest that the state is a spent force in global politics, as some early literature on globalization seemed to conclude. Rather, although the state remains a significant player on the global stage, within the context of globalizing capitalism, the traditional theorization of the state as possessing absolute sovereignty appears anachronistic. Instead, the transformation of sovereignty has seen the state adopt the task of oiling the wheels of global capital, providing services associated with surveillance and data collection, and supplying the means of violence against groups resistant to capitals aims. As Scholte notes, "the post-sovereign state has not abjured militarization so much as deployed armed force differently."[37] The view that the globalization of capital reduces the possibility of international war has not seen the state exercise restraint against those peoples and social movements who take a stance against the relentless march of economic globalization. Social movements that offer a human rights defense for actions taken against projects aimed to further economic "progress" are not tolerated.

As Robert Cox has argued, the traditional politics of state sovereignty is "no longer about alternatives, but about who is best equipped to manage the "irresistible" progress of globalization." For Cox, all that is left is personality politics, which signifies the "death of the citizen as a subject of politics, thus the death of politics as the forum for active citizens, and by implication the end of democracy."[38] In a world where values associated with "market discipline" provide the guiding values for action, where socioeconomic decisionmaking is conducted by unaccountable private and public institutions (referred to by Cox as the *nébuleuse*),[39] issues of democracy and human rights are displaced by concern to achieve ever-greater market efficiency. For practicing politicians and world leaders, the claim that further economic globalization is irrevocable and irresistible appears to support this view.[40]

The argument that sovereignty is limited by the state's new global role as administrator and "transmission belt" from the local to the global, rather than an independent political unit exercising choice, is now recognized in the literature.[41] Appeals to protect state sovereignty, such as those often heard in the politics of the European Union, no longer focus upon absolute authority but instead upon struggles to gain a greater voice in negotiating processes for managing the global economy. Moreover, although it is sometimes argued that the state voluntarily relinquishes sovereignty to further the interests of the nation, an alternative interpretation is that states are more concerned with gaining a stamp of approval from international organizations as competent facilitators for global capital. Competence here implies the capability to reduce welfare budgets of all kinds to ever-lower levels, including trimming health, unemployment, and housing assistance, and reducing taxation. The only exceptions to this are budgets that externalize corporate costs; for example, where education policy is focused upon training for employment, rather than the pursuit of knowledge.

In sum, when the state claims sovereignty on grounds that it represents the democratic will of the people, it is assumed that the legitimately constituted government is accountable for its actions. In this traditional account, the state assumes external sovereignty within the context of classical economic theory, where trade and investment imply transfers across borders. This approach sits uncomfortably in the emerging context of economic globalization, where production and finance are organized on a transnational basis. The emergence of transborder production, finance, markets, and business, in which the state plays an administrative role, offers ample opportunity to equivocate over controls intended to protect democratic systems or the values expressed in the international human rights regime.

As we shall see in the next section, while new forms of communication technology have enabled the spread of ideas like human rights and democracy, paradoxically that same technology has contributed to creating a global order in which claims for human rights remain unheard and where participation in the political process is less meaningful. Given these changes in the character of sovereignty and the role of the state, proposals flowing from traditional discourses of democracy and human rights appear unworkable. There is a deepening void created as the social bonds represented by the sovereign state decline and interest in human rights and democracy increases. However, so far no mechanisms have been devised "to guarantee transparency, open debate and accountability in the relationship between the states and their supraterritoral constituents."[42] The violence perpetrated by state governments against those who resist the force of economic globalization, together with reductions in public social expenditure, as the state seeks to adjust to prevailing global free mar-

ket conditions, suggests that the state no longer possesses the neces·
ities to fulfill the economic, social, and political needs of terr
stituents.[43]

State Sovereignty and Human Rights

The last section presented arguments about the necessity to reflect upon sovereignty in the current socioeconomic global order. The tradition of viewing the state as the central actor within global politics and as the main actor for delivering human rights seems to avoid pressing questions concerning sovereignty in a globalized order, which can no longer be described as Westphalian.[44] This section will look more closely at the assumed role of the state within the human rights regime and raise questions about whether the state can successfully discharge that role, given the changing nature of the sovereign state in a globalized world order.

Human rights are often promoted as a challenge to the internal sovereignty of the state by offering the individual a bulwark against state initiatives to violate human freedoms. The revolutionary character of this claim was recognized by those engaged in early preparations to create the human rights regime following the end of World War II and is often cited in the literature today.[45] Indeed, the superimposition of universalism on an existing commitment to an international society composed of politically separate states is sometimes seen as providing the unique character of the postwar order.[46] In future, it was argued, control over territory, the existence of central government, and a monopoly over the use of violence would not be sufficient to gain or sustain membership within international society. Internal sovereignty, the claim that the state could treat its own citizens as it willed, was outlawed. The modern state had thus evolved to include human rights as an additional and necessary feature for receiving recognition and sovereign equality. Accordingly, it was argued that political leaders would no longer be able to act with impunity. Instead, while nonintervention remained a central element in the construction of sovereign statehood, legitimacy also demanded evidence of a good human rights record. The failure to respect human rights therefore offered the prospect of delegitimation, loss of sovereignty, and the potential for intervention.[47]

However, as we saw earlier, the project for universal human rights may also be seen as a revolutionary move that seeks to define particular freedoms necessary for developing capitalist relations on a global scale. The promotion of natural rights as the foundation for this project supports the division between the public and private spheres, where the former is concerned with citizenship and the latter with economic life. In this respect, some have argued that rights offer an illusion of egalitarianism by masking the power relations that reside in the capitalist class system. Whereas claims for human rights are often presented as a radical tool for mounting resistance against tyrannical, oppressive, and despotic governments, for critics human rights represent a symbol of "normal-ization" that legitimates the voice of interests represented by the state. Critics thus argue that "rights have become rewards for accepting the dominant order"[48] and that the move toward global economic growth and development necessar-ily brings with it aspects of rights associated with the dominant order.[49]

Pae' acknowledged this view in his cost-benefit analysis of human rights. In this approach, sovereignty and human rights are treated as a tradable prop-erty,[50] subject to use-limitations as much as any other form of property. Any at-tempt to transgress these limitations attracts negative externalities, including instability, population movements, international disapprobation, economic sanc-tions, and, in some cases, direct intervention. A market approach to these exter-nalities is said to allow states to negotiate on human rights issues in exchange for other goods; for example, recognition as a full member of international so-ciety, improved terms of trade, and a voice in important international economic organizations and decisions. However, as the costs of adjusting policies for re-ducing human rights violations succeeds in attracting less international con-demnation, further economic gains become marginal. At this point of economic efficiency, no further action is judged necessary to reduce instances of human rights violations.[51]

Furthermore, this liberal economic approach argues that negative external-ities can be reduced by creating international machinery dedicated to protect-ing human rights. The benefits of institutionalization include a reduction in the costs of defining human rights standards, a reduction in the costs of enforcing those standards, and economies of scale. For example, if an abusing state gen-erates mass population movements across borders, international institutions may take responsibility for providing food, shelter, and healthcare to refugees. In this case, according to the liberal economic view, the abusing state faces lim-ited costs for its actions and will continue its policy of violation. Although some costs are carried by the receiving state, the burden falls mainly upon interna-tional institutions created to assist refugees, often in cooperation with NGOs. The policy of human rights abuses therefore carries fewer costs than might have been the case had the abusing state had to bear the full cost of violations. Thus, although institutionalization may reduce transaction costs, "if the abusing state was required to pay damages to the affected states or if the affected states could have stopped such abuses by compensating the abusing state, then the actual level of abuses would have been lower than the current level."[52] In short, the lib-eral economic approach advocates a "free market" in human rights, where states negotiate to reduce violations to economically efficient levels that satisfy the need of concerned state parties.

In this view, human rights may be underprotected by shifting responsibil-ity from the state to international institutions because the move makes threats by states to take action against a violating state less credible. This risk is height-ened if the cost to the "savior" state is to violate international law that is widely accepted by other members of international society; for example, ignoring a

Security Council resolution that forbids intervention. Since effective enforcement procedures are rarely included in international law, and whatever procedures there are remain weak, treaties may act to underline the centrality of sovereignty while simultaneously placing less responsibility for human rights on the state, closing off the possibility of developing an overarching system of global governance for human rights.

The liberal economic approach is therefore concerned with calculations to determine whether intervention in the name of human rights is efficient in free market terms. It is concerned with the marginal benefits of enforcement against the marginal costs of violations. In this way, human rights represent a "commodified" good to be traded, bargained, bought, and sold in the global marketplace. It is important to note here that liberal reason requires no normative or moral input. All that is required are economic calculations concerning the net benefits and costs to the state.

A less radical approach can be found in the argument on basic rights, the best-known exponent of which is Henry Shue, in *Basic Rights: Subsistence, Affluence, and US Foreign Policy*.[53] Shue defends human rights from a broadly liberal perspective, but one that attempts to ameliorate the real inequalities that underlie the formal equalities offered in civil and political rights. Shue's novel approach is to add subsistence rights to the basic liberal claims for life and liberty, an approach that reflects citizens' rights developed through the policies of the welfare state in the postwar years. These additional rights include minimum levels of food, unpolluted air, clothing, shelter, and elementary healthcare.[54] This can be seen as a reversal of standard liberal arguments, which assert that the right to life and liberty are prerequisite rights for the enjoyment of all other rights. However, Shue insists that the right to subsistence does not imply that there is a duty for others to provide the material means of subsistence to those unable to provide for themselves, although he concedes that this may be necessary on occasion. Rather, a human right to subsistence may simply mean a duty to

> stay out of people's way while they take x for themselves, or a duty to teach them to read so they can figure out how to make or grow x, or a duty to let them form a political party so that they can effectively demand that the government stop exporting x (instead of having the CIA arm their police so that they can suppress all dissent).[55]

In particular, Shue points to structural faults within the existing liberal order that may prevent people from achieving their basic rights.

While at first sight this formulation seems to provide a way of promoting the full range of human rights, including economic and social rights, many questions about implementation within a global liberal order remain unanswered. Shue suggests a global "division of moral labour," or what he terms "waves of duty-bearers," aimed at empowering people to engage in activities that allow them to secure their own future, free from local, national, regional and global structural barriers that exist in the current order. He acknowledges that this would demand a move to "limited sovereignty," as successive "waves" intervene to exercise their responsibility for securing human rights, including international and global institutions. Shue offers very limited discussion on the exact nature of his proposed new institutional arrangements for integrating state duties with those of other global actors, making it difficult to assess just how these arrangements would work in practice. Moreover, he has nothing to say about the tensions created by the right to private property; nor about freedoms associated with the global free market; nor about the right of new institutions to exercise their duty when clashes of interest occur. What we are left with is recognition that economic globalization presents a new order where the sovereign state cannot any longer be thought of as capable of regulating the actions of other actors, but a solution where the state continues to play a leading role. It remains unclear how these two apparently contradictory views can be reconciled.[56]

In similar vein, students of the European Union (EU) have investigated the changing nature of the relationship between rights and sovereignty within a liberal world order. Developments in the EU, in particular, are said to demonstrate a growing interest in exploring new forms of citizenship in a "post-Westphalian" order. Linklater, for example, attempts to promote the notion of transnational citizenship that enables a multilayered commitment to local and international institutions. Within the context of economic globalization, which challenges old Westphalian ideas of sovereignty, the EU has sought to create an innovative form of politics in response to the tensions found between new forms of government and individual freedom. Linklater argues that given the now widely accepted right to political participation, together with a duty to provide general welfare for the community as a whole, there is a need to imagine new notions of citizenship not exclusively tied to the state. Within the emerging context of the global order—an order where the sovereign state seems less capable of maintaining the welfare and livelihood of its citizens, and where a democratic deficit is created as the right to withdraw support from decisions made by multilateral organizations is itself withdrawn—Linklater claims there exists an opportunity to create a form of international citizenship through which human rights can be realized. The aim of such a project, according to Linklater, would be to extend citizens' rights in two directions—extend them "higher" to the institutions of global governance and extend them "lower" to local institutions—creating the conditions for citizens to participate in decision-making processes about their own future, including questions of rights and duties.[57]

Several issues are raised by this attempt to resolve the tension between old and new notions of state citizenship. First, as Hutchings has pointed out, so long as state citizenship remains integral to developing international citizenship, "international citizenship appears to depend on the idea of the state-citizen, with other notions of political identity and rights effectively only developing via the permission of the state."[58] Given that the idea of international citizenship is presented as a response to the demand for greater levels of participation under conditions of globalization, the statecentric focus seems ambiguous.

Second, international citizenship is offered as a solution to the weakening social bonds that the altered face of sovereignty represents. While this suggests nurturing new loyalties based upon social bonds associated with globalization, recent interest in new forms of citizenship fail to note the profoundly undemocratic nature of many networks associated with the move to globalization.[59] Indeed, some networks appear to generate loyalties that may not be conducive to new forms of democracy and citizenship, instead encouraging the very practices that democracy and citizenship are supposed to ameliorate.[60]

Third, the social and political developments found in the EU are offered as the outcome of a political choice: the exercise of agency alone brings Europeans to conclude that international citizenship offers a solution to problems of representation and rights. The motivation for engaging in the discourse of citizenship is concerned with preserving and developing freedoms associated with citizenship, freedoms that are increasingly challenged within a global context. The individual, as an end in itself, is the focus for this concern. However, the globalization of capital, production, and finance noted earlier provides a context in which the individual is seen as a means to an end, and that end is increased profits. Recent concern for citizenship may therefore provide a mask for new forms of exploitation rather than new opportunities to strengthen the rights of citizenship. Linklater seems to recognize this danger when be observes that international relations represents a "thin conception of citizenship which brings an international civil society into existence rather than the thicker conception of citizenship in which active membership of a political community is normally thought to imply."[61]

Fourth, the human rights regime is built upon the principle that the state is the subject of international law. Complex questions therefore arise concerning the status, role, and authority of international law in a multilevel form of citizenship.[62] Would it be possible or desirable to preserve existing international law on human rights or would there be a need to develop a new form of transnational law, which saw the international citizen as its subject? If new forms of law would be necessary, in what ways would it differ from international law, particularly on enforcement issues? And how would relations between the state and the international citizen be constructed?

Attempts to resolve issues to do with the changing nature of the global order are therefore open to the criticism that globalization has weakened the prospect for protecting human rights through mechanisms associated with the sovereign state. If the principles of the Westphalian order no longer hold, if the state's claim to sovereignty is in doubt, if the state cannot any longer claim sufficient capabilities to represent the people, and if, as will be argued in the next section, international law does not offer a viable solution, how can we pursue the project to protect human rights?

This question comes into sharp focus when human rights are promoted as a condition for receiving economic assistance aimed at gaining a place within the global economy, where civil and political rights associated with citizenship and national democracy assume central importance. In this arrangement, human rights are defined as the freedoms necessary for the individual to invest time, energy, and resources in entrepreneurial projects, which is seen as a necessary step toward engaging in global markets. However, the move from traditional systems of production that fulfill the needs of a local community to a system aimed at production for export goods sold on global markets brings consequences for human rights. As Thomas explains, the rights extended through market discipline offer "the appearance of extending individual choice and control over the products which capitalism successfully generates," while simultaneously increasing "inequalities and the resultant differential enjoyment of such benefits."[63] While the rights associated with the individual's civil and political freedoms are prioritized, other equally valid claims for economic, social, and cultural rights are marginalized. As discussed in Chapter 2, this process can act to stimulate social unrest that attracts coercive action and the consequent denial of civil and political rights.[64]

McCorquodale observes that there is strong evidence that neoliberal model for economic development often leads to greater national wealth at a social cost to the majority. In a global order where the imperative of market discipline "must be allowed to flourish while states are relegated to the role of assisting this flourishing," the opportunities for advancing human rights are incidental and fragmentary.[65] Human rights thus become, at best, a secondary consideration. All that is required to advance interests associated with economic globalization is strong state leaders prepared to propel their nation toward ever-higher levels of integration with the global capitalist order. Whether a state polity is described as dictatorship, authoritarian, absolute monarchy, or oligarchy is of little consequence, provided governments maintain stability in the interests of expanding global capital. As Hoogvelt notes, for example,

> when one is only interested in a raw material such as oil, and not in labour or consumer markets, one's profit strategy at that stage dictates a preference for dictatorships rather than democracy regimes. A sovereign ruler is all that is wanted: *Oil and dictatorship go together.*[66]

Even when it is claimed that the state represents the will of the people through democratic government, human rights can remain vulnerable. Beginning with the claim that liberal democracy cannot be dissociated from capitalist relations, some scholars have argued that although democracy is presented as an end in itself, the promotion of democracy should be seen through the lens of its political and economic purpose. That purpose is fulfilled when the introduction of democracy preempts either revolutionary change or a progressive reform in pursuit of interests that threaten to "abrogate the political and economic power of business and military elites."[67] Success and failure following the introduction of democratic institutions is measured not as levels of justice and social reform, but by achieving political stability. The reward for maintaining stability is continued economic and political support, even when "repressive abuses of human rights continue, usually against the familiar targets of labour, students, the left and human rights activists,"[68] who challenge the institutionalization of inequality. In cases where democratic freedoms are used by popular movements in the struggle for a more egalitarian society, few influential voices are raised against the mobilization of the police and the military.

What Gills, Rocamora, and Wilson refer to as "Low Intensity Democracy" therefore becomes a tool in the move to create the necessary reforms for opening markets and creating compliant governments prepared to pursue the twin goals of economic growth and development within a framework of market discipline.

> The new "democratic" regime, which temporarily enjoys increased legitimacy, can in fact undertake economic and social policies of "adjustment" that impose new hardships on the general population and compromise economic sovereignty. The paradox of Low Intensity Democracy is that a civilianized conservative regime can pursue painful and even repressive social and economic policies with more impunity and with less popular resistance than can an openly authoritarian regime. From the point of view of the US and conservative domestic elites in these countries, this quality must make it an interesting and useful alternative to traditional overt authoritarianism.[69]

In this way, calls to exercise tolerance and restraint toward democratic states, particularly newly created democracies, should be understood as part of the architecture of globalization and the pursuit of global market discipline.

A further defense of the human rights benefits of globalization offered by many authors is founded upon claims of a global civil society. In this view, civil society is understood as a means through which groups vulnerable to structural violations can mount and sustain protest. Social movements, it is argued, particularly those represented by NGOs, are developing the capacity to challenge the prevailing order through campaigns designed to change public perceptions, through lobbying, and through gaining a voice in high-level negotiations on a wide range of issues, including human rights, democracy, and the environment.[70] However, organizations associated with social networks rarely challenge the institutional framework within which such negotiations are conducted. Rather, problems are identified and their solutions sought in the old institutions of the Westphalian order. Indeed, it is a condition that NGOs embrace these values before gaining recognition by international forums. The system devised by the United Nations for recognition of NGOs offers some evidence of this, as do attempts to remove recognition from NGOs that offer too stringent critiques of political economic structures.[71] Accordingly, it comes as no surprise that states and NGOs often find it possible to reach a compromise agreement on global issues like the environment and human rights. The radical credentials for many NGOs are thus in doubt as they engage with state and corporate interests within the principles and values that describe global neoliberalism.[72]

For many authors, moreover, the myth of the global society can be sustained only by overlooking the incompatibility of community and individual rights.[73] Economic globalization has facilitated the exploitation of labor, as capital "shops around" for the cheapest source. It has also added to the increasing difficulties for trade unions to organize in an economic environment where the state, as a unit of administration, seeks to provide the best conditions for attracting investment. Paraphrasing Gramsci, Nef argues that "the crisis consists in that the old is dying and the new cannot be born."[74] The crisis of sovereignty, together with the failure to replace old notions of democracy and statehood with new ways to offer populations a sense of belonging, identity, and empowerment, has added to the emasculation of any real threat of resistance. As Nef argues, an examination of the architecture of the emerging global political economy reveals a "common ideology and professional socialization on the part of national and international 'experts'" that links global and domestic management through international agreements that legitimate economic action.[75]

The harmony of interests and values at the level of transnational networks, which consist in a transnational class of affluent, mobile, and influential voices located in both the developed and developing world, provides an image of progress, order, and stability that is not inclusive. While those closest to the center of economic globalization enjoy rights and privileges, those at the periphery become increasingly marginalized and impoverished. Within these marginalized groups, people are deprived of even the basic necessities to maintain life—food, water, shelter, meaningful employment, and access to basic healthcare. While those closest to the center of economic globalization enjoy shared experiences, the heterogeneous, fragmented strata at the periphery have no voice in social, economic, political, and cultural debates about their own future. Thus, for critics, where squalor "makes possible the prosperity of the few," destabilization, conflict, and violence follow, creating conditions that are a "direct threat to everyone's security."[76]

The discussion so far has focused upon issues to do with the nature of the sovereign state under conditions of economic globalization. Critics argue that the Westphalian tradition of sovereignty seems increasingly inappropriate in a global society that today bears little resemblance to an order that in the past saw the state as the only significant actor.[77] Within the contemporary global order, the sovereign state has become a unit of administration, with the primary task of managing the global political economy in the interests of global capital.[78]

International Human Rights Law

As noted earlier, questions about the nature of sovereignty were raised during early discussions to create an international human rights regime. At both the

Dumbarton Oaks Conversations (1944) and the San Francisco Conference on International Organization (1945), the tension between the principles of sovereignty and those of universal rights were sometimes raised but never fully resolved.[79] Within the context of postwar international relations, political leaders were acutely aware of the need to respond to the demand for human rights, but equally aware of the need to reaffirm the centrality of the sovereign state within the postwar order. For many legal scholars, the issue was not one of choosing between state sovereignty and human rights but whether the introduction of human rights represented a new kind of law, perhaps more appropriately labeled transnational, rather then international law.[80] The purpose of this move would be to resolve the contradictions between the cosmopolitan claims of human rights and the principles of sovereignty, nonintervention, and domestic jurisdiction, upon which the tradition of international law is built. Although the noble motives of this move are recognized by critics, Chinkin argues that it "impedes the application of basic international legal doctrine to human rights law, impedes its central and academic development and obscures conflicts between the two."[81] However, the tensions created by attempting to express legal rules on universal claims within a system founded upon the principles of state sovereignty present a puzzle that remains unresolved today.

Questions over the sovereignty/human rights international law nexus are made more complex by the advent of globalization and its impact on state sovereignty. Any argument asserting that international law does not diminish sovereignty must account for changes in the socioeconomic context in which states are said to take decisions. For example, for most states, the only realistic way of gaining a voice in rule- and norm-making processes associated with global governance practices is to ratify a treaty that provides institutional privileges in, say, the WTO or other international governmental organizations. Within the field of human rights, the state gains several advantages by ratifying a treaty. These include reinforcing claims for state legitimacy; the moral acclaim of both internal and external publics (even when that acclaim is confined to rhetoric rather than action); a demonstration of independence as the choice to ratify is exercised, and an increase in the moral standing of state leaders.[82]

However, while the necessity to ratify important treaties may encourage an ethos of "one world," it also adds to the creation of a standardized, homogeneous, and uniform order where difference is seen as a threat. For states seeking to establish their independence, like those created following the collapse of the USSR, entering into a treaty may attract recognition externally but may also appear as a threat to national identity internally. In the case of human rights in particular, international law may also provide the means for citizens to challenge governments struggling to build a national identity that strengthens the postcolonial state.

The legal tradition for defining state sovereignty is found in Article 1 of the Montevideo Convention. According to this tradition, to achieve legal personhood the state should possess a permanent population, a defined territory, a central government, and the capacity to enter into relations with other states.[83] Article 8 asserts: "No State has the right to intervene in the internal or external affairs of another." Moreover, the convention assumes equality between states, allowing these criteria to be presented as objective, neutral, value-free, and unconnected to power relations found in the political sphere of international relations. An alternative to this definition, and one that offers a view of limited sovereignty, is offered by the Permanent Court of Justice, which argued that the "jurisdiction of the state is *exclusively* within the limits fixed by international law—using this expression in its widest sense, that is to say, embracing both customary law and general as well as particular treaty law."[84] In a later passage, the court asserts that the jurisdiction of the state "is limited by the rules of international law."[85] The application of these legal principles attracts the conclusion that sovereignty is, in fact, conditioned by developments in international law. Thus, the UN Charter, the major human rights covenants, and regional human rights treaties should be read as imposing conditionalities upon claims to sovereignty.

Two questions arise when adopting this view. First, the recognition of a sovereign state depends upon the political acts of other states, through applying subjective political criteria rather than the objective criteria claimed for international law.[86] This is seen in the practice of awarding recognition to states that fall far short of complying with universally agreed human rights standards, even when, paradoxically, domestic populations are persecuted for attempting to claim their human rights. Second, although human rights are presented as neutral claims, in a globalizing world order the Judeo-Christian foundation of this claim, and its association with the liberal democratic state, leave space for challenges. Given doubts about the validity of international law's claim to provide neutral criteria for sovereignty, and further doubts about the neutrality of the idea of human rights, arguments about the legal definition of sovereignty—including the obligations that states must undertake in processes associated with recognition—might be seen as little more than an article of faith. In this way, international law assumes an authority that it could only possess in a more cosmopolitan world order.[87] For Watson, what we are left with is a "breathtaking naïve over generalization," an unspoken but nonetheless discernable call for the abolition of the sovereign state and its replacement with some form of central world government.[88]

Following the well-established legal definitions of state sovereignty, some have attempted to construct arguments that retain the authority of the sovereign state and the authority of cosmopolitan claims for human rights simultaneously. These arguments stress the voluntary nature of ratifying a human rights treaty, the weak enforcement procedures included in all treaties (with the possible exception of the European Convention), and the lack of any correlation between ratifying a treaty and improved human rights performance. Accordingly, the inclusion of universal human rights as an additional feature within international politics serves only to confirm the robust nature of the Westphalian order, at least as a legal construct. According to Krasner, "human rights agreements have never violated international legal sovereignty, which stipulates that juridically independent territorial entities have the right to free choice."[89] Although it could be argued that human rights treaties could compromise sovereignty, the fact that government representatives are recognized as competent to give the state's consent to be subject to international law is seen as recognition by other international actors as a reaffirmation of sovereignty, not a challenge to it. Crucially, Krasner acknowledges that the creation of international law may also reflect changing values within the international order, including changes in the nature of sovereignty, but has nothing to say about the cause of change.

This view is modified by those who understand world order as a society of states. For these scholars, the fundamental rationale for international law is found in the realization that it is unfeasible for any state, no matter how powerful, to coerce all others into adopting its own preferences and values. However, to avoid the risks associated with international anarchy and to ensure the continuation of mutually beneficial transactions between states, there is a need to agree on the rules of practical association. In contrast to the common purpose that motivates domestic law, international law offers a functional approach, based upon restraint and accommodation, rather than common purpose.[90] International law therefore has no pretensions about moral purpose and shared values. Its rationale is to provide an orderly context within which "normal" international relations can function. Seen in this way, international law appears to be morally problematic. Its purpose is not to challenge the values and social practices found within judicially equal states but to draw clear boundaries between the internal and external, emphasizing the principles of nonintervention and sovereignty. Given this understanding of international law, it remains unclear whether it offers an appropriate institutional way for promoting and protecting human rights, which have clear moral purpose.

More recently, and in the context of economic globalization, Gill has argued that although the state retains a legal obligation to promote and protect human rights, state authority is sufficiently in thrall to global economic interests that the capacity for fulfilling this obligation is severely emasculated.

However, as previous chapters have noted, in the current period, the dominant conception of human rights finds its authority in subjective values associated with market discipline and the global political economy. This raises questions about the much-vaunted "progress" on human rights, a claim that is predicated on the development of a corpus of international law developed in the decades since the Universal Declaration. For Gill, there is no connection between claims that human rights are part of a progressive move to "civilization" on a global scale.[91] Instead, international human rights law, like all international law, should be understood as a major tool for underpinning the power of global capital, as a means for imposing modernity on a global scale, and universalizing the values of "market discipline," a concept we encountered in Chapter 2.

From this view, Gill argues that market discipline acts as a "counter-law" that stands above the rules that describe the international human rights regime. This claim does not imply that the regime is of no consequence within the context of market discipline. On the contrary, international law in general and international human rights law in particular play a pivotal role in an emerging constitutional global order, which is characterized by a growing concern to promote sets of common rules that guide economic, social, and political action.[92] The constitutive nature of human rights law, which defines both the limits of human rights and the constitution of the human subject, acts to reify the freedoms necessary for legitimating market disciplinary processes and actions by providing a framework that is promoted as inalienable and binding.

Gill concludes that while the rights associated with the protection of private property legitimate claims for ownership, no legal mechanism exists to address the ethical and moral validity of property. International human rights law is not, therefore, the proclaimed civilizatory development that it is often claimed to be, but merely a simple expression of the imposition of modernity designed to encompass the world. For some critics, this failure identifies the law as an empty vessel that cannot attend to the social structures in which people must live their lives and in which violations occur.[93] Although criticism of the legal human rights regime is not hard to find, it is criticism largely confined to disagreements within a legal framework of rights, rather than an attempt to engage in a critique of the foundations of international law.[94] In short, the politics of human rights is mostly framed within a set of assumptions about social change and dynamism while the framework itself remains unquestioned. Thus, while Dietrich takes human rights and dignity as important values that deserve protection, he rejects "the prejudice, however self-evident it may seem on the surface, that law is the only possible form to communicate and to protect this dignity."[95]

The standard objection to this argument is that the legal regime also includes many rights that are often seen as antithetical to market discipline. The often repeated claim for the unity of all rights, regularly reinforced through resolutions passed within the UN system, cannot be denied, at least not at the formal level represented by international law. However, this argument fails to take full account of the distinction between legal obligation and political action—between the norms found within the pages of international law and those expressed in "normal" activity found in the prevailing global order. The intellectual gymnastics conducted by way of avoiding this distinction include the claim that while all rights are equal, economic and social rights should be considered as "aspirations," rather than as real rights to be honored immediately; that economic and social rights are of a different order from civil and political rights; that economic and social rights are not justicable; and that economic and social rights cannot be implemented before establishing civil and political rights.[96] These arguments point to market discipline as a framework for action designed to secure compliance and conformity to particular values that are counterposed to the prohibition model of law.[97] In this way, the international human rights regime acts as a mask for structural inequalities characteristic of market discipline.[98] In the contemporary global order, the arena in which rights are exercised is defined by the mechanisms of discipline, rather than the rule of international law.[99]

Although some scholars have attempted to resolve the tension between legal and political recognition, arguing that the rights set out in the human rights regime represent the most recent addition to the principles that define statehood and that international human rights law does represent a limitation on the jurisdiction of state sovereignty, "the reality is more sobering."[100] For all the legal and bureaucratic energy invested in creating the global human rights regime, the standards set out in international law continue to be infringed widely. The intensive effort to stimulate greater commitment to international law, the adoption of more sophisticated legal procedures for implementation, and the utilization of communications technology for highlighting gross violations of human rights "have not reduced the scale or intensity of violations to which the world has inexcusably become accustomed."[101] While, on one hand, human rights are presented as central to arguments over recognizing an independent Zimbabwe (former Southern Rhodesia), South Africa, and states formed following the collapse of the USSR, on the other, tolerance is extended to Musharef's Pakistan, Saudi Arabia, and Kuwait.[102] Such inconsistency implies that questions of human rights are more subject to political analysis than legal reason, no matter how robust the law may be or how legal reason is applied.

Inconsistency is also found when the rules of other international legal regime collide with those of the human rights regime. For example, Howse and Mutua ask "what is to be done when there is a clear conflict between, say, a particular human right and a principle or provision in international trade law?"[103] Both the UN Charter and the rules of the WTO appear clear on this issue. The UN Charter, which places at its center the principles of security and human rights (Art. 103), states that these principles should prevail when conflicts occur. Article XX of the GATT, which remains central to the WTO, provides that nothing in the treaty "shall be construed to prevent the addition or enforcement by any contracting party of measures . . . necessary to protect public morals." This seemingly unequivocal statement suggests that the state continues to possess sovereign rights that trump universal human rights. However, when conflicts do arise the assumed consensus on human rights can quickly subside into a struggle over the purpose of social and economic action, between claims for human rights and liberal freedoms necessary to pursue profit.[104] Furthermore, although the United Nations and international political, economic, and financial institutions have begun to develop a consensus on a wide range of issues and processes discussed earlier in Chapter 5, including human rights, the celebration of this consensus may be premature. In many situations, the relationship between these bodies is so poorly defined that diametrically opposing policies often create conflict and confusion, rather than order and clarity.

Finally, the tradition of individualism is reflected in international human rights regime. Within human rights talk, scholars and practitioners routinely take the individual as both the victim and perpetrator of violations. The priority given to civil and political rights supports the interests of free market principles, which seek to promote a socioeconomic environment in which innovation, endeavor, and enterprise are highly prized. It follows that we must also hold the individual responsible for all of his or her actions, including violations of human rights. This convention, which has its roots in the Judeo-Christian notion of sin, tends to deflect attention from those economic and social structures that support the interests of particular groups. Consequently, investigations into the causes of human rights violations seldom go beyond the assumption that all violations can be explained by reference to wilful acts perpetrated by the powerful on the less powerful, excluding the possibility that, for example, trade rules or the principles of the global economic order may also lead to human rights violations.[105]

* * *

Questions of sovereignty remain at the center of much human rights talk. This can be seen in the difficulties encountered in formulating a human rights regime during discussions on the Universal Declaration, when the primacy of the sovereign state was beyond question. Today, however, with the advent of economic globalization, many claim that the changing nature of sovereignty raises many questions about the state's potential for fulfilling its obligations under international human rights law. Moreover, the changing nature of sovereignty raises questions about the potential authority of international law in a world order where power seems to no longer reside exclusively in the state.

Notes

1. David Held et al., eds., *Global Transformations: Politics, Economics, and Culture* (Cambridge, UK: Polity, 1999).

2. Examples include Joseph A. Camilleri and Jim Falk, *The End of Sovereignty? The Politics of a Shrinking and Fragmenting World* (Aldershot, UK: Edward Elgar, 1992); Barry Gills, Joel Rocamora, and Richard Wilson, "Low Intensity Democracy," in *Low Intensity Democracy*, ed. Barry Gills, Joel Rocamora, and Richard Wilson (London: Pluto, 1993); Andrew Linklater, *The Transformation of Political Society* (Cambridge, UK: Polity, 1998); Leo Panitch, "Rethinking the Role of the State," in *Globalization: Critical Reflections*, ed. James Mittelman (Boulder, Colo.: Lynne Rienner, 1995); Justin Rosenberg, *The Empire of Civil Society: A Critique of the Realist Theory of International Relations* (London: Verso, 1994); Jan Aart Scholte, "Globalization and the State," *International Affairs* 73, no. 3 (1997).

3. Jose A. Lindgren Alves, "The Declaration of Human Rights in Postmodernity," *Human Rights Quarterly* 22, no. 2 (2000).

4. Held et al., eds., *Global Transformations*.

5. Simon Chesterton, "Human Rights as Subjectivity: The Age of Rights and the Politics of Culture," *Millennium* 27, no. 1 (1998).

6. Richard Devetak and Richard Higgott, "Justice Unbound? Globalization, States, and the Transformation of the Social Bond," *International Affairs* 75, no. 3 (1999).

7. Ibid.

8. Held et al., eds., *Global Transformations*.

9. R. B. J. Walker, "Security, Sovereignty, and the Challenge of World Order," *Alternatives* 15, no. 1 (1990).

10. Thomas Hobbes, *Leviathan* (London, Penguin, 1981).

11. John Locke, *Two Treatises of Government* (Cambridge, Cambridge University Press, 1962).

12. Antonim Wagner, "Redefining Citizenship for the 21st Century: From the National Welfare State to the UN Global Compact," *International Journal of Social Welfare* 13 (2004).

13. Hedley Bull, *The Anarchical Society* (London: Macmillan, 1977).

14. The best-known attempt to place sovereignty and the state within historic context is found in Rosenberg, *Empire of Civil Society*.

15. Cynthia Weber, *Simulating Sovereignty* (Cambridge: Cambridge University Press, 1885).

16. Ulrich Beck, *What Is Globalization?* (Cambridge, UK: Polity, 2000).

17. Camilleri and Falk, *The End of Sovereignty?*

18. John Vincent, "The Idea of Rights in International Ethics," in T. Nardin and D. R. Maple, eds., *Traditions of International Ethics* (Cambridge, Cambridge University Press, 1992).

19. In Paul Gordon Lauren, "'To Preserve and Build on Its Achievements and to Redress Its Shorcomings': The Journey from the Commission on Human Rights to the Human Rights Council," *Human Rights Quarterly* 29 (2007): 311.

20. Ibid.

21. John Hoffman, *Sovereignty* (Minneapolis: University of Minnesota Press, 1998); Louis Henkin, *International Law, Politics, and Values* (London: Martinus Nijhoff Publishers, 1995).

22. Richard Falk, *Human Rights Horizon: The Pursuit of Justice in a Globalizing World* (London: Routledge, 2000).

23. Weber, *Simulating Sovereignty*.

24. Anthony Woodiwiss, *Globalization, Human Rights, and Labour Law in Pacific Asia* (Cambridge: Cambridge University Press, 1998).

25. Camilleri and Falk, *The End of Sovereignty?*

26. Stephen Krasner, *Sovereignty: Organized Hypocrisy* (Princeton, N.J.: Princeton University Press, 1999).

27. Rosenberg, *The Empire of Civil Society*.

28. William Robinson, *Promoting Polyarchy: Globalization, US Intervention, and Hegemony* (Cambridge: Cambridge University Press, 1996); Mark Rupert, *Producing Hegemony: The Politics of Mass Production and American Global Power* (Cambridge, Cambridge University Press, 1997).

29. V. T. Tamilmoran, *Human Rights in Third World Perspective* (Ithaca, N.Y.: Cornell University Press, 1992).

30. Janet Dine and Andrew Fagan, eds., *Human Rights and Capitalism* (Cheltenham, UK: Edward Elgar, 2006).

31. Boutros Boutros-Ghali, *Agenda for Peace—Preventive Diplomacy, Peacemaking, and Peace-Keeping,* UN Doc. A/47/277=S/24111 (1992).

32. Boutros Boutros-Ghali, "Agenda for Peace" (New York: United Nations, 1992).

33. World Bank Report, 1997.

34. Boutros-Ghali, "Agenda for Peace."

35. Mauro F. Guillen, "Is Globalization Civilizing, Destructive, or Feeble? A Critique of Five Key Debates," *Annual Review of Sociology* 27 (2001); Malcolm Waters, *Globalization* (London: Routledge, 1995).

36. Mustapha Kamel Pasha and David L. Blaney, "Elusive Paradise: The Promise and Perils of Global Civil Society," *Alternatives* 23, no. 1 (1998).

37. Scholte, "Globalization and the State."

38. Robert Cox, "Democracy in Hard Times: Economic Globalization and the Limits to Liberal Democracy," in *The Transformation of Democracy*, ed. Anthony McGrew (Cambridge, UK: Polity, 1997).

39. Ibid.

40. Tony Blair, "Speech at the WTO," May 19, 1998.

41. Robert Cox, "Civil Society at the Turn of the Millennium: Prospects for an Alternative World Order," *Review of International Studies* 25, no. 3 (1999); Cox, "Democracy in Hard Times."; Scholte, "Globalization and the State."

42. Scholte, "Globalization and the State."

43. Ibid.

44. Peter Jones, *Rights* (Basingstoke, UK: Macmillan, 1994).

45. Tony Evans, *US Hegemony and the Project of Universal Human Rights* (Basingstoke, UK: Macmillan, 1996).

46. Andrew Linklater, *Man and Citizen in the Theory of International Relations* (Basingstoke, UK: Macmillan, 1990).

47. R. J. Vincent, *Human Rights and International Relations* (Cambridge: Cambridge University Press, 1986).

48. Costas Douzinas, *Human Rights and Empire: The Political Philosophy of Cosmopolitanism* (Abingdon, UK: Routledge-Cavendish, 2007).

49. Chesterton, "Human Rights as Subjectivity."

50. JoonBeom Pae', "Sovereignty, Power, and Human Rights Treaties: An Economic Analysis," *Northwest Journal of International Human Rights* 5, no. 1 (2006).

51. Ibid.

52. Ibid.

53. Henry Shue, *Basic Rights: Subsistence, Affluence, and US Foreign Policy*, 2nd ed. (Princeton, N.J.: Princeton University Press, 1996).

54. It can be argued that the periodic interest in welfare rights arises only during periods of economic prosperity, waning as the economy moves from boom to bust. See Alex Kirkup and Tony Evans, "The Myth of Western Oppostiion to Economic, Social and Cultural Rights: A Reply to Whelan and Donnelly," *Human Rights Quarterly* 31, no. 1 (2009): 221–238.

55. Shue, *Basic Rights*.

56. Ibid.; see the afterword.

57. Linklater, *The Transformation of Political Society;* Andrew Linklater, "What Is a Good International Citizen?" in *Ethics and Foreign Policy*, ed. Paul Keal (Canberra: Allen & Unwin, 1992).

58. Kimberly Hutchings, "The Idea of International Citizenship," in *The Ethical Dimensions of Global Change*, ed. Barry Holder (Basingstoke, UK: Macmillan, 1996).

59. Pasha and Blaney, "Elusive Paradise."

60. Caroline Thomas, "International Financial Institutions and Social and Economic Rights: An Exploration," in *Human Rights Fifty Years On: A Reappraisal*, ed. Tony Evans (Manchester: Manchester University Press, 1998).

61. Linklater, *Transformation of Political Society*.

62. Tony Evans and Jan Hancock, "Doing Something Without Doing Anything: International Law and the Challenge of Globalization," *International Journal of Human Rights* 2, no. 3 (1998).

63. Thomas, "An Exploration."

64. Quoted in Robert McCorquodale and Richard Fairbrother, "Globalization and Human Rights," *Human Rights Quarterly* 21, no. 3 (1999).

65. Ibid.

66. Ankie Hoogvelt, *Globalization and the Postcolonial World: The New Political Economy of Development* (Basingstoke, UK: Palgrave, 2001) (emphasis in original).

67. Gills, "Low Intensity Democracy."

68. Ibid.

69. Ibid.

70. Cox, "Civil Society at the Turn of the Millennium."

71. Oxfam, in particular, has been threatened several times with expulsion from the UN for engaging in "political" lobbying. For critiques of the status of NGOs in global civil society, see Gary Teeple, *The Riddle of Human Rights* (Aurora, Canada: Garamond Press, 2005). Further critiques can be found in Devetak and Higgott, "Justice Unbound?" and Scholte, "Globalization and the State."

72. Cox, "Civil Society at the Turn of the Millennium."

73. Kees van der Pijl, "Transnational Class Formation and State Forms," in *Innovation and Transformation in International Studies*, ed. Stephen Gill and James Mittelman (Cambridge: Cambridge University Press, 1997).

74. Jorge Nef, "Globalization and the Crisis of Sovereignty, Legitimacy, and Democracy," *Latin American Perspectives* 29, no. 6 (2002).

75. Ibid.

76. Ibid., p. 66.

77. Sorcha MacLeod and Douglas Lewis, "Transnational Corporations: Power, Influence, and Responsibility," in *Global Ethics and Civil Society*, ed. John Eade and Darren O'Byrne (Aldershot, UK: Ashgate, 2005).

78. Stephen Gill, "Constitutionalizing Inequality and the Clash of Civilizations," *International Studies Review* 4, no. 2 (2002).

79. Evans, *US Hegemony.*

80. Antonio Cassese, *Human Rights in a Changing World* (Oxford: Oxford University Press, 1990).

81. Christine Chinkin, "International Law and Human Rights," in Evans, ed., *Human Rights Fifty Years On*, at p. 106.

82. Tony Evans, *The Politics of Human Rights: A Global Perspective*, 2nd ed. (London: Pluto Press, 2005), pp. 72–74.

83. *Montevideo Convention on the Rights and Duties of States*, December 26, 1933.

84. International Court of Justice (ICJ), "Advisory Opinion" (ICJ, 1923) (emphasis in original).

85. Ibid.

86. Chinkin, "International Law and Human Rights."

87. J. S. Watson and vol. 3 Illinois Law Forum, 1979, "Legal Theory, Efficacy, and Validity in the Development of Human Rights Norms in International Law," *Illinois Law Forum* 3 (1979).

88. Ibid., p. 619.

89. Krasner, *Sovereignty: Organized Hypocracy.*

90. Terry Nardin, *Law, Morality, and the Relations of States* (Princeton, N.J.): Princeton University Press, 1983).

91. Gill, "Constitutionalizing Inequality and the Clash of Civilizations."

92. Ibid.

93. Douzinas, *Human Rights and Empire.*

94. For the distinction between criticism and critique, see Chapter 1.

95. Wolfgang Dietrich, *A Structural-Cyclic Model of Developments in Human Rights,* Human Rights Working Papers, 2000; available at www.du.edu/humanrights/workingpapers (cited January 20, 2001).

96. For these criticisms and responses to them, see Kishore Mahbubani, "The West and the Rest," *The National Interest* (Summer 1992); Mahmood Monshipouri, "Islamic Thinking and the Internationalization of Human Rights," *The Muslim World* 84, nos.

2–3 (1994); V. J. Staples, "What Are Human Rights?" *The Lancet,* www.sciencedirect.com, May 8, 1999 (cited November 2001); Daniel J. Whelan and Jack Donnelly, "The West, Economic and Social Rights, and the Global Human Rights Regime: Setting the Record Straight," *Human Rights Quarterly* 29, no. 4 (2007).

97. Alan Hunt and Gary Wickham, *Foucault and Law: Towards a Sociology of Law and Governance* (London: Pluto Press, 1994).

98. Johan Galtung, *Human Rights in Another Key* (Cambridge, UK: Polity, 1994).

99. Michel Foucault, "Two Lectures," in *Critique and Power: Recasting the Foucault/Able Debate*, ed. Michael Kelly (Cambridge, Mass.: MIT Press, 1994).

100. Chinkin, "International Law and Human Rights."

101. Ibid.

102. Ibid.

103. Robert Howse and Makau Mutua, "Protecting Human Rights in a Global Economy: Challenges for the World Trade Organization" (Rights and Democracy, 2000).

104. Ibid.

105. Galtung, *Human Rights in Another Key.*

7

International Institutions for the Protection of Human Rights

Previous chapters have looked at the shifting terrain of human rights as an idea and as a characteristic associated with the move to economic globalization. Although critique has been offered throughout the history of human rights, for the most part these voices have been marginalized or simply ignored. The precedent for this practice was established during early discussions for a postwar international order that featured human rights. For Eleanor Roosevelt, the first chairperson of the Commission on Human Rights, progress meant drafting international law and creating the machinery for promoting and protecting human rights, not engaging in protracted discussions on the philosophical and conceptual foundations of rights claims.[1] Such discussions, Roosevelt feared, could only widen and deepen irresolvable differences, diminishing the prospects for the promotion and protection of human rights for many decades to come. Pragmatic politics therefore triumphed over conceptual politics. The major international agreements on human rights, including the Universal Declaration and the two major covenants, were therefore created in a milieu where silence on important conceptual differences ruled.[2]

However, the long-term dangers of continuing with developing UN human rights machinery that "largely pirouetted around a missing centre" were recognized by some, even in the early days.[3] During preparation for the Declaration, the United Nations Educational, Scientific, and Cultural Organization (UNESCO) sought to address conceptual questions on the nature and foundation of rights, the distinction between negative and positive rights, and the limits of international law in any program to protect human rights.[4] A further paper prepared for the secretariat by Charles De Visscher was widely distributed to members of the commission. De Visscher urged the commission to defer organizational and legal discussion before exploring the social and political values that were inevitably in flux following the momentous changes brought by the war. What, he asked, does the conscience of the civilized world look for today?

Undoubtedly something more than technical improvements of rules whose formal validity only too frequently contrasts with their disregard in practice. Something more, too, than the proliferation of organizations and proceedings which can only have a beneficial effect in so far as they are supported and associated with a spirit of international society.

Furthermore, De Visscher warned the commission that, historically, human values had always been sacrificed to political demands. The failure to learn this lesson, he argued, would see the commission fall far short of fulfilling its responsibilities.

> It is a pure delusion to expect a better international order to emerge simply and solely as the result of the establishment of direct relations between states, [since the state], as the historical center of national exclusivism, must, by its own nature, constantly seek to strengthen its own power and the unlimited extension of its own sovereignty.[5]

The failure to respond to such warnings and exhortations, by enabling a period of reflection upon conceptual issues, may be explained by the moral outrage against Nazism that pervaded many discussions in the immediate postwar period. As the full horror of the war was revealed—concentration camps, summary executions, medical experimentation using human subjects, slave labor, and forced population movements—many of those engaged in the project for human rights were driven by a sense of urgency. Despite Roosevelt's view that the Declaration was a "statement of basic principles of inalienable human rights setting up a common standard of achievement for all the peoples of all the nations,"[6] the two years between the creation of the commission and the General Assembly resolution that accepted the Universal Declaration of Human Rights saw little discussion on the issues raised by De Visscher and UNESCO. Paradoxically, the failure to engage in such discussions can be seen as a cause of the Declaration's success. Its quasi-legal language, its political mix of eighteenth-, nineteenth-, and twentieth-century European political philosophy, and its openness to broad interpretation provided something for everyone. Even those who abstained could argue that the values expressed in the Declaration did not go far enough.[7]

If the rationale for ignoring important conceptual and contextual issues was to avoid political, philosophical, and conceptual conflict, then it proved a successful strategy, at least in the short term. In the long term, however, the decision saw the commission develop into an arena for ideological disagreements, where each side accused others of failing to measure up to internationally agreed human rights standards.[8] Importantly, the UN human rights machinery developed as an organizational structure with little thought for potential future changes either of or within world order. The rapid move to decolonization, which saw the globalization of the state as the only acceptable form of political organization, Cold War struggles, and, more recently, developments in economic globalization have each provided new contexts for the promotion and protection of human rights. As we saw in earlier chapters, the last of these, the dynamics and complexity of globalization, has provided the setting for critique from postmodernism, feminism, neo-Marxism, and non-Western cultures, each of which seeks to engage with the changing face of sovereignty, international law, and claims for universal truths. It might therefore be argued that the time is ripe to engage anew with philosophical and conceptual debates before undertaking more institutional and organizational changes that replicate past faults.

With this in mind, this chapter looks at some of the most recent changes to the global human rights regime. In particular, it focuses upon the abolition of the UN Commission on Human Rights and its replacement with the Human Rights Council. A further section looks at the creation of the International Criminal Court. Before I undertake these discussions, however, I briefly discuss the potential capabilities of the United Nations and its agencies to act for the promotion and protection of human rights within the structures of a globalized world order. Although the UN remains the focus of much attention, and is often cited as evidence of "progress" in the field of human rights, complex questions about agency and structure remain largely unasked.

International Human Rights Institutions as Agents of "Progress"

There is a clear disjuncture between the aims of UN institutions and de facto improvements in human rights.[9] From the early days of the Commission on Human Rights, every additional institutional arrangement has been recommended as a progressive improvement to the growing network of international law, monitoring procedures, deliberative committees, and advisory offices that we know collectively as the global human rights regime. From an examination of texts or formal procedures that describe the workings of these institutions, it would be difficult to fault their contribution to improving human rights globally. However, for all the academic and legal industry devoted to "progress" at the formal level represented by the United Nations, the rights of people in many parts of the globe remain unprotected and unclaimed. Indeed, for some commentators, the significance afforded to the formal regime has meant that "the voices that problematize the idea of human rights and point to its difficulties from a normative, institutional, and multicultural perspective" are largely lost.[10]

Explanations for this disjuncture allude to a number of issues: the shift to economic globalization, which prioritizes trade and finance over all other issues;[11] clashes of culture;[12] the tensions between cosmopolitan rights and the international system;[13] the failure to develop new systems of law more appropriate for the current world order;[14] and the tendency to promote human rights as politically neutral in a global political arena.[15] What all these approaches seem to point to is the failure to recognize fully that the formal regime developed at the UN, which operates at the level of diplomacy and the texts of international law, remains largely independent of the socioeconomic structures that provide the framework in which people live their lives. In short, international machinery and international law for the protection of human rights have largely failed to reconcile the principles upon which they are founded (the state, sovereignty, nonintervention) with the newly emerging order represented by economic globalization.

It might be said, then, that there are two worlds of human rights: one at the United Nations, where "progress" is understood as the creation of international law and institutions, and the other within the structures of the global political economy, where violations remain common. This distinction was recognized by Secretary-General Kofi Annan, who called for the full integration of human rights issues within all international organizations, including the World Bank, the International Monetary Fund, and the WTO.[16] Although Annan's approach has seen many international organizations reflect upon ways of integrating rights in their current policies,[17] an issue discussed further in Chapter 8, these organizations continue to argue that their primary obligations are governed by economic principles, not the principles of human rights.

The UN world of human rights is predicated upon a set of assumptions concerning diplomatic norms and procedures. Most centrally, within the tradition of diplomacy and mainstream international relations, the state is understood as a singular unit, possessing identifiable objectives, aspirations, and dispositions. These characteristics imply a shared identity within the state; a set of commonly held values and associated social institutions that distinguish the internal from the external order. Potential or real conflicts found within the state can be safely disregarded when considering the conduct of international relations. In this way, the unitary state is understood to possess reflective qualities, including the potential for intervention, reason, and the pursuit of interests within a dynamic global milieu. Most significantly, and from the perspective of universal human rights, the state is assumed to possess an ethical dimension expressed through rational, responsible actions, and the capability to place these actions within a moral framework. Crucially from the perspective of the legal human rights regime, the state assumes a legal personality, including the capacity and capability to take decisions and undertake actions to fulfil its obligations. In this sense, there is no distinction between the representatives of the state engaged in diplomacy and the state itself.[18] The state is personified: the "individual writ large."[19] Although the state remains an abstract notion, and cannot therefore be said to "act" as an independent agent, without making this assumption the idea of international society under the rule of law makes little sense.

While this analysis may provide a description of commonly held beliefs about the conduct of diplomacy and international relations, it provides no explanation for the relationship between the individual claiming human rights and the state. What it describes is a community or network of diplomacy, where legitimate membership is constructed within social ties defined in terms of norms and cultural practices.[20] John Vincent aptly referred to the diplomatic network as being like a grand lodge of freemasonry, dedicated to "mutual aid and the promotion of good feeling among its members."[21] The primary tool in achieving this objective is communication among states aimed at developing common interests in trade and economic development, not in areas of domestic policy. Crucially, if the first function of diplomacy is communication among states, then it may be argued that a concern with human rights obstructs the fulfilment of that function. If a state with a poor human rights record is to be excluded socially [or] lectured at, communications suffer.[22]

Thus, following Roosevelt's earlier concerns, those engaged in the UN institutions remain apprehensive about the potential for conflict should they engage with fundamental questions that have remained unasked since the creation of the United Nations; for example, the tensions between universalism and particularism, between cosmopolitanism and state sovereignty, and between the unity of rights and the need to prioritize in a world of scarcity. Thus, it might be argued that pragmatic politics can function only in the absence of conceptual clarity.

There is, therefore, a dichotomous quality about human rights diplomacy. On the one hand, the diplomatic network of human rights is outward looking, working tirelessly toward creating an institutional framework in which universally agreed rights can be protected and promoted. On the other hand, it is a "closed" network, ordered through the application of diplomatic manners and conventions. As such, the institutions associated with the global human rights regime operate as an independent network governed by the logic of diplomacy, which seeks to avoid conflict and tension over fundamental questions, particularly where trade and economic exchange is concerned. The UN world of human rights might therefore be understood as a closed order, removed from the real world of human rights embedded in the global political economy.

From the Commission to the Human Rights Council

The diplomatic context outlined in the preceding section, in which the global human rights regime was created and subsequently developed, has changed little during past decades. Roosevelt's concern to avoid conflict and disagreement over conceptual politics held sway for much of the commission's life. The failure to engage in the fundamental idea of human rights, including the contemporary political context in which rights emerged as a central concern for international relations, "obscures its true character and the identity of the norms it seeks to universalize."[23] In short, because of the failure to engage with conceptual disagreements on human rights, liberal rights provide the intellectual basis for the regime by default. At the end of the Cold War, this assumption was reinforced by the End of History thesis, which legitimated the practice of marginalizing conceptual politics, asserting instead the arrival of a final, unmatched "truth";[24] the triumph of liberalism and global capitalism was completed.

Several issues stood against the success of the commission throughout its life. First, the quality of the membership did not encourage confidence, either because members were ill informed or because their politics suggested contempt for human rights. The first director of the UN human rights secretariat, for example, recalls that nominations to its membership were so poorly scrutinized that he believed at least one successful nomination was a Nazi sympathizer.[25] Moreover, states that had placed themselves at the center of the push to establish a postwar global human rights regime were soon adopting policies that could only be seen as hypocritical. For example, the United Kingdom supported political rights provided such claims did not extend to the colonies and colonial economic interests. Similarly, the United States used its considerable postwar authority to press for human rights provided segregationist policies remained untouched.[26] For its part, the USSR's commitment to human rights stretched only to the point where rights offered a threat to its sociopolitical system and the ambitions of Stalin.

Second, during the years of the Cold War the commission offered a battleground for playing out ideological differences between Eastern and Western blocs. While the Eastern bloc regularly accused the West of failing to honor economic and social rights, the Western bloc accused the East of failing to implement civil and political rights. Many of these conflicts focused upon conditions in less-developed states and the appropriate path these states should take in the move to modernization, particularly in light of rapid decolonization from the mid-1960s onward. Put simply, the struggle was between those who claimed that economic development should take priority over human rights—at least until the less-developed had achieved considerable progress toward modernization—and those who claimed that human rights provided the conditions for achieving modernization and should thus take priority over economic development.[27]

Third, the expansion of the commission's membership, from the original eighteen to fifty-three, may have lent greater democratic legitimacy to the commission, but it also created greater opportunities for members to create regional and ideological groupings designed for mutual protection against accusation of human rights violations. Increasingly, meetings degenerated into a "circus of confusion" as members stalled for time, in the knowledge that the next meeting of the commission was a year in the future.[28] The increased membership also generated a greater workload for the already overstretched UN staff, particularly the underresourced Directorate of Human Rights.

Fourth, as discussed in Chapter 6, there is a tension between the principles of sovereign statehood, upon which the United Nations is built, and those of universal human rights. One solution to this problem, which was suggested during negotiations for the Declaration but rejected, was to appoint commission members for their expertise in human rights, rather than as state representatives, thus breaking the state-representative norm adopted throughout the UN structure. The compromise was to create a commission composed of "experts" nominated by states that had gained a seat on the commission.[29] The failure to satisfactorily solve the tension between universalism and particularism meant that commission members were faced with the choice of serving the national interest or serving the interests of humankind. Unsurprisingly, given this choice, most commission members routinely chose the former over the latter.

Fifth, existing political conflicts within the commission were intensified following the attack on the World Trade Center in 2001. This attack inspired the so-called "war on terror," marking a new period of conflict where groups opposed to oppressive governments could be legitimately oppressed in the name of security and order, values that now took priority over all other considerations. Although the tone of many policymakers was regretful, an argument gained ground that acts previously considered as violations of human rights must be tolerated in the effort to overcome global terrorism. In offering this defense against allegations of torture, extraordinary rendition, illegal detention, and violence against civilians, many states—the United States, in particular—set a new standard for human rights that others were pleased to emulate. For instance, court proceedings have exposed practices adopted by British security and intelligence services that permitted them to interrogate a British resident in another country, knowing him to have been tortured using practices that are outlawed in Britain.[30]

Against this background, the commission became increasingly dysfunctional, assuming instead the image of a jury composed of abusing states, who used it to deflect attention from their poor human rights records in a cynical game of international politics.[31] Noting this in a 2005 report, Amnesty International argued that the commission was increasingly used to shield its members from human rights scrutiny, rather than protect and promote the universal values for which it was created. Amnesty concluded that in the conflict between universalism and the principle of state sovereignty, the state had won.[32] While this conclusion should not be rejected, it may offer an oversimplified view of human rights at the beginning of the twenty-first century. It represents a continued faith in a traditional statecentric world order that does not recognize the significance of globalized economic interests, particularly where energy is an issue.

Program for Change

In response to these criticisms, Secretary-General Kofi Annan convened a High-Level Panel, "Threats, Challenges, and Change," which identified the ten most important problems that faced the organization.[33] The panel's report, which was completed in December 2004, included far-reaching recommendations on the United Nations future response to human rights.

Under the title "A More Secure World," the High-Level Panel noted the commission's capacity to perform its tasks had been severely undermined. It argued that by "eroding credibility and professionalism" states had failed to demonstrate a commitment to the promotion and protection of human rights. Instead, states had used the commission to "protect themselves against criticism or to criticize others," rather than to seek to fulfill obligations undertaken in the

UN Charter. Calling for change, the report found that the "Commission has become a source of heated international tension, with no positive impact on human rights and a negative impact on the Commission."[34] In light of these findings, the report recommended that the commission be abolished and replaced by a council, a move intended to reassert the organization's commitment to human rights set out in the UN Charter. Other recommendations included universal membership of the council, which would avoid conflicts over the allocation of seats, the requirement that designated delegates should be prominent and experienced human rights figures, and the creation of an advisory group of fifteen independent experts (three from each of the five regions) with the task of advising on country-specific issues, the rationalization of thematic mandates, and support for research, standard setting, and definitions.[35]

Taking up the High Level Panel's recommendations, Secretary-General Kofi Annan presented *In Larger Freedom,* a reforming report that offered new measures for achieving the UN's goals of security, development, and human rights.[36] Significantly, after noting that the current organization of the UN was "built for a different era" and that "not all our current practices are adapted to the needs of today," Annan called for wide-ranging reforms, including the creation of a Human Rights Council and the abolition of the commission. What this call overlooked was that the standards and norms that the proposed reforms were intended to implement were also created in another period and therefore reflect a particular global economic, social, and political order that no longer exists. *In Larger Freedom* does not, therefore, offer a radical program for renegotiating human rights in the age of globalization, but a program for improving the implementation of human rights negotiated before the advent of economic globalization.

This important distinction has received attention in the literature on social organization and social networks. Thompson, for example, suggests two possible ways of understanding organizational networks: technological and social.[37] Technological networks should be understood as providing formal structures within which interactions take place designed to achieve particular outcomes. The success of technical organization depends upon the existence of generally agreed values and principles found within particular networks, including social, business, economic, and nongovernmental networks. Technical organization thus represents an attempt to operationalize shared values by agreeing formal constituted processes intended to achieve particular goals. Social networks, on the other hand, provide more fluid sets of relations concerned with defining and redefining social ties, as norms and cultural practices are challenged by dynamic social, economic, and cultural processes. The social network of rights, for example, which I have referred to earlier as human rights talk, moves away from accepting the values upon which the current human rights regime is built and, instead, attempts to critique those values. The aim of this process is to respond to the dynamics of social change, which today includes global relations associated with economic globalization. *In Larger Free-*

dom is clearly constructed as a technological network, with its rules of procedure, commitment to international law as the central means for achieving goals, and a realist ethos providing the framework within which the rhetoric of rights operates. There is, therefore, a disjuncture between the creation of new technical networks and the dynamic social networks that are central to processes of economic globalization.

Throughout *In Larger Freedom,* Annan continues with the practice of avoiding conceptual politics. The report assumes that broad, global agreement on what is meant by human rights already exists. This assumption is based upon the development of a vast corpus of international human rights law, created by the Commission on Human Rights and ratified by most states. However, as was argued in Chapters 3 and 4, this assumption attracts increasing criticism. To reiterate, feminists have argued that the human rights regime is gendered, potentially excluding 50 percent of the world's population.[38] Similarly, recent debates on Islam, Asian Values, Confucianism, and cultural relativism have built upon the idea that although the concept of human rights is now widely shared, there are many competing conceptions.[39] Postmodernist explanations of developments in social, political, and economic life have also impacted upon the generally accepted meaning of human rights, exposing all projects for discovering universal truth to the charges of deceit.[40] These critiques, which have gained considerable credence in the decades following the Declaration and the creation of major pieces of international law, are largely ignored. Furthermore, the report also refers to "human dignity," which also remains undefined, vague, contestable, and confusing.[41]

A further assumption in the report is found in paragraph 131, which assumes a strong link between human rights and democracy. While this relationship is widely accepted, it raises many questions, which the report does not address. Indeed, some have argued that the assumption that human rights and democracy are "two sides of the same coin" often serves to legitimate economic relations with known violators. This occurs when a previously undemocratic state introduces the machinery and formal practices for democratic elections and representation but continues to practice oppressive measures that deny opposition to the existing government. In this way, trading partners can claim to support only those who practice democracy while simultaneously overlooking the partner's human rights record. While there may be a strong relationship between human rights and certain readings of democracy, this is not self-evident.[42]

Although any UN report must necessarily reflect the statecentric membership of the General Assembly, the Security Council, and other UN bodies, *In Larger Freedom* offers no detailed discussion of structural constraints on delivering universal human rights in an age where the role of the state in contested.[43] Linked to this are questions about relying on international law as the main tool for delivering human rights, an issue we encountered in Chapter 6. Although the global human rights regime is largely a legal construct, international human rights law does nothing to change socioeconomic structures that are the cause of many human rights violations. The fanfare that accompanied the creation of the International Criminal Court, for example, overlooks the fact that it is not possible to arrest, prosecute, and punish a social and economic structure, which may be the cause of many, perhaps most, human rights violations.[44]

Despite these critiques, there is some allusion to alternatives to the state-centric and international law approach to human rights. *In Larger Freedom* suggests that solutions to problems of development, security, and human rights can be found within an "active civil society and private sector" (Para. 20), because states alone no longer have the capacity to undertake the necessary actions. However, looking to civil society and the private sector for achieving greater protection of human rights brings its own problems. Civil society includes powerful economic actors with an interest in profiting from the freedoms associated with the global free markets. Given the earlier discussion on the impact that such actors have upon achieving human rights, this aim seems, at best, confused. The literature has recognized this confusion on many occasions.[45] Furthermore, although the report proposes to "strengthen the contribution of states, civil society, the private sector and international institutions to advancing a vision of larger freedom" and ensure that "all involved assume their responsibilities to turn good words into good deeds" (Para. 22), the UN's record of developing clear responsibilities for global economic actors in the field of human rights remains poor.[46]

While the report acknowledges that rich nations have the resources to ensure basic economic rights globally, it remains unclear exactly how this can be achieved. In a global political economy characterized by free markets, the pursuit of redistributive policies seems an unlikely choice. An alternative is to continue along the path first set out by Franklin D. Roosevelt in his famous Four Freedoms speech. Rejecting the redistribution option, Roosevelt proposed that freedom from want be achieved by promoting a global liberal economic system in which the poor could exercise the choice to help themselves.[47] Since in the current global order this second choice has already been made, many questions remain outstanding. As many commentators have argued, the poor are an integral part of the current global political economy, without which the capitalist economic system would collapse.[48] How then can we expect to improve economic and social rights within an order that is itself described, in part, by the violation of those rights?

However, notwithstanding these potential problems, in May 2006 the General Assembly adopted the resolution that brought the Human Rights Council into existence.[49] The forty-seven-member council, elected by overall majority vote in the General Assembly, convened for its first meeting in June of the same year. Unlike the commission, which convened only once each year, the council meets year-round, potentially allowing it to keep a closer watch as crises develop. The council has also retained many of the processes previously found in the commission; for example, the role of NGOs and complaints procedures. Furthermore, the council can also draw upon the wisdom of the Advisory Committee, a think tank that offers expertise and advice on thematic issues, rather than specific instances of violations.

From well before its creation as the replacement for the commission, the council received considerable criticism. Most importantly, throughout the process preparatory to creating the council, the United States ambassador to the United Nations, John Bolton, continued to display contempt for the new institution.[50] In his opposition to the creation of the council, Bolton asserted that the proposal included many inadequacies, but seemed unable to identify with any clarity exactly what these were.[51] Although not entirely incapable of offering some constructive ideas, Bolton missed nearly all the negotiation meetings, but

> then fiercely complained in holier-than-thou tones about the "manifest deficiencies" of any reform proposals other than his own, persistently introduced new amendments and tried to reopen the text of the operative resolution in ways that were widely regarded by other delegations as crude delaying tactics, argued that the United States and the other permanent members of the Security Council were entitled to automatically possess "guaranteed seating" on the new Human Rights Council . . . and constantly denied in the face of overwhelming evidence to the contrary that the United States employed double standards and was engaged in serious human rights abuses in its war against Iraq or its "war on terrorism."[52]

Giving evidence to the US Senate Foreign Relations Committee, Peggy Hicks alleged that Bolton's performance during negotiations for the council, particularly his attempts to offer mischievous amendments, "detracted from the goal of building a stronger Council."[53] Furthermore, the failure of the United States to ratify core human rights treaties, for instance, the Convention on the Rights of the Child and the Covenant on Economic, Social, and Cultural Rights, and recent actions in the name of the "war on terror"—the Iraq war, Guantanamo, secret prisons, torture, and "extraordinary rendition"—all contributed toward a growing belief that human rights were low on its international agenda.

During the General Assembly vote on the council, many states regretted the US stance. In a speech before the vote, for instance, the Cuban ambassador noted US reluctance to agree to the creation of the council because "no matter how much its interests are satisfied, the super-power always wants more in its own craving for hegemony and dominance." He continued by accusing the United States of seeking to create a council that provided an opportunity for powerful states to gain a "strengthened tribunal of inquisition against the peoples of the South," while simultaneously ensuring the "impunity they already enjoy in the Commission on Human Rights." Will it be possible, he asked, for the new council to "adopt a resolution demanding that the United States be accountable and assume responsibility for torture and other serious human rights violations perpetrated in the illegal United States naval base in Guantanamo, in Abu Ghraib prison or on flights to secret detention centres operated in Europe by the Central Intelligence Agency?"[54] Although the rationale for abolishing the commission and replacing it with the council was to bring an end to political conflicts that had mired progress on human rights for many decades, the conflicts expressed in the General Assembly during the debate promised continuity rather than change.

The Council for Human Rights: No Change? Or Worse?

The rationale for creating the council was that the commission had developed into a club for those who sought to avoid criticism of their own human rights record. Introducing the resolution to create a Human Rights Council, the president of the General Assembly sought to highlight the contribution to the protection of human rights the new body would make, in contrast to the now dysfunctional commission. In particular, he stressed that the draft resolution would "make universality, impartiality, objectivity and non-selectivity, constructive international dialogue and cooperation guiding principles of the work of the Council."[55] Furthermore, he stressed the importance of shifting responsibility for human rights from a Commission of the Economic and Social Council to a council in its own right, a move designed to improve the status of human rights within the UN system. Of particular note was the increased frequency of meetings, the establishment of efficient mechanisms to convene special sessions, and the stipulation that states seeking membership of the council would be considered for their commitment and engagement with human rights issues.

However, within the first year of its existence, the council began to develop many of the traits that it was supposed to suppress. Indeed, given the anticosmopolitan nature of the state, the General Assembly's realist credentials, and the acceptance of the state as the primary actor for delivering human rights, expressed through the corpus of international human rights law, any other outcome would have been surprising. As the High Commissioner for Human Rights observed, the conflictual nature of the council should have been no surprise, since "to suggest that an intergovernmental human rights body should be apolitical is like criticising spring for coming after winter."[56]

UN Watch's assessment suggests that the council has not delivered the improvements that its formal constitution promised, and may have contributed to making matters worse.[57] Following the example of the commission, observers report that the council is increasingly dominated by alliances between states seeking to undermine mechanisms intended to support human rights. While 53 percent of the membership might be considered as from states where the rule of law and human rights have achieved an advanced level, the remaining percentage includes states that are widely recognized as persistent human rights violators. Although some have argued that "change is a process not an event,"[58] implying that the formal transference of human rights responsibilities from the commission to the council should be seen as the start, not the resolution, of change, the reemergence of old habits and politics that protect the interests of member states from criticism and the use of the council as a tool for conflicts between competing interests fall far short of expectations.

At the center of recent criticism is the predominance of Israel on the council's agenda. Although the attack on Gaza during the early weeks of 2009 would justify a period of particular attention,[59] even before these events more than 50 percent of all special sessions and 80 percent of all resolutions were devoted to Israel, while other situations (for example, Sudan, Tibet, and Zimbabwe) were virtually ignored. During 2006, the council institutionalized its focus on Israel and Palestine by giving the situation a permanent place on the agenda under the heading "Human rights situation in Palestine and other occupied Arab territories."[60] This might be seen as a proxy or displacement mechanism for waging retribution against the United States and its open contempt for the council during its creation, tempered further by the protection Israel receives from the United States in the Security Council.[61] Whatever the cause, the time allotted to Israel limits the time devoted to other human rights situations, offering a shield for those who are perpetrating violations elsewhere.

Two further examples illustrate the return of old commission habits. First, an Expert Group was asked to investigate the situation in Darfur, Sudan. Although the situation in Sudan can be understood as a conflict among religious, racial, and ethnic groups, oil resources found in the south of the country, 70 percent of which are currenlty exported to China, adds further complexity. The discovery of oil in southern Sudan, and the prospect of finding further deposits in the region of Darfur, attracts the interest of major political economy actors in ways that might otherwise not transpire.[62] In its report to the council, the Expert Group concluded that while the "process of cooperative engagement with the Government of Sudan has worked well in procedural terms," there was little evidence of implementation that had a "tangible impact on the ground."[63] The report notes that many of the recommendations could, however, have been implemented within three months given that they did not require lengthy legal, constitutional, or administrative resources. In many cases, the government of Sudan had failed to show any response to recommendations. Overall, the group concluded that barring a few exceptions, no improvement in human rights could be reported. In response to the report, the council expressed some concern that progress on implementing many of the recommendations had not been undertaken. However, in the resolution accepting the report, the council was content to acknowledge "the cooperation of the Government of Sudan and welcomes the open and constructive dialogue between the Government and the Expert Group."[64] Furthermore, the council took the decision to replace the Expert Group with a special rapporteur, with access to fewer resources and limited staff. Thus, according to Human Rights Watch, the council "rewards Khartoum's failure to take the steps to address the Darfur crisis identified by a group of experts appointed by the Council."[65]

A further investigation of the situation in Sudan was conducted by a High Level Mission, led by Nobel Peace Prize Laureate Jody Williams. The government of Sudan, however, refused to cooperate with the mission by the simple expedient of refusing to issue visas. Undeterred, the mission went to Addis Ababa, where it conducted interviews and collected documentation from past officials in the Sudanese government and UN representatives. The mission also traveled to Chad to gather material from refugee camps to which many Sudanese had fled. On the mission's return, and during the process of drafting the mission's report, Williams was approached by two Western governments and asked not to be too damning of the government of Sudan, it being argued that such a report would damage the council. One delegation took the view that the report should be couched in terms that "keeps everyone happy." Williams declined to respond to this suggestion, publishing the report in March 2007.[66]

On receiving the mission's report, which was condemned by the government of Sudan as irrelevant because no visas had been issued, leaving the mission with only secondary data, the council declined to respond to the mission's recommendation.[67] Instead, the council, in expressing "its deep concern regarding the seriousness of the ongoing violations of human rights and international humanitarian law in Darfur," decided to set up a monitoring group "to work with the Government of Sudan and the appropriate human rights mechanisms of the African Union."[68]

A third example suggesting that the character of the council may not be so dissimilar to its predecessor can be seen in the system of Universal Periodic Reviews (UPRs), which began in April 2008 with a review of the United Kingdom's human rights record. More recently, China was the subject of the review system. During the three-hour session, Chinese officials dismissed the suggestions of many highly developed states, mostly aimed at reforms for improving civil and political rights—for example, the abolition of labor-camp sentencing, the continued use of the death penalty, child labor, torture, and the failure to support freedom of religion. In contrast, many less-developed states "hailed" China as a "beacon" of economic development to be followed and criticized Western members for "politicizing" the discussion.[69] Cuba urged China to act decisively to control "self-appointed" human rights activists, who were a danger to state security and the people of China. Similarly, Pakistan blamed criminals with external links for protests in Tibet, while Sri Lanka applauded the independence and self-determination of the Chinese people following a long period of colonialism when colonial powers "tore China into little pieces."[70] In this way, socioeconomic conflicts subverted the original intentions of the council and the UPR system, imitating similar conflicts identified in the commission as the reason for its dysfunction.[71]

While there is a growing body of criticism of the council's early work, some commentators remain optimistic, arguing that more time is needed for the new institutional arrangements to reach their full potential. Lawrence Moss, for example, argues that the council still has the potential to achieve its mandate to protect human rights, provided civil society groups and governments fully engage in its work.[72] President Obama's recent decision to reverse past US policy and take a seat on the council is also seen as an encouraging sign.[73] The United States' long tradition of human rights advocacy and its considerable political influence will, it is hoped, enable the council to overcome its early failings and, instead, achieve some progress toward the aims articulated by Annan and others during the early years of the twenty-first century. Just how other members of the council will respond to the United States, with its recent well-publicized history of detention without trial, torture, and the continued use of the death penalty, remains to be seen.

Moss's optimistic assessment assumes that the council's current difficulties are institutional and organizational rather than political, overlooking the reality of the UN system, which is built upon a membership of self-interested sovereign states. However, evidence suggesting a contrary view is not hard to find. For example, an open letter sent to the council by thirty-five prominent human rights NGOs, drawn from all parts of the world, complains that council members have sought to intimidate several special rapporteurs engaged in investigating freedom of expression, extrajudicial killings, and arbitrary executions. The irony of this is not lost on many NGOs, who accuse state members of attempting to deny freedom of expression in an institution given the explicit purpose of ensuring such a freedom.[74] Where the promotion and protection of human rights are concerned, political expediency thus overcomes integrity and credibility.

The International Criminal Court

On July 17, 1998, 120 states adopted the Rome Statute, providing a legal basis for creating a permanent International Criminal Court (ICC).[75] The statute entered into force on July 1, 2002, when it received its sixtieth ratification. It is the "first permanent, treaty based, international criminal court to help end impunity for the perpetrators of the most serious crimes of concern to the international community."[76] Following its creation, it was hailed as the most important advance in the protection of human rights, adding further to a shift in focus from setting standards for human rights, which characterized the previous period, to that of implementation.

The creation of the ICC has been seen as the culmination of a historic process dating back to the trials of Bonapartists in 1815, although the accused were then viewed as enemies, rather than criminals. During the twentieth century, the idea of recognizing international crime gained ground, first with the Hague Convention of 1907, which recognized respect for life, property, and religion, and later in the botched trials of German war criminals following World War I, the failed prosecution of "Young Turks" over Armenian genocide, and the Nuremberg and Tokyo war trials after World War II. These trials, however, are often seen as a "victor's justice," a process for legitimating vengeance following conflict, made possible not through the exigency of international law but through the political will of powerful states. This was recognized at the Paris peace talks at the end of World War I, when the United States argued that to prosecute the defeated for crimes was post facto justice and therefore a moral rather than legal judgment.[77] Such trials may therefore have less to do with justice than with retribution.[78]

Following the growing interest in human rights inspired by the Universal Declaration, the principles of sovereignty as the foundation for international law were increasingly challenged by those of universalism. The creation of the ICC, which is the latest symptom of this shift in principle, seeks to establish rules based upon global community, world society, and the brotherhood and sisterhood of humankind. By adopting the principles of universalism over those of particularism, some acts are seen as so heinous that we must now accept that those who commit them should be prosecuted and, if found guilty, punished no matter where they seek to hide in the world. The claim of sovereign immunity is no longer legitimate where human rights is concerned. Moreover, the doctrine of universality asserts that the violation of certain core crimes can be prosecuted by any state on behalf of the international community of states. Although this doctrine is already incorporated in some aspects of international law—for example, acts that have serious consequences for state security and certain acts undertaken by nationals outside the state—the creation of the ICC is intended to strengthen state obligations and to extend responsibility for bringing perpetrators of certain crimes to justice through international institutions. This implies a decisive break from past conventions of international law, where the principles of sovereignty, domestic jurisdiction, and nonintervention were often seen as inviolable.

The final impetus for establishing the ICC was provided by the end of the Cold War. In 1994, the International Law Commission was asked to prepare a draft statute for an international criminal court. This draft, which covered largely organizational and procedural matters, was followed in 1996 by a draft code that sought to define international crime.[79] These proposals later became the basis for the creation of the Tribunal for the Former Yugoslavia, which further reinforced the growing consensus that impunity was no longer acceptable in a globalized world order.[80] The Rome Statute, which provides the legal foundations for establishing the permanent International Criminal Court, may therefore be seen as the latest response of the international community to historic changes in world order. The consensus reached by the international community focuses upon three types of international crime: genocide, crimes against humanity, and war crimes.[81] Although the court has not been in existence for sufficient time for it to make clear how these crimes will be understood in detail, they are crimes more likely to fall under civil and political rights, rather than economic, social, and cultural rights. Crimes over which the court has jurisdiction also include the "crime of aggression," but this cannot be exercised until some definitional agreement has been reached (Art.5.2).[82] Under Article 8 of the statute, the court assumes jurisdiction only over "serious" war crimes. Random instances of violations are therefore excluded unless these are defined as representative of a planned policy. To guard against vexatious or spurious actions, Article 15 calls for the ICC prosecutor to submit complaints made by signatories of the statute to a pretrial chamber before continuing with an investigation.

The statute claims jurisdiction through a dual-track system. The first track is established under Article 13(b) of the Rome Statute, which permits the UN Security Council to refer a situation to the ICC under Chapter 7 of the UN Charter. In this way, states are placed under an obligation to surrender indicted persons. In the case of the failure to comply, the Security Council has enforcement powers, including embargoes, freezing the assets of members of government and their backers, and the authorization of force. Significantly, under Article 16 of the statute, the Security Council has powers to postpone an investigation for up to a year, although this can be renewed annually. In effect, within this first track, the Security Council has the power to control the proceedings of the prosecutor and thus impact on the court's authority.[83]

The second track deals with cases referred to the court by state parties to the statute or the ICC prosecutor (Arts.13[a] and 13[c]). Having no enforcement powers, this track relies upon the cooperation and good faith of parties to the statute. It is this track that causes some states the most concern, notably the United States. While the powers invested in the Security Council are well known and well practiced, the statute's second track is seen by some as having the potential to expose nationals of nonparty states to indictments inspired by political motives rather than legal reason. For a powerful hegemonic state, like the United States, which assumes for itself tasks associated with global policing, this track is therefore unacceptable. The United States argues that this objection is valid because military and diplomatic personnel engaged in dangerous and exacting missions cannot perform efficiently when placed under threat of criminal proceedings. The inclusion of this track therefore presents powerful states with the intractable problem of fulfilling the role of global leader while simultaneously protecting its citizens from the threat of criminal proceedings.[84]

The statute also accepts the principle of "complementarity," which establishes the court as a last resort. Article 17(1) calls for the court to take action when a state is unwilling or genuinely unable to initiate proceedings under its own legal machinery. For some states, this is seen as undermining the principle of domestic jurisdiction insofar as the court takes to itself the power to determine whether a state is acting honorably, rather than shielding an individual from possible court action. In rejecting this argument, "the international community as a whole articulated and defended its entitlement to engage in international constitutional law-making."[85] Furthermore, under Article 18 of the statute, the ICC prosecutor is obliged to notify a state with an interest in a potential prosecution of the intention to start investigations. Should a notified state respond by informing the prosecutor, within one month, that it has taken internal action through its own legal system, the prosecutor must defer to the state's investigation. However, if there is evidence that the state in question is undertaking a "sham" investigation, there is provision for the prosecutor to continue.

In rejecting arguments concerned with violating domestic jurisdiction, Broomhall points out that the ICC does not demand that states transfer an important aspect of state sovereignty to a supranational body, as some fear. Instead, the successful operation of the court relies upon the freely given cooperation of state parties to the statute. As evidence for this claim, Broomhall notes that a number of states have already passed legislation to enable cooperation with the ICC, including the transfer of suspects, the supply of witnesses, and systems for accepting convicted prisoners. Any legislation that inhibits cooperation with the court could also be seen as a violation of the statute. While the court does have a number of options for enabling cooperation—for example, requesting the Security Council to assist—political expediency limits the use of such tools.[86]

The most active critic of the court has been the United States. Although President Clinton signed the Rome Statute on the last day of his presidency, this decision was "suspended" by his successor, the newly elected President George W. Bush. This action did not merely signal the intention of the United States not to participate in the ICC, but rather the beginning of a campaign to undermine the Rome Statute and all that it stood for. US resistance to the ICC hardened following the attack on the World Trade Center on September 11, 2001. According to the Bush administration, this event further demonstrated the need for the United States to remain free of institutional restraints like the ICC, if it was to respond quickly and efficiently to such threats.[87] At the center of US opposition to the court was the conviction that it would expose US troops and officials to gratuitous and politically motivated charges, rather than pursue those who had engaged in criminal acts.

The United States argued against the Rome Statute on five grounds. First, as the single most powerful state in the current world order, the United States could not support international law that sought to restrain its capabilities for policing world order. Second, the statute would expose US citizens to judicial proceedings and mechanisms to which the US government had not given its consent. Third, the establishment of a supranational court challenged the principle of sovereignty, in particular the right to self-defense and to freely participate in humanitarian or antiterrorist operations. Fourth, there were insufficient checks and balances in the statute to overcome the prospect of abuse as enemies of the United States sought use of the court for political purposes. Fifth, the second track of the court's two-track jurisdiction, which permits situations to be considered when reported by a state party or the prosecutor, undermined the authority of the Security Council. Without a failsafe, so the argument ran, the statute amounted to a "palace revolution," challenging the competence of the UN as a statecentric organization, its principles and Charter, and, most importantly, undermining the authority of the Security Council.[88]

In hearings on the US approach to the draft statute, conducted before President Bush took office, the Senate Foreign Relations Committee had sought to establish why the United States was so strongly opposed to the statute, while other states felt able to support it. The central argument that emerged from the hearings was based upon US exceptionalism and uniqueness as the world's single, most powerful military and economic power. While the overwhelming majority of states accepted that no individual should receive immunity from prosecution for war crimes, crimes against humanity, and genocide, no matter their country of citizenship, the United States was expected to use its considerable resources in all manner of disputes and conflicts, to create the conditions for world peace and security. If the United States became party to the statute, citizens would be exposed to an international court for actions undertaken in fulfillment of the United States' historic destiny as the global hegemon.[89]

In his testimony to the hearing of the Senate Foreign Relations Committee, then assistant secretary of state for international organizational affairs John Bolton portrayed the Rome Statute as an attempt to bind nations together in a web of institutional structures designed to restrain the use of US power. He concluded that the United States should not only resist any temptation to become party to the statute but, crucially, that the United States should adopt policies actively aimed at undermining the ICC, a strategy he hoped would see the court first wither and then collapse. Four avenues were suggested for operationalizing this approach. First, the United States should demand that its troops and personnel were given immunity from the court's jurisdiction in US-sanctioned missions. Without this agreement, the United States should threaten to withdraw from existing missions and refuse to participate in any future decisions to provide peacekeeping and peacemaking proposals.

Second, although under Article 13 of the statute the Security Council can refer crimes to the court, in accordance with the US policy of noncooperation, referral should be blocked by all and every means.

Third, noting that the conditions set down in the then-proposed statute "may not proceed with a request for surrender which would require the requesting state to act inconsistently with its obligations under international agreements pursuant to which the consent of a sending State is required to surrender a person of that state to the Court," Bolton proposed that the United States seek bilateral immunity agreements for US troops and personnel with all other countries.[90]

Last, in cases where other countries refused to cooperate in granting immunity to US personnel, the United States should consider withdrawing military and economic aid. Although, later, Ambassador Pierre-Richard Prosper promised not to take any action that would undermine the ICC, the United States announced its intention to "unsign" the statute, signaling an intention to follow the advice proferred by Bolton.

For many on the Senate Foreign Relations Committee, it was not sufficient to protect the national interests of the United States by voting against the Rome

Statute. Senator Helms, for instance, argued that the "United States must aggressively oppose this Court each step of the way, because the treaty establishing an international criminal court is not just bad, but I believe is also dangerous," since it undermined the threat of military action. For others on the committee, the threat to sovereignty presented the greatest objection to the court. Senator Ashcroft argued that sovereignty included the authority of the state to define crime and punishment, a right that no state or international institution can challenge. Accordingly, he argued that the "Court strikes at the heart of sovereignty by taking this fundamental power away from individual countries and giving it to international bureaucrats."[91]

During the Rome Conference, considerable effort was made to overcome some of the United States' objection to the creation of a court. For example, Article 12, which describes preconditions to the exercise of jurisdiction, was added, but it failed to appease the United States. In a further attempt to gain US approval, Article 124 was crafted to permit a state to delay accepting the jurisdiction of the ICC for a period of seven years with respect to war crimes set out under Article 8. Neither of these concessions was sufficient to persuade the United States to become party to the statute. Consequently, as David Scheffer, US ambassador-at-large for war crimes, argued, so long as prosecutions could to go ahead if "either the state territory where the crime was committed or the state of nationality of the perpetrator of the crime were a party to the treaty or have granted voluntary consent to the jurisdiction of the court," the United States would not become party to the statute. Scheffer, continuing, said that official action of a nonparty state "should not be subject to the Court's jurisdiction if that country does not join the treaty, except by means of Security Council action under the UN Charter."[92] As Rothe phrases it, the United States "continued to take the dubious position that humanity is best served by the US remaining free from the limitations imposed by the Rome Statute."[93] While this stance maintained the liberal principle that freedom is secured when we are subject to the minimum of legal and regulatory restraint, for many other countries it served to further enhance an image of the United States as a power unable to respond to developing conditions in an emerging world order.

The US Response

Starting in 2002, President George W. Bush set about implementing the proposals formulated by Bolton during the Senate Foreign Relations hearing on the statute. In August 2002, for example, he signed a supplementary appropriations bill that brought the American Servicemember's Protection Act into law, an act that restricts US cooperation with the ICC, participation in UN peacekeeping, and the provision of military assistance to countries that ratify the Rome Statute. In particular, the restriction on participation in UN peacekeeping missions provides "coercive" legislation that forbids US involvement unless certain demands are met.[94] Among these demands is that the Security Council agrees to immunity from ICC jurisdiction for US personnel and to restrictions on the deployment of troops in countries that are party to the statute. Furthermore, the act authorizes the president to take "all necessary action" to obtain the release of US service personnel and citizens detained by the ICC, a power that has become known as the "Hague invasion" clause.[95]

A further measure designed to undermine the ICC was the introduction of bilateral immunity agreements, sometimes known as Article 98 agreements. Under these agreements, the United States may provide troops only if the receiving state guarantees the protection of US personnel from ICC intervention. Although there is some variation in the conditions of bilateral Article 98 agreements, the aim remains the same in each case: to deny the possibility of US personnel being turned over to the ICC, either to answer criminal charges or to act as a witness. In July 2003 the Bush administration announced the suspension of US military aid to thirty-five countries that were party to the statute, threatening not to resume aid until Article 98 agreements had been concluded. By the end of 2008, Article 98 agreements had been completed with nearly one hundred countries, although some ICC member-states have refused to cooperate.[96]

Contradictions in the US policy on the ICC were exposed following the UN Commission of Inquiry on Darfur, Sudan, which reported to the Secretary-General in January 2005. The commission's report determined that although the government of Sudan had sanctioned indiscriminate violence against the population of Darfur, this did not amount to genocide. The definition of genocide requires evidence of intent to eliminate a national, ethnic, racial, or religious group, which the authors of the report had not found. However, the report concluded that there was good reason to bring those responsible for acts of rape, mass killings, torture, and forced displacement of civilians to account. Furthermore, the report recognized that the Sudanese judicial system had "proved incapable and the authorities unwilling" to bring to justice those responsible for crimes committed in Darfur, including military personnel, government officials, rebels, militia, and foreign army officials.[97] It therefore recommended that the Security Council refer the situation of Darfur to the International Criminal Court, under Article 13(b) of the Rome Statute, noting that the Security Council had repeatedly recognized that the situation constituted a threat to international peace and security. The report concluded that prosecution by the ICC of persons allegedly responsible for the most serious crimes is Darfur would contribute to the restoration of peace.

This proposal put the United States in a difficult position. Either it would have to breach its policy of obstructing the work of the ICC and vote in the Security Council to support the commission's recommendation or it would have to veto such a resolution and risk eroding its moral authority. To avoid this difficulty, the United States offered a counterproposal, which included the creation of a special court based at the existing headquarters of the tribunal for Rwanda in Tanzania. The US secretary of state, Condoleezza Rice, made great efforts to persuade European governments to support this proposal.[98] However, according to the majority of members of the Security Council, the urgency of the situation in Darfur did not lend itself to the creation of a special tribunal, which would have taken, at best, a full year in preparation before it could realistically consider any case.

On March 31, 2005, the Security Council passed Resolution 1593 (2005), which "referred the situation in Darfur since 1 July to the Prosecutor of the International Criminal Court" and called for the full cooperation of all parties, including the Sudanese government. As a concession to US fears that citizens of states not party to the Rome Statute would be exposed to the jurisdiction of the court, Resolution 1593 confirmed that nationals, officials, and personnel from contributing states outside Sudan would remain within the "exclusive jurisdiction of that contributing State for all alleged acts or omissions arising out of or related to operations in Sudan established or authorized by the Council."[99]

Four states abstained on the vote, including the United States. Following the vote, the US representative, Anne Woods Patterson, reiterated her country's opposition to the ICC, but acknowledged the violation of human rights in Darfur, noting that the creation of a special tribunal remained the preferred option of the United States. However, Woods Patterson noted with satisfaction that as a substantial contributor to peacekeeping and the humanitarian effort in Sudan, US personnel would benefit from the immunity set out in the resolution. Importantly, Woods Patterson asserted that protection given to personnel from non-state parties to the statute was "precedent-setting." Furthermore, the United States noted that the resolution recognized that none of the expenses incurred in the referral would be borne by the United Nations, setting a further precedent; instead, all costs would be borne by state parties to the Rome Statute or those who contributed voluntarily. So important was this that any "effort to retrench on this principle by the United Nations or other organizations to which the United States contributed could result in its withholding funding or taking other action in response."[100]

Structural, Legal, and Political Limitations of the ICC

Three conclusions can be drawn from the discussion in this section. First, it is clear that the court aims to deal with individuals identified as perpetrators of internationally recognized crime. Individuals are totally responsible for their actions and must be punished. Within this approach, there is little recognition that all individuals live their lives within social, economic, and political settings that condition their actions. Although individuals can be criticized for failing to recognize the potential for violations within particular social, economic, and political settings, the emphasis on personal responsibility overlooks the context in which action takes place. Individuals may therefore become scapegoats that act to obscure the guilt of those who created the social context in which people live their lives. Thus, while the individual may be punished, the social setting remains and may continue to provide the stage for further violations in the future. This raises the question of how we might distinguish between the criminal acts of individuals at the sites of crimes and those who create and maintain the social framework in which those acts are committed, a question that remains largely unaddressed.

One possible approach to this question has been offered by Agnes Heller, who offers a concise rearticulation of the problem. For Heller, "one is the author of one's own deeds, good or bad, [but] one is not necessarily the author of the conditions under which they are committed."[101] Given this distinction, Heller argues for a separation of what she calls "historic crimes" from "heinous crimes." While the first concept includes those crimes conducted within a prevailing moral and legal framework, the latter are perpetrated by those who propose and encourage the "evil maxims" that influence the behavior of the community by creating that framework. For Heller, those who perpetrate "heinous crimes" should always be pursued and punished, while perpetrators of "historic crimes" should be treated sympathetically or even forgiven. This conclusion is reached because while "heinous crime" is concerned with achieving objectives in the domain of morals, "historic" crime is merely the response of people within the context of the extant social order. However, according to Heller, the prosecution of those who commit "heinous crimes" may not be possible because those responsible for creating the structures within which the crimes are committed may be long dead.

Second, and following from the emphasis on individual responsibility for "historic crimes," is the observation made in earlier chapters that the overemphasis on the individual as the violator deflects attention from structural violations, most importantly those seen in the global political economy. The practice of searching for the savage violator of human rights offers a mask for the causes of violations found in existing socioeconomic structures that support particular interests. While much energy and time are spent on developing legal institutions for punishing violators, those who continue to suffer economic deprivations, social exclusion, and political isolation from the decision-making processes that define the global political economy are largely neglected. Other than moral suasion, excluded groups are offered limited means to achieve justice. As Tucker observes, advocates of the court "err in confusing law with politics and in expecting from a court results, whether remedial or deterrent, that at best can only be consequences of a functioning political order."[102] Legal institutions like the ICC therefore reinforce ideas associated with individual responsibility and thus divert attention from the causes of many violations and the remedies that could be explored to prevent them.[103]

Third, if hegemony is defined as the exercise of both coercion and consensus, there is a need for the hegemon to gain respect based upon moral, normative, and ethical grounds.[104] The consensus element is best achieved by projecting a set of defining moral values and principles, which are claimed as the basis for the hegemon's successful rise to power. The adoption of particular ways of thinking, knowing, and acting is presented as "common sense"— as in the best interests of others, not just those of the hegemon. The success of the consensus element can be judged by reductions in human and financial costs to the hegemon, associated with the coercive element. In the current period, the success of the hegemon in codifying particular values and principles under international law has become the central tool for binding others to the interests of the hegemon.[105] However, although the hegemon will always strive to achieve a global consensus, there will always be a need for coercive capabilities to put down pockets of dissent and resistance. In the exercise of its global policing role, the hegemon will always reserve the right to use coercive measures as it sees fit.

There is, of course, a tension between coercive force and consensus through international law, particularly when law is developed as part of a moral and normative code. On the one hand, the hegemon wants to project its role as moral leader and thus promote its own values as shared values in the interests of all, while on the other hand it demands freedom to act at liberty in the cause of global order. From this perspective, US policymakers were not impressed by the prospect of a court that threatened to circumscribe the potential for coercion. The US objection to the court should not therefore be seen as an objection to particular aspects of the Rome Statute, but a reaction against universalism as a principle, at least as that principle would be applied to the United States.[106] As a former UK foreign secretary observed, during the years that preceded the Rome Statute, the administration of George W. Bush pursued a "relentless pogrom against the Court," which achieved a level of hostility that came "to occupy a totemic role in its belief that US freedom of action must never be constrained by international jurisdiction."[107] For a global hegemon, if the maintenance of global order demands a policing role, then no impediment should stand in its way, including laws that seek to restrain the use of power.

The failure to reconcile the tensions between coercion and consensus severely weakened the ICC. If the most powerful state—and the state that self-consciously projects itself as the embodiment of human rights—refuses to participate in a system created to bring those guilty of genocide, war crimes, and crimes against humanity to justice, then why should others subject their citizens to the jurisdiction of an international criminal court? Indeed, the failure to become party to the Rome Statute, and the pursuit of policies intended to undermine the court, signal a contrary commitment to human rights. Evading the law by claiming exceptionalism suggested to many that while the US government moralizes about the rule of law as the basis for developing human freedoms, "it clearly has not accepted the norm that the international community has the right to enforce these laws on citizens of the United States."[108] US policy may therefore have added to existing perceptions of hypocrisy, double standards, and the paucity of moral and normative commitment that plays an important role in the maintenance of hegemony. How damaging this may be for the future of human rights remains an interesting question.

As a footnote to these conclusions, and earlier remarks concerning the US attitude toward the ICC, the change from the Bush to the Obama presidency does not seem to have brought a change in policy. At the recent review confer-ence on the Rome Statute, a major issue was the current provision that permits a signatory member to suspend the jurisdiction of the court for a period of seven years for war crimes committed by their citizens (Art. 124). Many states ar-gued that the provision has served its purpose, including several states experi-encing ongoing armed conflict. However, powerful states pushed for retaining the provision, including the United States, Russia, and China, none of which are parties to the statute. The success of these states in retaining the article rested on the argument that it was necessary to offer this concession to attract non-members to sign the statute, a device that so far has failed to encourage this small group of powerful states to engage with the ICC.[109]

$$* \quad * \quad *$$

Attempts to devise institutional arrangements for the protection and promotion of human rights at the global level seem to have achieved only limited progress. The tension between the principles of universalism and particularism has pro-duced seemingly insurmountable problems. The failure to recognize the polit-ical ethos of human rights talk, particularly in international forums like the United Nations, and instead to focus on legal solutions has created an institu-tional framework that fails to meet the enormity f the global human rights situ-ration. For the Human Rights Council, in particular, the early years of its existence do not seem to have solved the problems that were given as the ra-tional for its creation. As for the International Criminal Court, it remains fo-cused on seeking and prosecuting the "wicked" perpetrators of violations. While this may be claimed as some "progress" toward fulfilling the promise of human rights, it fails to offer anything for the countless millions who suffer because they are deprived of their basic economic rights.

Notes

1. Eleanor Roosevelt made a series of notes prior to the first meeting of the commis-sion. One of these reads simply, "The job is to complete a draft Bill in Two weeks time." See Box No. 5487, Papers of Eleanor Roosevelt, Roosevelt Library, Hyde Park, N.Y.

2. For recollection of early meetings of the commission's drafting group, see Eleanor Roosevelt, *The Autobiography of Eleanor Roosevelt* (London: Hutchinson, 1962).

3. Moses Moskovitz, *International Concern with Human Rights* (Dobbs Ferry, N.Y.: Oceana Publications, 1974).

4. UNESCO, *The Grounds for an International Declaration of Human Rights*, Paris, July 31, 1947.

5. Eleanor Roosevelt certainly received and read a copy of this document (E/CN.4/40 1947). See her annotated copy in Box No. 4595, Roosevelt Library, Hyde Park, N.Y.

6. UN General Assembly, *Official Records,* 3d Committee, 98th meeting, p. 32.

7. For a more detailed discussion on the background to the Declaration, see Tony

Evans, *US Hegemony and the Project of Universal Human Rights* (Basingstoke, UK: Macmillan, 1996).

8. Ibid. See esp. Chapters 3 and 4.

9. United Nations Development Programme, *Human Development Report, 2000—Human Rights and Human Development* (Oxford, UK: UNDP, 2000). This report acknowledges the depth and breadth of human rights violations in both developed and less-developed countries. For example, it notes that 790 million people lack adequate nourishment, 250 million children are used as child labor, 1.2 million women and girls under eighteen are trafficked for prostitution each year, and that there is continued denial of women's rights in many countries.

10. Makau Mutua, *Human Rights: A Political and Cultural Critique*, ed. Bert B. Lockwood, Pennsylvania Studies in Human Rights (Philadelphia: University of Pennsylvania Press, 2002).

11. Robert Howse and Makau Mutua, "Protecting Human Rights in a Global Economy: Challenges for the World Trade Organization" (Rights and Democracy, 2000).

12. Stephen Gill, "Constitutionalizing Inequality and the Clash of Civilizations," *International Studies Review* 4, no. 2 (2002); Samuel P. Huntington, *The Clash of Civilizations: Remaking of World Order* (New York: Touchstone, 1997).

13. Onora O'Neill, "Agents of Justice," *Metaphilosophy* 32, nos. 1 and 2 (2001).

14. B. S. Chimini, "Marxism and International Law," *Economic and Political Weekly* 34, no. 6 (1999).

15. Mutua, *Political and Cultural Critique*.

16. Kofi Annan, "Secretary-General's Address to the World Economic Forum" (Davos, World Economic Forum, 2004); Kofi Annan, "The United Nations Cannot Stand Still, Because the Threats to Humanity Do Not Stand Still" (Davos: World Economic Forum, 2006).

17. See, for example, World Bank, "Equity and Development," in *World Development Report, 2006* (Washington D.C.: World Bank, 2006).

18. Rosalyn Higgins's comments on this issue are reported in J. S. Watson and vol. 3 of Illinois Law Forum, 1979, "Legal Theory, Efficacy, and Validity in the Development of Human Rights Norms in International Law," *Illinois Law Forum* 3 (1979).

19. Colin Wight, *Agents, Structures, and International Relations: Politics of Ontology*, ed. Steve Smith, Cambridge Studies in International Relations (Cambridge: Cambridge University Press, 2006), pp. 183–199.

20. Grahame Thompson, "Is All the World a Complex Network?" *Economy and Society* 33, no. 3 (2004).

21. R. J. Vincent, *Human Rights and International Relations* (Cambridge: Cambridge University Press, 1986). p. 132.

22. Ibid.

23. Mutua, *Political and Cultural Critique*, p. 1.

24. Francis Fukuyama, "The End of History," *The National Interest* (Summer 1989).

25. John Humphrey, *Human Rights and the United Nations: The Great Adventure* (Dobbs Ferry, N.Y.: Transnational Publishers, 1984).

26. For a brief discussion on the attempt to include a "Colonial Clause" in the covenant, see Evans, *US Hegemony,* pp. 138–142.

27. Kishore Mahbubani, "The West and the Rest," *The National Interest* (Summer 1992).

28. Paul Gordon Lauren, "'To Preserve and Build on Its Achievements and to Redress Its Shortcomings': The Journey from the Commission on Human Rights to the Human Rights Council," *Human Rights Quarterly* 29, no. 2 (2007).

29. Tony Evans, "US Hegemony, Domestic Politics, and the Project of Universal Human Rights," *Diplomacy and Statecraft* 6, no. 3 (1995), esp. Chapter 3.

30. "Torture and the Missing Paragraph," *Guardian*, London, editorial, February, 11, 2010, p. 32.

31. Lauren, "'To Preserve and Build on Its Achievements."

32. For a brief discussion of the commission's decision that the membership should be representatives of states, rather than experts in the field, see Evans, *US Hegemony,* pp. 86–89.

33. United Nations, "A More Secure World: Our Shared Responsibilities" (United Nations, 2004), www.un.org/secureworld.

34. Ibid.

35. For Secretary-General Annan's presentation of the report to the General Assembly, see General Assembly, "Kofi Annan Speech Presenting the Report of the High-Level Panel on Threats, Challenges, and Change, GA Fifty-Ninth Session: Agenda Item 55" (New York: United Nations, 2004).

36. General Assembly, "Draft Resolution (a/60/L.48)," in *Report of the Fifth Committee (A/60/271)* (New York: United Nations, 2006).

37. Thompson, "Is All the World a Complex Network?"

38. Hilary Charlesworth, Christine Chinkin, and Shelly Wright, "Feminist Approaches to International Law," *American Journal of International Law* 85, no. 4 (1991); Simon Chesterton, "Human Rights as Subjectivity: The Age of Rights and the Politics of Culture," *Millennium* 27, no. 1 (1998); Mutua, *Political and Cultural Critique;* V. Spike Peterson and Laura Parisi, "Are Women Human? It's Not an Academic Question," in *Human Rights Fifty Years On: A Reappraisal,* ed. Tony Evans (Manchester: Manchester University Press, 1998).

39. Joanne R. Bauer and Daniel A. Bell, *The East Asian Challenge for Human Rights* (Cambridge: Cambridge University Press, 1999); Barry K. Gills, "The Crisis of Postwar East Asian Captialism: American Power, Democracy, and the Vicissitudes of Globalization," *Review of International Studies* 26, no. 3 (2000); Mahbubani, "The West and the Rest"; Diane K. Mauzy, "The Human Rights and 'Asian Values' Debate in Southeast Asia: Trying to Clarify the Key Issues," *Pacific Review* 10, no. 2 (1997); Anthony Woodiwiss, *Globalization, Human Rights, and Labour Law in Pacific Asia* (Cambridge: Cambridge University Press, 1998).

40. Jose A. Lindgren Alves, "The Declaration of Human Rights in Postmodernity," *Human Rights Quarterly* 22, no. 2 (2000); Zuhtu Arslan, "Taking Rights Less Seriously: Postmodernism and Human Rights," *Res Publica* 5 (1999); Alan Hunt, *Explorations in Law and Society: Towards a Constitutive Theory of Law* (New York: Routledge, 1993); Alan Hunt and Gary Wickham, *Foucault and Law: Towards a Sociology of Law and Governance* (London: Pluto Press, 1994); Mutua, *Political and Cultural Critique.*

41. K. Anthony Appiah, "Citizens to the World," in *Globalizing Rights,* ed. Matthew Gibney (Oxford: Oxford University Press, 2003); Chandra Muzaffar, "From Human Rights to Human Dignity," in *Debating Human Rights: Critical Essays from the United States and Asia,* ed. Peter Van Ness (London: Routledge, 1999); Issa Shivji, "Constructing a New Rights Regime: Promises, Problems, and Prospects," *Social and Legal Studies* 8, no. 2 (1999).

42. Thomas Carothers, "Democracy and Human Rights: Policy Allies or Rivals?" *Washington Quarterly* 17, no. 3 (1994).

43. Ulrich Beck, *What Is Globalization?* (Cambridge, UK: Polity, 2000); Chimini, "Marxism and International Law"; Hunt, *Explorations in Law and Society;* Robert McCorquodale and Richard Fairbrother, "Globalization and Human Rights," *Human Rights Quarterly* 21, no. 3 (1999).

44. Johan Galtung, *Human Rights in Another Key* (Cambridge, UK: Polity, 1994).

45. Robert Cox, "Civil Society at the Turn of the Millennium: Prospects for an Alternative World Order," *Review of International Studies* 25, no. 3 (1999); Robert Cox, "Democracy in Hard Times: Economic Globalization and the Limits to Liberal Democ-

racy," in *The Transformation of Democracy*, ed. Anthony McGrew (Cambridge, UK: Polity, 1997); Tony Evans, *The Politics of Human Rights: A Global Perspective*, 2nd ed. (London: Pluto Press, 2005); McCorquodale and Fairbrother, "Globalization and Human Rights"; Mutua, *Political and Cultural Critique*.

46. Noam Chomsky, "'Recovering Rights': A Crooked Path," in *Globalizing Rights: The Oxford Amnesty Lectures, 1999*, ed. Matthew J. Gibney (Oxford: Oxford University Press, 2003); Joyce V. Millen, Evan Lyon, and Alec Irwin, "Dying for Growth: The Political Influence of National and Transnational Corporations," in *Dying for Growth: Global Inequality and the Health of the Poor*, ed. Jim Young Kim et al. (Monroe, Maine: Common Courage Press, 2000); Henry Shue, *Basic Rights: Subsistence, Affluence, and US Foreign Policy*, 2nd ed. (Princeton, N.J.: Princeton University Press, 1996).

47. President Franklin D. Roosevelt, Annual Message to Congress, January 6, 1941, in S. Shepard Jones and Denys P. Myers, eds., *Documents on American Foreign Policy*, vol.1 (Boston: World Peace Foundation, 1941).

48. Cox, "Democracy in Hard Times"; Tony Evans, *The Politics of Human Rights: A Global Perspective*; Caroline Thomas, "Global Governance, Development, and Human Security," in *Human Security*, ed. Caroline Thomas (London: Pluto Press, 2001); Susan George, *The Lucano Report* (London: Pluto, 1999); Gill, "Constitutionalizing Inequality and the Clash of Civilizations."

49. Votes for, 170; against, 4 (Israel, Marshall Islands, Papua, USA). There were three abstentions (Belarus, Iran, Venezuela).

50. Lauren, "To Preserve and Build on Its Achievements."

51. Human Rights Watch, "New Council Opposed by Unusual Duo: U.S. and Cuba" (2006), www.hrw.org/en/news/2006/03/12/new-council-opposed-unusual-duo-us-and-cuba.

52. Lauren, "To Preserve and Build on Its Achievements," p. 333.

53. Peggy Hicks, "The UN Human Rights Council: Testimony Delivered to the US Senate Foreign Relations Committee" (2007).

54. General Assembly, "Draft Resolution (a/60/L.48)."

55. Ibid.

56. Quoted in D. D. Raphael, "The Liberal Western Tradition of Human Rights," *International Social Science Journal* 18, no. 1 (1966).

57. UN Watch, "Dawn of a New Era? Assessment of the United Nations Human Rights Council and Its Year of Reform" (Geneva: UN Watch, 2007).

58. General Assembly, "Draft Resolution (a/60/L.48)." See speech by Mr. Maurer (Switzerland).

59. UN action following the Gaza attack included a move to set up a commission with the remit to examine accusations of Israeli war crimes and its responsibilities for human rights violations, see A/HRC/12/48 for the final report (September 2009); also the ICC prosecutor in The Hague started preliminary analysis of the military conduct of Israeli forces participating in the offensive. See http://www.presstv.ir/detail.aspx?id=85225&sectionid=351021701.

60. Human Rights Council, decision 1/106, 24th meeting, June 30, 2006.

61. BBC, *The Investigation: The Human Rights Council*, Radio 4, broadcast January 15, 2009.

62. Julie Flint and Alex de Waal, *Darfur: A New History of a Long War* (London: Zed Books, 2005).

63. Human Rights Council, 6th session, A/HRC/6/L.11/Add.1, December 19, 2007.

64. Ibid.

65. Human Rights Watch, "An Unacceptable Compromise by Rights Council on Darfur," hrw.org/English/docs/2007/12/14/sudan17584.htm.

66. Report of the High-Level Mission on the situation of human rights in Darfur pursuant to Human Rights Council decision S-4/101.

67. (A/HRC/4/L.7/Rev.2), follow-up to the decision of December 13, 2006, by the Human Rights Council at its fourth special meeting, entitled "Situation of Human Rights in Darfur" (S-4/101).

68. See UN document (A/HRC/4/L.7/Rev.2).

69. Reuters, February 12, 2009, http://news.yahoo.com/s/nm/20090211/wl_nm/us_un_rights_china

70. See *Herald Tribune,* February 11, 2009. http://news.yahoo.com /s/ap/20090211/ap_on_re_eu/un_un_china_rights

71. Most recently, the council chose to congratulate the government of Sri Lanka on its victory over the Tamil Tigers, rather than seek to investigate widespread reports of human rights violations perpetrated by both sides during the conflict.

72. Lawrence Moss, "New Human Rights Council Requires Greater Political and Diplomatic Effort to Realize Its Potential," in *Commentary* (Human Rights Watch, 2007).

73. See AFP at http://www.google.com/hostednews/afp/article/ALeqM5jGxKsxx rGLY7OmXNT53QwGYg0Ew.

74. See Amnesty International at http://www.amnesty.org/en/library/asset/IOR41/024/2009/en/df63060b-e9ac-443f-a800-24438da05c3c/ior410242009en.html.

75. The Rome Statute, A/CONF.183/9.

76. International Criminal Court website, http://www.icc-cpi.int/Menus/ICC/About+the+Court/.

77. Gary Jonathan Bass, *Stay the Hand of Vengeance: The Politics of War Crimes Tribunals* (Princeton, N.J.: Princeton University Press, 2002).

78. Spyros Economides, "The International Criminal Court: Reforming the Politics of International Justice," *Government and Opposition* 38, no. 1 (2003); William A. Schabas, *An Introduction to the International Criminal Court,* 2nd ed. (Cambridge: Cambridge University Press, 2004).

79. For history of the ILC report and code, see http://www.un.org/law/ilc/.

80. Security Council resolution S/Res/827 (1993).

81. For detailed analysis of definitions of these categories of crime, see, Schabas, *Introduction to the International Criminal Court.*

82. Some agreement on defining the crime of aggression was achieved at the review conference for the Rome Statute, held in Kampala, Uganda, May 31 to June 11, 2010. However, no progress was achieved on procedures for punishing such a crime.

83. Ibid., for a full explanation of the ICC's powers.

84. John P. Cerone, "Dynamic Equilibrium: The Evolution of US Attitudes Towards International Criminal Courts and Tribunals," *European Journal of International Law* 18, no. 2 (2007); Economides, "The International Criminal Court: Reforming the Politics of International Justice"; Robert C. Johansen, "The Impact of US Policy Toward the International Criminal Court on the Prevention of Genocide, War Crimes, and Crimes Against Humanity," *Human Rights Quarterly* 28, no. 2 (2006); Hans-Peter Kaul, "Construction Site for More Justice: The International Criminal Court After Two Years," *American Journal of International Law* 99, no. 2 (2005); Dawn Rothe and Christopher W. Mullins, "The International Criminal Court and United States Oppostion," *Law and Social Change* 45 (2006); Schabas, *Introduction to the International Criminal Court.*

85. Marc Weller, "Undoing the Global Constitution: UN Security Council Action on the International Criminal Court," *International Affairs* 78, no. 4 (2002).

86. Bruce Broomhall, *International Justice and the International Criminal Court: Between Sovereigty and the Rule of Law* (Oxford: Oxford University Press, 2005).

87. Cerone, "Dynamic Equilibrium."

88. Mark A. Hall, "The Scope and Limits of Public Health Law," *Perspectives in Biology and Medicine* 46, no. 3 (2003); Weller, "Undoing the Global Constitution."

89. For a report on the hearing by Michael P. Scharf, who gave evidence, see *American Society of International Law,* www.asil.org/insights/insigh23.htm, August 1998.

90. The Rome Statute, A/CONF.183/9, Article 98.

91. Senate Foreign Relations Committee, July 23, 1998. During the hearing on the Rome Statute, Senator Gramm commended Ambassador Scheffer for voting against the treaty, a vote that he claimed was contrary to the Clinton administration's instructions.

92. Ambassador Scheffer, Senate Foreign Relations Committee, August 1998, http://www.asil.org/insights/insigh23.htm.

93. Rothe and Mullins, "International Criminal Court and United States Opposition."

94. Ibid., where Rothe and Mullins point out that the act provides "legitimate legislation" for a coercive tool to delegitimize the efficacy of the ICC.

95. Weller, "Undoing the Global Constitution."

96. For the most recent figures, see http://www.globalsolutions.org/issues/bia_resource_center.

97. Report of the International Commission of Inquiry on Darfur, January 25, 2005, www.un.org/news/hd/sudan/com_ing_darfur.pdf, para. 569.

98. Robin Cook, *Guardian,* London, February 11, 2005.

99. Security Council Resolution 1593, adopted at the 5158th meeting, March 31, 2005, S/Res/1593(2005). Votes in favor, 11; against, 0. There were four abstentions—Algeria, Brazil, China, and the United States.

100. UN press release SC/8315, Security Council 5158th meeting (night). In July 2008, a warrant was issued for the arrest of Omar Hassan Ahmad Ali Bashir, president of the Sudan. On June 6, 2010, the ICC review conference president insisted that Uganda must arrest Bashir if he attended the AU summit in Kampala in July. Uganda is a party to the Rome Statute and therefore has a legal obligation to make the arrest.

101. Agnes Heller, "The Limits to Natural Law and the Paradox of Evil," in *On Human Rights: The Oxford Amnesty Lectures, 1993,* ed. Stephen Shute and Susan Hurley (New York: Basic Books, 1993).

102. Robert W. Tucker, "The International Criminal Court," *World Policy Journal* 18, no. 2 (2001): 80.

103. Mark J. Osiel, "Why Prosecute? Critics of Punishment for Mass Atrocities," *Human Rights Quarterly* 22, no. 1 (2000); Rothe and Mullins, "The International Criminal Court and United States Opposition."

104. Antonio Gramsci, "Selections from the Prison Notebooks," ed. Quinton Hoare and Geoffrey Smith (London: Lawrence & Wishart, 1996).

105. Terry Eagleton, "Deconstruction and Human Rights," in *Freedom and Interpretation: The Oxford Amnesty Lectures, 1992,* ed. Barbara Johnson (New York: Basic Books, 1992); Hunt, *Explorations in Law and Society*; Kirsten Sellars, *The Rise and Rise of Human Rights* (Stroud, UK: Sutton Publishing, 2002).

106. Weller, "Undoing the Global Constitution."

107. Robin Cook, *Guardian,* London, February 11, 2005, p. 28.

108. Johansen, "Impact of US Policy."

109. Chandra Lekha Sriram, "ICC Hypocrisy Over War Crimes," *Guardian,* London, www.guardian.co.uk/commentisfree/2010/jun/22/icc-hypocrisy-article-124-war-crimes.

8

Human Rights as Resistance to the Global Political Economy

In earlier chapters we have looked at theoretical and practical challenges to established ideas and institutions for the protection of universal human rights. From a conservative perspective, which has sought to establish and maintain a set of rights that legitimate particular interests, the global project for human rights provides a moral foundation that legitimates the dominant order. Although the Universal Declaration is often claimed as a radical challenge to the existing order, the argument that "it accurately reflected the conservative social mores and liberal economic values of the immediate post-war era" has been encountered several times in the course of this book.[1] Opposed to this understanding of the modern human rights regime is the view that human rights continue to offer a radical challenge to the existing order. Whereas in the past those who violated human rights could find safety by invoking the principles of sovereignty, nonintervention, and domestic jurisdiction, today, it is argued, the rise of a rights-based global order denies this defense.

In political struggles between conservatives and radicals, therefore, human rights offer a strong defense "against interests as well as a means by which interests are advanced."[2] This tension is explored in this chapter, which points to the conservative ethos of many civil society groups, and in Chapter 9, which looks at the potential for change. During the eighteenth century, for example, voicing support for human rights was seen as sedition, a charge leveled at Tom Paine that forced him to flee Britain.[3] During the nineteenth century, both conservatives and radicals opposed human rights—conservatives because the idea was seen as too egalitarian and subversive, and radicals because the focus on civil and political freedoms suggested an endorsement of wealth inequalities.[4] In the decades following World War II, human rights were often proclaimed as the defining image of the age, where "amazing progress" was achieved in generating international law and new institutions for the protection of human rights.[5] Much of this period was characterized by conflicts over prioritizing either civil and political rights or economic and social rights, with Western-bloc states championing the former and Eastern-bloc states the latter. Today, with the end of the Cold War, human rights are increasingly presented as a central plank in the construction of what Fukuyama famously termed "the end of history,"[6] which is said to achieve democracy and freedom for all.

Yet, the tension between radical and conservative approaches to human rights remains. While, today, the universality of human rights is widely accepted, conflicts over rights issues continue to provide a focus for many political struggles. The distinction between *concept* and *conception,* first encountered in Chapter 2, provides an insight into these tensions. Whereas the former expression suggests a generic term that has achieved widespread acceptance, the latter acknowledges the existence of competing definitions and understandings of a term. What this implies is that while there may be wide agreement on taking action for the promotion and protection of human rights, differences over what counts as a human right, and how that right should be secured, remain a rich field for political protest and struggle. Although globalization has fostered greater awareness of the suffering of unknown others, which "is becoming an integral part of our consciousness and paving the way for a vague but unmistakable sense of a global moral community,"[7] this is often at odds with the values that describe the structures and institutions that constitute the global order.

The language of rights has thus claimed a predominant place in contemporary social and political thought and action. From more frivolous claims like the "human right" to keep a pig in a suburban garden[8] to the commercial use of rights as seen in a mobile-phone company's advertising campaign based on the slogan "Freedom of Speech"[9] and to the policies and practices of governments, international organizations, and transnational business and finance, legitimate action is filtered through the prism of human rights to define questions of moral worth, justice, and fairness. This wide range of claims for human rights demonstrates the readiness with which people turn to the lingua franca of human rights when seeking to resist perceived injustices found in economic globalization. As Fiona Robinson observes, today "the idea that we are human beings first, and citizens second—an idea upon which the concept of human rights depends—resonates with increasing strength around the world."[10]

Against this, however, are continued disagreements over the idea and practice of human rights in a global political economy that exhibits widespread instances of social deprivation and injustice. Such injustices, which are increasingly placed within the context of neoliberal globalization, have inspired many civil society groups to take up human rights as a central tool for political struggle. No matter the subject of self-designation—whether it is peace, poverty, the environment, or rights—protesters "voice their resistance using the moral, legal and political language of human rights."[11] In this way, coalitions are formed by otherwise disparate groups, with the image of human rights serving as the common denominator.[12] In particular, globalization has inspired a shift of focus for protest from the national to the global, from a narrow, parochial, and local interest to a broader vision of common interests opposed to neoliberal globalization and from "normal" politics expressed through the state and interstate relations to exploring new forms of political expression and struggle. Summing this up, Teeple argues that, today, open resistance is found everywhere and at all levels of society.

Since the 1980s no part of the world has been free of significant manifestations of counter-reaction to the assertion of global corporate rights and the corresponding neo-liberal policies. There are as many demands and pretexts as there are transgressions and negations of rights. Although they are met variously with armed force, political and legal repression, or ideological censure, both the resistance and the consciousness of unrealized human rights that it spawns continue to expand.[13]

For some commentators, such campaigns are a response to the failure of the state and interstate system to deliver a form of democratic decisionmaking through which populations can express their preferences.[14] In other words, the centers of power associated with globalization are increasingly remote, while the decisions made within these centers increasingly touch people's lives.

For all the general agreement that the idea of human rights defines the ethical and moral standards of the current world order, the tension between conservative and radical versions of rights emerges in reactions to campaigns waged by international nongovernmental organizations (INGOs). Tolerance of many campaigns is extended only insofar as resistance movements express their discontent through established social and legal institutions.[15] To challenge those institutions themselves, which is tantamount to suggesting that the dominant order itself is the cause of many human rights violations, risks counterresistance in the form of oppressive measures, including the use of police and military force.[16] From a conservative perspective, protest remains legitimate only when it is aimed at gaining entry to the existing order with the aim of reform, rather than as a radical challenge that threatens to damage or bring down that order.[17] In accepting this version of tolerance, groups that are feted by the dominant order move away from their radical potential and settle for acting as the moral conscience of existing dominant interests.[18]

The context for the current tensions between radical and conservative approaches to human rights is inspired by several issues peculiar to globalization. Although these have been discussed earlier in this book, it is worth briefly reiterating them here. First, the technology that supports the rapid expansion of the global political economy has also enabled a wider and deeper understanding of socioeconomic injustices that motivate expressions of discontent, resentment, bitterness, and resistance. Armed with this knowledge, social movements are able to generate networks around common interests and concerns that flow from processes of globalization. Second, the now largely discredited Western project for the philosophy of rights has deprived the human rights regime of the firm foundations upon which its postwar construction was built. Interest in postmodernist, feminist, and neo-Marxist critiques of human rights under conditions of globalization are, in part, cited as the cause of this foundational challenge.[19] Equally important is the greater exposure to non-Western ideas of rights that is enabled by globalization, some of which we encountered in Chapter 4.

Third, the erosion of Western philosophy's claim to have revealed a set of universal human rights, together with the argument that the claim for individual rights was little more than a necessary adjunct to "market discipline," revitalized human rights talk. In particular, the right to private property within the context of economic globalization offered a central focus for critique. The defense against this potential avenue of critique was to shift the focus of human rights talk from philosophical foundationalism to the technical language of the law. In this way, the legal discourse set the parameters for the future of human rights, leaving a sense of "closure" that excluded further investigation of the philosophy of rights and, thus, marginalizing the politics of rights found in dissenting voices. Fourth, following from the preceding point, "progress" in protecting human rights is measured by the generation of international law, rather than by real social and political improvements in people's lives. Thus, while the attempt to reify rights in international law generates cause for celebration in some quarters, reports of gross violations of civil, political, economic, and social rights continue.

As a characteristic of modernity, the current manifestation of human rights talk is claimed by conservatives and radicals alike, reflecting both support for, and a challenge to, the current global order.[20] Apart from the intellectual critiques outlined in Chapters 3 and 4, the development of transnational social movements and INGOs with an interest in using claims for human rights within their campaigns has attracted considerable attention. It is to these that we now turn.

Global Civil Society Actors

Walker notes that in traditional international relations theory, social movements are conceptualized as but a "mosquito on the evening breeze," but he then reminds us that some mosquitoes "can have deadly effects."[21] Similarly, Oscar Wilde is reported to have remarked that if you think something is insignificant because it is small, you have never shared a bed with a flea.[22] In recent years, the assumption that global civil society actors represent the embodiment of Walker's mosquito or Wilde's flea has gained ground.[23] Today, there exists a commonly held perception that the authoritative power of global civil society actors has increased parallel to the expansion of globalization. The growing number and authority of these groups, it is said, is subverting the existing state system. In particular, whereas in the past state security remained the central concern for international relations, today, these groups argue that globalization has enabled the growth of complex social networks sharing a common interest in the pursuit of justice and rights. This claim is often framed within the context of some form of "global citizenship," which is seen as the evolution of institutions for global governance or world politics.[24]

According to this view, the clearest evidence for the existence of global civil society is seen in the activities of INGOs and the formation of global social movements. The rationale for these organizations is to challenge decisions made at both the national and international level in an attempt to influence fu-

ture policy or to encourage the full implementation of existing policy and obligations made under international law. In recent decades, many of these organizations have gained access to policymakers, are regularly invited to participate
in international conferences on a wide range of social and economic issues, and
hold consultative status at the United Nations.[25] On some occasions, more radical organizations turn to direct action, particularly where issues related to globalization are concerned. The most vivid examples of this form of protest are
seen in the 1999 so-called "Battle in Seattle,"[26] the 1998 protests in Geneva
that saw McDonald's restaurants ransacked, and protests at the 2009 G20 meeting in London.[27] INGOs are therefore cast in the role of transmission belts
bridging the state/society divide and promoting alternative and diverse approaches to the problems that face humanity.

   For many commentators, the impetus for the increasing number and influence of global civil society actors is found in changes in the nature of sovereignty associated with the rise of globalization.[28] Crucially, critics argue that
globalization has seen a decline in the prospect for expression of political preferences at the national level, since "non-corporate sectors in the emerging global
civil society have few means of countervailing leverage."[29] In the wake of the
shift to a globalized world order, the transfer of many decision-making
processes from the national to the international level, the globalization of production and finance, and the move to create new institutions for global governance, global civil society is said to signal a realignment of interests. This
realignment focuses on the distinction between the interests pursued by states
and the interstate system and those pursued by an emerging global civil society
formed of transnational social relations created and maintained through the use
of new technology. Within this context, global civil society actors turn to lobbying and political protest as their only available means of political expression.
Global civil society is thus presented as a sphere of freedom that enables the
pursuit of issues outside the traditional security interests of the state and international system: poverty, deprivation, humanitarian crises, human rights, and
global warming, for example. Although global civil society is populated by
disparate groups with very different aims and agendas, what they have in common is a belief that the institutions of global governance, created to manage
processes of economic globalization, are at the root of many ills found within
the global order. The idea of universal human rights, which focuses attention on
humanity rather than wealth and security, offers a rallying call for many of these
protests and thus provides a common purpose.

   In this way, the idea of human rights assumes the form of resistance against
the exclusionary effects of globalizing capital and the "the environment of
vested beliefs,"[30] which threatens the very identity of all other societies by recasting them in its own image. While for many global civil society groups it is
sufficient to press for the implementation of human rights standards already
agreed under international law, for others the cause of human rights violations
is found within the ideological structures of globalization itself. For the most

part, resistance to globalization is passive, rather than violent. That is to say, resistance often appears as an irritant, expressed as words or deeds, but an irritant that seeks to capture public attention, garner wider support, popularize a cause, and thus force change. While the poor, in particular, are mostly unable to organize open revolt against an opposition that can call upon the support of the military and police, "silent" resistance by thousands, perhaps tens of thousands of individuals is intended to erode the existing political order.[31]

The problems with conceptualizing global civil society are well known. In particular, the idea of civil society was first developed as part of a methodology for gaining insights into state/society relations at the domestic level.[32] In its original conception, it was concerned with contrasting social politics with politics conducted through the state and its agencies. The move from civil society within the state to civil society that claims to represent some global or universalizing set of relations is not, therefore, so easily achieved.[33] However, proponents appear to assume that under conditions of globalization, where social actors are not constrained by the state, appeal to some kind of universalizing discourse can be conceptualized through notions of a global civil society. While global government does not exist, proponents argue that the advent of globalization signals new forms of governance regimes against which to juxtapose global civil society. In response to this new order, new forms of democracy and participation have emerged, a phenomenon that proponents see in the increasing influence of INGOs dedicated to making states and the society of states accountable for their actions.[34] However, globalization has enabled wider recognition that the European tradition of political thought, which reflects a particular notion of civility, coexists with other traditions and cannot continue to claim ownership of any universal "truth."[35] Therefore, the idea of universal human rights, which is claimed as constitutive of global civil society, may not be as clear as proponents claim. The undertone of moral superiority that is present in the literature on global civil society and INGOs may not, therefore, be justified.

A further problem for conceptualizing relations between global civil society and INGOs is agency. Since INGOs are mostly focused on policy processes and the implementation of policy, there is little room for reflection upon existing socioeconomic structures that play an important role in creating the very problems that INGOs seek to address. Furthermore, including all INGOs under the umbrella of global civil society not only obscures differences between their aims and objectives but also their differential relations of power in regard to the institutions of governance within the global order.[36] As Wood has argued, the "conceptual portmanteau" that characterizes the literature on global civil society and INGOs "indiscriminately lumps together everything from households and voluntary associations to the economic system of capitalism" and serves only to "confuse and disguise as much at it reveals."[37]

The problem of conceptualizing global civil society, social movements, and INGOs, and explaining the relationship between the three, is increasingly recognized in the literature. Fischer, for example, notes that the diversity of interests and functions of INGOs is so great that the use of the term is little more than "a shorthand for a wide range of formal and informal associations."[38] To add further to this lack of clarity, some have defined global civil society actors in terms of formal organizations and institutions, while others take a less formal view, preferring to define them as loose networks that share particular ideas and goals.[39] The failure to establish clearer and more parsimonious definitions for terms like *social movements* and *INGOs* has not served the literature well and has led some to conclude that few distinguishing characteristics exist beyond the simple juxtaposition between government and nongovernment actors.[40] In spite of these difficulties, ideas of global civil society, social movements, and INGOs have found a place in the lexicon of political activism as it becomes increasingly clear that the move to regional and global decision-making challenges national democratic institutions. In this sense, claims for civil society are contrasted to the remote decision-making institutions of global governance.

The failure to provide clear conceptual boundaries has weakened any claim that INGOs and social movements have emerged as influential actors within global civil society. For all the academic industry directed at demonstrating the links between INGO activity and changes in policy and social attitude, verification for such links has proved elusive. As Saunders argues, the diversity of interests and approaches within any particular issue area (e.g., conservative, reformist, radical) complicates judgments on effective influence.[41] Furthermore, the arguments presented in earlier chapters, that the status of human rights is contested on many fronts, suggests that consensus within civil society groups is mostly lacking.[42] Where agreement is claimed on so-called "core values," this often reflects a set of norms and principles that support existing interests associated with the global political economy. Claims for women's rights, for example, do not go beyond questions of nondiscrimination, are rarely acknowledged as a means to an end (empowerment), and for liberal feminists reflect a gender bias that prioritizes rights of most concern to men.[43] Thus, the activities of global civil society actors may not offer evidence of a counterhegemonic force but, instead, reflect conservative values that describe the dominant global order.

Global Civil Society Actors as Resistance

There is, however, an alternative view of civil society, first encountered in Chapter 3. In this alternative view, civil society is cast as a private sphere within which the individual enjoys rights associated with private property.[44] In this reading, the state's central role is to guarantee the private sphere in which the egoistic, atomized individual pursues private desires and interests. The role of the state is to fabricate a set of institutions for protecting the individual against the violation of these rights, which today are claimed as universal. In particular, the institutions for participation through democracy and citizenship provide images of equality that conceal real inequalities within the economic sphere.[45] Seen in this way, civil society does not stand in opposition to the state or the international system, which is often suggested in the literature on social movements and INGOs, but, rather, invests the state with political powers for maintaining social order, ensuring "fair play" within a set of values and principles that civil society has itself created. However, in a globalized world order, where old boundaries that previously constrained the private sphere are considerably weakened and where the state now acts as an administrative unit for global interests, the legitimacy of government as representing the wishes of the people through democracy and citizenship are increasingly questioned. In an attempt to reaffirm legitimacy, political leaders turn to the claim that some as yet undefined form of "cosmopolitan democracy" emerges from global civil society, and it is to this that they respond.[46]

This conclusion recalls Gramsci's analysis that the role of civil society is to provide the central site for creating consensus, and thus a central role in maintaining class hegemony.[47] In this analysis, consensus provides a form of latent coercion sufficient to ensure that ways of thinking and acting are conducted in the interest of the dominant class. The material success of the current hegemonic order, first built across Europe and North America and now expanding to encompass the globe, is promoted vigorously in many less-developed countries. Part of this program requires traditional social and cultural values to be abandoned in favor of those that promise a single, integrated world economy based upon the individual and private property. To achieve this goal demands a passive revolution within less-developed states that legitimizes new ways of thinking and acting, ways that are appropriate for engaging with the hegemonic order. The promise of universal human rights, defined as the rights of the individual to engage freely in the private sphere of global civil society, thus becomes a proxy for previously shared community and national identities.

Human rights may therefore reflect a "common sense" authority that is now widely accepted within global civil society. As Walker notes, "claims about ethics have too often become a way of avoiding questions about the political conditions under which ethical claims can be sustained." Using this approach, analysis of INGO and social-movement campaigns may reveal the extent to which particular groups "do, or do not, conform to what are taken to be already constituted ethical traditions rather than to ask how emerging political practices challenge and reconstruct such claims."[48] Similarly, Conor Gearty reminds us that human rights are "the phrase that comes to mind when we want to capture in words a particular view of the world that we share with others and that we aspire to share with still greater numbers of people."[49] Thus, where global civil society actors do emerge in response to the unfortunate consequences of globalization, their demands are mostly framed within a logic that articulates "conventional liberal accounts of human rights, which merge, at a general level, with expectations and policy goals of powerful states."[50] The "widespread use and proliferating scope" of human rights therefore reflects a view of rights that "cannot provide the necessary discursive or strategic tools to mount serious resistance to globalization for those who are most vulnerable to it."[51]

This should, perhaps, offer no surprise, because the discourse of rights is dominated by governmental and nongovernmental organizations based in neoliberal societies. In cases where global civil society groups have sought to project alternative socioeconomic formations, and thus acted to resist the march of globalization, coercive counterresistance has occurred. Amoore notes that when states employ counterresistance measures, perhaps by utilizing the police or military, this provides the space for reinforcing the claim that "legitimate" politics takes place within the established "natural" order, simultaneously rendering alternatives illegitimate and legitimating the use of coercion where necessary.[52] For example, as we saw in Chapter 4, for many Islamic thinkers "change had to be total, comprehensive, and revolutionary" because there was "no possibility of coexistence between Islam and other political and social systems."[53] This thinking brings forth counterresistance, as exampled by military action against states where Islam is the most widespread religion, but has also been used to justify curbs on freedoms at the domestic level in many developed states.[54]

The use of human rights as counterresistance, as the central moral image motivating recent military action by Western states, is seen clearly in preparations for intervention in Iraq. Prime Minister Tony Blair, for example, asserted that the "best defence of our security lies in the spread of our values,"[55] which it is the responsibility of global institutions to promote, and which other governments need to recognize as universal. In this sense, if, as Blair asserts, the "essence of a community is common rights," then those who fail to accept "our" values make themselves vulnerable to whatever measures are necessary to secure those values. Thus, the existence of a global community

> does not mean that industrialized countries should adhere to global rules, should take into account the views of non-Western states on human rights, or should take the right to development seriously. It means that the West has the right to intervene on foreign soil in order to defend self-defined values that it feels should be respected globally. The result is a groundswell of disaffection in communities excluded by the discourse.[56]

Similarly, Mutua refers to the major human rights INGOs as "conventional doctrinalists," suggesting that their primary concern is to promote the values associated with market discipline. For Mutua, rather than organize to expose the existing order as the cause of many human rights violations, the mission of many INGOs is to conduct a crusade for the rights associated with globalization by "crafting organizational mandates that promote liberal ideas and norms."[57] Their mission, he agues, is to "civilise" those who have not yet embraced the dominant order: the so-called "backward" countries that are judged to have a poor civil rights record. Amnesty International, for example, supports the idea of human rights that is a characteristic of the prevailing socioeconomic global order. Its high profile, based upon a self-defined mandate that obscures the importance and significance of many socioeconomic rights, including the rights of women, children, aboriginals, marginal peoples, and the protection of the environment. In particular, Amnesty's concentration on prisoners of conscience divorces the individual's rights from the sociopolitical context that gave rise to violations. Thus, Amnesty separates the victim from the circumstances of the violation and projects a picture that sees many thousands of violations as peculiar occurrences, rather than the outcome of a particular world order configuration.[58]

The potential for INGOs to offer radical criticism is therefore self-limiting. The strategy of the most prominent INGOs is to integrate within the existing socioeconomic global order and its particular view of human rights, rather than engage with questions concerning the idea that the relations of economic globalization may be the source of the problems. To promote such ideas "would be little short of biting the hand that feeds them."[59] The claim that INGOs represent a neutral challenge, which simply seeks to ensure compliance with international law, exposing those who fail to do so along the way, is therefore questionable.

> No one should be expected to believe that the scheme of rights promoted by INGOs does not seek to replicate a vision of society based on the industrial democracies of the North. Only after openly conceding that INGOs indeed have a specific political agenda can the discussions be had about the wisdom, problems, and implications for the advocacy of such values, And only then can conversations about the post-liberal society start in earnest.[60]

Counterresistance and Pacification

The global demand for human rights, as expressed in the growing number of INGOs and the iconic status given to several of these organizations, raises the question of why so few global civil society actors offer a radical critique of human rights talk and institutions. From the perspective of human rights as the dominant ethical and moral claims that help sustain globalization, the assault on human rights by "intellectuals of the postmodernist and deconstructionist sort" is of little significance.[61] From this view we might also assume that the claims of neo-Marxists, Islamists, feminists, or any other form of critique are equally rejected. In light of the wide acceptance of the idea of human rights as the central ethical and moral plank in global politics, proponents remain confident that the intellectual resistance offered by these groups cannot be sustained.[62] This "common sense" view assumes the proven existence of some metaphysical rationale for human rights—a universal agreement on the foundations for human rights to which all but a few disgruntled intellectuals now subscribe. In this sense, it might be argued that we have, indeed, reached the end of history. Terms like *democracy, civil society, liberalism, free markets*, and *human rights* can now be used interchangeably, or at least as interconnected policy objectives. That INGOs and social movements confine their activities to criticism of inconsistencies within current ideas and arrangements for implementing human rights, rather than offering critique, should therefore come as no surprise.

To maintain the human rights discourse in the image of neoliberalism demands a significant commitment by what Chomsky has referred to as "compliant intellectuals."[63] The task of this group is to interpret the actions of governments and international institutions as right and just or, when public opinion and protest become so great that it cannot be assuaged, to point to mistakes when benign intentions go awry. For Chomsky, the historic record suggests that it is not difficult to find those who would justify almost any action, a view that appears to be supported by recently released CIA top-secret memos offering reasons why particular interrogation practices are definitely not torture.[64] Similarly, arguments that neoliberal states are as committed to economic and social rights as they are to civil and political rights, even in the face of evidence that stands against this claim, are part of the mainstream diet of academic journals.[65]

The media has also encouraged the widely held view that INGOs are engaged in a continuous struggle against injustices consequential to the global political economy. Supporters of those engaged in such a struggle may therefore view INGOs as taking the moral high ground above those whose ambition is to promote and develop a neoliberal order in every corner of the world. However, as we have seen in arguments encountered in previous chapters, such an approach fails to interrogate important questions to do with the distribution of power within the global political economy. Crucially, it fails to take full account of mechanisms for maintaining and reproducing existing power relations. The image of INGOs locked in a constant struggle with powerful economic actors may therefore offer an illusion of resistance that has no substance, since struggle implies opposition to interests associated with the existing global order, rather than an attempt to seek reform within a framework that supports those interests. This illusion is encouraged by those closest to the center of globalization, who do not sit idly by in the face of potential resistance.[66] Instead, as Chomsky has observed, the practice of co-option—reshaping potential resistance through integrating it into the dominant order—is readily achieved because the "sponge of neo-liberalism" soaks up all revolutionary ideas, refashioning them in the service of the dominant order.[67] Thus, many prominent INGOs, feted as a bulwark against the unwanted consequences of globalization, offer only passive resistance rather than a critique of an order that is itself the cause of many human rights violations.

The argument that the logic of global capitalism, with its attendant values expressed as universal freedoms, utilizes the idea of human rights as a tool for impelling all peoples to engage fully in the global political economy has been a central argument for this book. This argument assumes that as an attribute of our common human nature, the individual's objective needs and interests are best realized through the observance of human rights. When encountering those who refuse to recognize this rationale for human rights, the more "enlightened" assume a duty to point ignorant dissidents to universal "truths," to save them from themselves. Those engaged in this line of thinking are at pains to remind critics that while principles and values are universal, their implementation can take a local form, drawing on past traditions and cultural mores. However, no matter the form of implementation, the subversion of universal principles that provide the moral foundations for market discipline cannot be tolerated. Counterresistance is therefore justified because, as Appiah argues, "the universe not human sentiment determines what is right and good," validating the moral realists' view that "if the universe is on my side, it will naturally be opposed to those 'Others' who disagree with me."[68]

Following this line of thought, the rationale for many conservative, counterresistance INGOs is to oppose the overzealous protection of human rights, particularly economic and social rights, on grounds that to do so inhibits the further expansion of capital. In particular, conservative INGOs cite the challenge that potential resistance brings to the free market, which they claim, if successful, would damage the prospects for developing a neoliberal world order that guarantees higher standards of living in every corner of the world.[69] Although it is not always easy to distinguish between resistance and counterresistance groups, because they utilize the same tools and strategies, one of the most significant differences is that counterresistance groups, who often gain corporate funding, have the greater potential to access resources essential for protecting and promoting interests associated with market discipline.[70]

An example of counterresistance can be seen in the campaign to persuade the United Nations to adopt strategies that favored the interests of corporations. During the 1980s, for example, the Heritage Foundation produced more than one hundred reports arguing that the UN favored regulatory and redistributive policies that damaged the prospects for expanding corporate interests within a neoliberal global order. Work on environmental programs (a threat to corporate practices), regulations on consumables (for example, a threat to the baby-milk industry), the UN's disarmament work (a threat to the arms industry), World Health Organization campaigns (a threat to the tobacco industry), and restrictions on labor (a threat to all corporations) were all seen as threats to the future of neoliberal economic growth on a global scale.[71] In each case, lobbying groups, like the International Chamber of Commerce, sought to "take back" the United Nations by "stamping out its socialistic and redistributive tendencies, crushing its 'anti-corporate' biases and populist impulses, and making it a trusty vehicle for globalizing capitalism and particularly for US-based investors and companies."[72]

Further strategies of counterresistance are managed by the UN. For example, Secretary-General Boutros Boutros-Ghali began to close down those social programs organized by the UN that were identified by corporations as a challenge to free market principles. Moreover, Boutros Boutros-Ghali dismantled the Centre on Transnational Corporations, which was condemned by the Heritage Foundation as the key player in "the campaign against multinational corporations."[73] As we saw in Chapter 7, in the wake of these successful campaigns to lessen the impact of UN involvement in corporate interests, business leaders, governments, and UN agencies developed the Global Compact as an alternative and acceptable means for continuing corporate involvement in policy-setting processes.[74]

The UN's policy for "globalization with a human face," first proposed by the UNDP and UN Secretary-General Kofi Annan in 1999 with the approval of many INGOs,[75] offers a further example of pacification. At the center of this proposal was the assumption that, if in fact some of the causes of human rights violations are found in the structures of globalization, particularly during the transition from traditional socioeconomic relations to those now found in the global order, all that is necessary is to undertake key reforms of existing programs. By undertaking reforms, the values that describe processes for the continued expansion of economic globalization are considered sound and are in no way responsible for violations. Consequently, it is sufficient to support those caught up in processes of change if they are offered transitional assistance by ensuring that the major international organizations take full account of human rights consequences in their policy planning. To fulfill this requirement, the WTO, for example, points to various articles in its constitution and those of other UN organs as evidence of reform. However, the WTO freely admits that these provisions are only loosely related to the protection of human rights and that there remains considerable debate among legal experts about how these provisions as a whole relate to other international treaties and law.[76]

Processes of co-option do not merely absorb any potential threat but also reinforce the institutions of the dominant order by contrasting the cooperative involvement of less radical INGOs to those that persist in mounting a radical challenge. Although the work of the most prominent INGOs is often cited as evidence of the dominant order's concern for human rights, the rights they are most concerned with are individual rights and freedoms essential for a free market political economy. For example, while in recent years both Amnesty International and Human Rights Watch have decided to include economic, social, and cultural rights in their missions, there is little evidence of activity aimed at protesting in support of these rights. Indeed, the 2001 attack on the Twin Towers in New York may have contributed to both INGOs keeping their focus on civil and political rights.[77] Similarly, the Roman Catholic Church has sought to defuse the fervor surrounding liberation theology established during the 1980s by claiming to embrace its values. At its height, liberation theology encouraged the poor to exercise their rights by participating fully in decision-making processes about their own future. Today, however, the church encourages the poor to appeal to the conscience of the rich for a greater share of the wealth generated by those whose good fortune it is to engage in economic globalization.[78]

A further technique deployed in the cause of co-option is the neoliberal practice of tolerance, which is extended only to those who confine their criticisms to legal and procedural matters, not to those who presume to challenge the dominant order. It is common to find proponents of market discipline arguing that the new "politics of recognition demands new expressions of sensitivity to difference and new possibilities for expanding the range of permissible disagreements."[79] This is the virtue of tolerance, which is a fundamental principle of social pluralism. However, market discipline does not extend tolerance to all groups, ideas, and values. Instead, tolerance is extended only to those who accept the general purposes of market discipline by adopting its values and following the "correct" procedures for realizing the "good life." Those who attempt to challenge the general principles of the dominant economic, social, and political order are tolerated only insofar as they "do not seek to make the transition from word to deed, from speech to action."[80]

This is the condition of "repressive tolerance," which Marcuse argues is little more than a "market-place of ideas" in which notions of the "good life" compete for attention within the confines of a particular version of social order, currently that described by market discipline.[81] Within this social order, the role of civil society is to defend the social and economic norms associated with the global marketplace. Normalization demands that the "individual who enters these civil spaces is expected to adopt a certain stance towards his or her own person and towards others."[82] Those who cannot or will not embrace the values embodied in civil society are treated as ignorant, ill-informed beings, lacking the moral capacity to engage fully in decisions about their own interests.[83] Tolerance and civility are therefore concerned with the preservation and management of a particular form of civil society, a narrowing of the political agenda, and the exclusion of actors whose voices appear as a threat. In neoliberal societies, tolerance is practiced by legitimating a set of civil liberties and freedoms that are granted to all citizens, regardless of "race, colour, sex, language, religion, political or other opinion, national or social origin, property, birth or other status."[84] Against this expression of formal equality and tolerance, however, is the actual practice of tolerance, which cannot be divorced from power relations, relations that determine what will or will not be tolerated. In the face of repressive tolerance and inequality, "the idea of available alternatives evaporates into an utterly utopian dimension" because the dominant world order is characterized by "indoctrination," "manipulation," and "extraneous authority."[85]

Summed up succinctly by Marcuse, progress toward tolerance is "perhaps more than before asserted by violence and suppression on a global scale," when tolerance is extended to "policies, conditions, and modes of behaviour which should not be tolerated because they are impeding, if not destroying, the chances of creating an existence without fear and misery."[86] Tolerance may therefore perform the task of "closure" by excluding alternatives that threaten the existing order; for example, by defining legitimate rights claims as a legal problem rather than one best understood within the context of the global political economy or by treating resistance to market discipline as perpetrated by "evildoers" rather than as a consequence of the prevailing socioeconomic global order.[87] From this perspective, Islam offers an example of the perceived failure to embrace market discipline as "common sense," and therefore a counterhegemonic threat to the global capitalist project.[88]

The distinctions between tolerance and intolerance are seen clearly in what is often presented as a trade-off between human rights and security. The actions of the United States and the United Kingdom following the events of 9/11, for example, suggest that human rights are now considered subservient to security interests. Although both states persist in proclaiming their human rights credentials, military intervention is presented as the right to intervene in other countries in the name of gaining global respect for self-defined, neoliberal values. Guantanamo Bay, where the legal and political status of prisoners remain unclear; the torture in Abu Ghraib; and the practice of moving detainees around the globe to interrogate them in states where torture is tolerated all attest to the contempt with which human rights is now treated in the name of security.[89] At the domestic level, established human rights law is amended, reinterpreted, or overturned in the name of new security threats. John Reid, as UK home secretary, argued that we live in times when it is necessary to "modify some of our own freedoms in the short term in order to prevent their misuse and abuse by those who oppose our fundamental values," and threaten our security.[90] The outcome of such action, according to some, is to foment greater disaffection in territories where a groundswell of discontent already exists.[91]

For many human rights advocates, the question of trade-off is best resolved by developing policies that promote human rights vigorously, thus creating the necessary and sufficient conditions for countering resistance and establishing social stability.[92] From this view, there should be no conflict between security and human rights because the former is achieved by implementing the latter. For others, however, evidence in support of the necessary-and-sufficient argument does not stand up to scrutiny. Firstly, critics point to the many examples where security remains strong while observance of human rights is weak; for instance, China, Vietnam, and Egypt. Secondly, from survey evidence it can be argued that many people are willing to accept restrictions of their human rights and freedoms against a trade-off for greater security.[93] Thirdly, the mere fact that a state boasts a democratic constitution does not guarantee either human rights or security. In the case of the United States, for example, the Presidential Order on Detention, Treatment, and Trial of Certain Non-Citizens in the War Against Terrorism, signed November 13, 2001, was condemned as an affront to normal standards of justice.[94] Similarly, Amnesty International dismissed the United Kingdom's Anti-Terrorism, Crime, and Security Act for the restrictions it imposed on freedoms in the name of "doing something" rather than increasing security.[95]

Together with tolerance, a further strategy deployed in processes of counterresistance and co-option is the professional and intellectual discourse of international law, which is presented as the authentic voice of human rights talk. While this voice has little to say about power and interests associated with the dominant idea of human rights, the legal discourse has succeeded in subordinating alternative voices with an interest in exposing the causes of human rights violations. The hegemony of international law therefore performs the task of "closure," shifting human rights talk from the political to the legal discourse, providing the space for forging a particular and singular view of rights expressed as a legal canon. Although human rights international law is presented as the greatest achievement of the postwar era, an alternative view might therefore be that it acts as a mask for protecting interests associated with globalization.[96]

Noting this potential, Gearty argues that the rise of popular democracy during the nineteenth and early-twentieth century was seen as a potential threat to the interests of capital. The common response was to create rights law, which offered capital the opportunity to reaffirm dominance through legislation based upon prepolitical claims, including property rights. Through this process, the justice of private property was delivered through rights law, turning an essentially political discourse concerned with investigating rights into a legal discourse concerned with implementing rights. In this way human rights became depoliticized. Furthermore, Gearty argues that once law is established, money drives the system, in the sense that lawyers, courts, human rights experts, and the cost of raising the profile of a case are beyond the pocket of the world's majority. Human rights law is not therefore accessible to everyone, because the law does not provide "routes that are open to the poor, the disadvantaged, [and] the voiceless for which 'human rights' is supposed to be a specially tailored and supportive language." Moreover, in the process of legal entrenchment, the poor see the language of rights taken from them and placed once again in hands of the "rich, the powerful, the already fortunate, to do with what they will to consolidate their own advantage."[97] Thus, although civil and political rights may imply the right to insurrection in response to governments that attempt to subvert constitutional rights—rights that are largely constructed upon the right to private property—groups that are degraded and impoverished as a consequence of accumulation are mostly excluded from the means to exercise those rights. Under these conditions "insurrection in the name of the common good would spell the end of private property, and hence the divide between civil society and the state."[98]

Furthermore, Gearty argues that human rights have been arrayed in order to exploit both people and the natural world. Although in the first instance, human rights talk focused upon generalities of rights claims, which brought greater depth and breadth to the discourse, it also exposed the many areas of socioeconomic life to which the law must respond. However, once the discourse moves from the political to the legal discourse of rights, the fluid ideas that were the stuff of the former focus now demand greater certainty. This step reinvigorates interest in rights and the rule of law, which in Western societies characterizes liberal democracy, placing human rights law at its center. Through this process, rights develop from the presocial claims found in Hobbes to achieve a set of trenchant ideological values that cannot be transgressed. Noting this, Gearty argues that this approach to law

> essentially sees the idea of human rights not as an emancipatory political concept at all but rather as a pre- or supra-political ideal, as reflective of a truth beyond politics to which politics ought to be subject. On this view, our core or essential human rights are made up of a number of rights that people have which *preceeds* politics or which are *above* politics. They are not rights which are achieved (and sustained) *through* politics.

In short, the politics of rights is determined and beyond discussion once the transition from the political to the legal discourse is completed, closing off further debate and forbidding already excluded voices from engaging in critique. In this way, the current crisis over human rights, which has engendered both great optimism and great pessimism in equal number, is created by the increased focus on the legislation of rights, on the one hand, and consequent decline in the politics of rights, on the other.

However, for many INGOs, the central tool in their campaign armory remains the law. Much of INGO work is concerned with pressing governments to implement existing human rights law and offering a critical review of proposed or new legislation. However, the mere drawing up of constitutions and laws for the protection of human rights fails to realize that human rights law is a means to an end, not an end in itself. For Gearty, the end is to treat people fairly, justly, and with dignity, simply because, as he expresses it, "we are."[99] De Fayter also notes that many INGOs are more concerned with documenting human rights abuses and engaging in legal redress on a case-by-case basis, rather than seeking the causes of violations. In this way, INGOs are drawn into processes that reinforce and legitimate the law as the most effective, if not the only, means for protecting human rights. While human rights advocates "may find comfort in the familiarity of the case file approach," it adds to deflecting attention from socioeconomic structures and processes, the investigation of which may reveal uncomfortable questions.[100]

According to Susan George, one of the clearest examples of this was seen during the days of decolonization, where the imperial powers sought to protect the property rights of European settlers by accompanying the new constitutions with a bill of rights. While the idea of rights commonly conjures images of torture, political prisoners, the massacre of civilians, and the denial of democracy, violations that provide the focus for many INGOs, a broader view that includes socioeconomic rights continues to press for attention. In particular, George notes that the framers of the Universal Declaration of Human Rights

> devoted their attention to the choices of society with regard to the *just distribution of material and non-material advantages*. The notion of "just distribu-

tion" includes inequalities both within and between nations; the shares allotted to different social classes in particular societies and also the disparities between rich and poor at the international level.[101]

Today, property rights are considered as an immutable set of values that legitimate any national constitution, even though, as George argues, "globalization has inexorably transferred wealth from the poor to the rich, [increasing] inequalities both within and between nations" [and creating] "far more losers than winners."[102]

These techniques and processes for mollifying potential resistance to globalization are seen clearly in the tension between the formal, legal human rights regime and the norms of market discipline. The notion of "civility" emanating from global civil society groups narrows the political agenda set by the regime and thus serves only to enhance the sense of grievance that motivates further resistance.[103] In other words, the more vigorously global civil society promotes market discipline and its associated human rights values, the greater the resistance, creating a "periodic and irresolvable problem of policing the non-civil in civil society."[104] Those groups that adhere to the norms of civility are included in decision-making processes that continue to favor the interests of global capital, while those that offend against "normal" politics, perhaps by taking direct action, are excluded. For the latter group, disapproval may be registered through violence, by labeling those engaged in resistance as "mad" or by introducing legislation that outlaws particular organizations.[105]

*   *   *

This chapter began by noting that, historically, the idea of human rights has been co-opted by both conservatives and radicals. Conservatives claim that human rights provide an essential set of moral values for achieving and maintaining the project of economic globalization, which is claimed as generating a "natural" form of social relations that benefits all humankind. Radicals, on the other hand, argue that the dominant conception of human rights serves only to legitimate free market discipline on a global scale, generating forms of social exclusion that lead to poverty, immiseration, and loss of cultural identity.

The past three decades have seen increasing levels of protest against the dominance of corporate interests in many parts of the world, in both the developed and less-developed states. These protests are in response to growing concerns over economic globalization and corporate power, which is supported by neoliberal policies adopted by the great majority of states. For many, protest and political struggle centers on the state's commitment to guarantee corporate rights at the expense of fulfilling obligations undertaken through international human rights law. While the manifestation of INGOs, social movements, and civil society groups has brought claims that we are living through a period where new forms of governance are emerging, and on a global scale, the evidence for these claims remains inconclusive, at least in the field of human rights. The concept of human rights provides a convenient focal point for otherwise disparate interests seeking a common cause that strengthens their collective influence. However, the cacophony of voices emanating from widely different interests does little to clarify fundamental disagreements over the idea of human rights.

Notes

1. Kirsten Sellars, *The Rise and Rise of Human Rights* (Stroud, UK: Sutton Publishing, 2002), p. 22.

2. R. J. Vincent, *Human Rights and International Relations* (Cambridge: Cambridge University Press, 1986), p. 122.

3. John Keane, *Tom Paine: A Political Life* (Boston Little, Brown, 1995).

4. Michael Freeman, *Human Rights* (Cambridge, UK: Polity, 2002).

5. T. Opsahl, "Instruments of Implementation of Human Rights," *Human Rights Law Journal* 10, no. 1 (1989): 33.

6. Francis Fukuyama, "The End of History," *The National Interest* (Summer 1989).

7. Bhikhu Parekh, "Principles of a Global Ethic," in *Global Ethics and Civil Society*, ed. John Eade and Darren O'Byrne (Aldershot, UK: Ashgate, 2005), p. 18.

8. Report on the BBC *Today* program on a woman who claimed it was her "human right" to keep a pig in her urban garden, a right that the courts should uphold, July 2008.

9. Koen De Feyter, *Human Rights: Social Justice in the Age of the Market* (London: Zed Books, 2005).

10. Fiona Robinson, "The Limits of a Rights Based Approach to International Ethics," in *Human Rights Fifty Years On: A Reappraisal*, ed. T. Evans (Manchester: Manchester University Press, 1998).

11. Fiona Robinson, "Human Rights and the Global Politics of Resistance: Feminist Perspectives," *Review of International Studies* 29, special issue (2003): 162.

12. Donatella della Porta, "The Global Justice Movement: An Introduciton," in *The Global Justice Movement: Cross-National and Transnational Perspectives*, ed. Donatella della Porta (Boulder, Colo.: Paradigm Publishers, 2007).

13. Gary Teeple, *The Riddle of Human Rights* (Aurora, Canada: Garamond Press, 2005), p. 164.

14. Mario Pianta and Raffaele Marchetti, "The Global Justice Movement: The Transnational Dimension," in *The Global Justice Movement: Cross-National and Transnational Perspectives*, ed. Donatella della Porta (Boulder, Colo.: Paradigm Publishers, 2007).

15. Herbert Marcuse, "Repressive Tolerance," in *A Critique of Tolerance*, ed. R. P. Wolff, Barrington Moore, and Herbert Marcuse (Boston: Beacon Press, 1969).

16. Robert Cox, "Democracy in Hard Times: Economic Globalization and the Limits to Liberal Democracy," in *The Transformation of Democracy*, ed. Anthony McGrew (Cambridge, UK: Polity, 1997).

17. Costas Douzinas, *Human Rights and Empire: The Political Philosophy of Cosmopolitanism* (Abingdon, UK: Routledge-Cavendish, 2007).

18. James Petras, "NGOs in the Service of Imperialism," *Journal of Contemporary Asia* 29, no. 4 (1999).

19. Terrell Carver, *The Postmodern Marx* (Manchester: Manchester University Press, 1998); Terry Eagleton, "Deconstruction and Human Rights," in *Freedom and Interpretation: The Oxford Amnesty Lectures, 1992*, ed. Barbara Johnson (New York: Basic Books, 1992).

20. Conor Gearty, *Can Human Rights Survive?* (Cambridge: Cambridge University Press, 2006).

21. R. B. J. Walker, "Social Movements/World Politics," *Millennium* 23, no. 3 (1994): 669.

22. Annie Taylor, "The Significance of Non-Governmental Organizations in the Development of International Environmental Policy: The Case of Trade and Environment," Ph.D. diss., University of Southampton, September 1998.

23. The term *global civil society actors* is used here to include what the literature refers to variously as nongovernment organizations, social movements, civil society, lobbying organizations, pressure groups, and a range of other labels. See Robert O'Brien et al., *Contesting Global Governance: Multilateral Economic Institutions and Global Social Movements*, ed. Steve Smith, Cambridge Studies in International Relations (Cambridge: Cambridge University Press, 2000), pp. 12–16. The aim of this chapter is to look at the ways in which these groups use the idea of human rights and the reactions of the state and international society to their activities, rather than to offer an analysis that attempts to distinguish between different types.

24. Mustapha Kamel Pasha and David L. Blaney, "Elusive Paradise: The Promise and Perils of Global Civil Society," *Alternatives* 23, no. 1 (1998). See also Tony Evans, "Citizenship and Human Rights in the Age of Globalization," *Alternatives* 25, no. 4 (2000).

25. For the rules governing NGO status at the UN, see http://esango.un.org/paperless/.

26. Jagdish Bhagwati, *Free Trade Today* (Princeton, N.J.: Princeton University Press, 2001).

27. *Times,* London, http://www.timesonline.co.uk/tol/comment/columnists/camilla_cavendish/article6024674.ece.

28. See, for example, Joseph A. Camilleri and Jim Falk, *The End of Sovereignty? The Politics of a Shrinking and Fragmenting World* (Aldershot, UK: Edward Elgar, 1992); Robert Cox, "Civil Society at the Turn of the Millennium: Prospects for an Alternative World Order," *Review of International Studies* 25, no. 3 (1999); Cox, "Democracy in Hard Times"; Andrew Linklater, *The Transformation of Political Society* (Cambridge, UK: Polity, 1998); G. B. Madison, *The Political Economy of Civil Society and Human Rights* (London: Routledge, 1998); Pasha and Blaney, "Elusive Paradise"; Justin Rosenberg, *The Empire of Civil Society: A Critique of the Realist Theory of International Relations* (London: Verso, 1994).

29. Teeple, *Riddle of Human Rights,* p. 122.

30. Noam Chomsky, "'Recovering Rights': A Crooked Path," in *Globalizing Rights: The Oxford Amnesty Lectures, 1999*, ed. Matthew J. Gibney (Oxford: Oxford University Press, 2003), p. 71.

31. Fantu Cheru, "The Silent Revolution and the Weapons of the Weak: Transformation and Innovation from Below," in *Innovation and Transformation in International Studies*, ed. Stephen Gill and James H. Mittelman (Cambridge: Cambridge University Press, 1997).

32. The notion of social movements is also found in the literature to indicate similar qualities to those found in INGOs. Social movements are said to be a subset of global civil society, a type of group action defined as informal social networks that focus on specific political and social issues with the intent of supporting, resisting, or reversing existing policy trends. The distinction between INGOs and social movements is not always clear. However, the distinction made between *institutions* and *organiza-*

tions—terms that are often used interchangeably in the literature—may offer some guidance. Organizations are empirical entities, possessing offices, personnel, budgets, and other material goods necessary to develop bureaucratic and procedural systems aimed at achieving particular ends; whereas institutions can be described as sets of social relations described by particular sets of norms and rules for behavior, possessed of no material or empirical assets. Similarly, while NGOs can be identified as having a material existence, institutions can be thought of as sets of ideas that influence ways of thinking and knowing.

33. David Chandler, *Constructing Global Civil Society: Morality and Power in International Relations* (Basingstoke, UK: Palgrave, 2005).

34. Anthony McGrew, "Globalization and Territorial Democracy: An Introduction," in *The Transformation of Democracy*, ed. Anthony McGrew (Cambridge, UK: Polity, 1997).

35. Cox, "Civil Society at the Turn of the Millennium."

36. Annie Taylor, "The Significance of Non-Governmental Organizations."

37. Ellen Meiksins Wood, *Democracy Against Capitalism* (Cambridge, Cambridge University Press, 1995), p. 244.

38. Willaim F. Fischer, "Doing Good? The Politics and Anti-Politics of NGO Practices," *Annual Review of Anthropology* 26 (1997): 447. See also O'Brien et al., *Contesting Global Governance*.

39. For a good discussion of the problems defining NGOs and social movements, see Clare Saunders, "Using Social Network Analysis to Explore Social Movements: A Rationalist Approach," *Social Movement Studies* 6, no. 3 (2007).

40. Petras, "NGOs in the Service of Imperialism."

41. Saunders, "Using Social Network Analysis."

42. Pasha and Blaney, "Elusive Paradise."

43. Radhika Coomaraswamy, "To Bellow Like a Cow: Women, Ethnicity, and the Discourse of Rights," in *Human Rights of Women: National and International Perspectives*, ed. Rebecca Cook (Philadelphia: University of Pennsylvania Press, 1994).

44. Karl Marx, "On the Jewish Question," in *Karl Marx: Selected Writings*, ed. David McLellan (Oxford: Oxford University Press, 2002).

45. F. Furet, *Marx and the French Revolution* (London: University of Chicago Press, 1995).

46. David Held, "Democracy: From City-States to a Cosmopolitan Order," *Political Studies* 40, special Issue (1992).

47. Antonio Gramsci, "Selections from the Prison Notebooks," ed. Quinton Hoare and Geoffrey Smith (London: Lawrence and Wishart, 1996).

48. Walker, "Social Movements/World Politics," p. 693.

49. Gearty, *Can Human Rights Survive?* p. 4.

50. Robinson, "Human Rights and the Global Politics of Resistance," p. 162.

51. Ibid.

52. Louise Amoore, "Global Resistance—Global Politics," introduction to *The Global Resistance Reader*, ed. Louise Amoore (Abingdon, UK: Routledge, 2005), p. 7.

53. Quoted in T. Butko, "Revelations or Revolution? A Gramscian Approach to the Rise of Political Islam," *British Journal of Middle Eastern Studies 31*, no. 1 (2004): 41–62.

54. Similarly, neoliberal action to neutralize the women's and environmental movements include legal solutions that promote nondiscrimination, rather than empowerment; Coomaraswamy, "To Bellow Like a Cow: Women, Ethnicity, and the Discourse of Rights."

55. Speech by Prime Minister Tony Blair, March 5, 2004.

56. De Feyter, *Human Rights: Social Justice in the Age of the Market,* p. 81.

57. Makau Mutua, "Human Rights International NGOs," in *NGOs and Human*

Rights: Promise and Performance, ed. Claude F. Welch (Philadelphia University of Pennsylvania Press, 2001), p. 153.

58. Teeple, *Riddle of Human Rights*. During the past few years, both Amnesty and Human Rights Watch have made some move toward promoting economic and social rights. While for the most part this set of rights has achieved only a lowly place on the agenda of these two INGOs, in May 2009 Amnesty's secretary-general, Irene Kahn, attempted to reposition the organization. Noting the world economic crisis and the growing problems of poverty and inequality throughout the world, Kahn accepted that "the world is sitting on a social, political and economic time bomb": an economic crisis that is also a human rights crisis. For a report on Kahn's statement, see http://www.amnesty.org/en/news-and-updates/feature-stories/economic-crisis-reveals-deeper-human-rights-problems-20090528.

59. Ibid., p. 101.

60. Mutua, "Human Rights International NGOs," p. 159.

61. Madison, *The Political Economy of Civil Society and Human Rights*.

62. K. Anthony Appiah, "Citizens of the World," in *Globalizing Rights*, ed. Matthew Gibney (Oxford: Oxford University Press, 2003).

63. Chomsky, "'Recovering Rights,'" p. 71.

64. For links to memos, see http://www.msnbc.msn.com/id/30270759/.

65. Daniel J. Whelan and Jack Donnelly, "The West, Economic and Social Rights, and the Global Human Rights Regime: Setting the Record Straight," *Human Rights Quarterly* 29, no. 4 (2007). For a reply to this claim, see Alex Kirkup and Tony Evans, "The Myth of Western Opposition to Economic, Social, and Cultural Rights? A Reply to Whelan and Donnelly," *Human Rights Quarterly* 31, no. 1 (2009).

66. Ellen Paine, "The Road to the Global Compact," in *Global Policy Forum* (2000); Jan Aart Scholte, "Globalization and the State," *International Affairs* 73, no. 3 (1997).

67. Chomsky, "'Recovering Rights.'"

68. Appiah, "Citizens of the World."

69. See, for example, Heritage Foundation, http://www.heritage.org/, and International Chamber of Commerce, http://www.iccwbo.org/.

70. Paine, "Road to the Global Compact."

71. Joyce V. Millen, Evan Lyon, and Alec Irwin, "Dying for Growth: The Political Influence of National and Transnational Corporations," in *Dying for Growth: Global Inequality and the Health of the Poor*, ed. Jim Young Kim et al. (Monroe, Maine: Common Courage Press, 2000); Paine, "Road to the Global Compact."

72. Paine, "Road to the Global Compact," p. 3.

73. See Heritage Foundation, heritage.org/Research/InternationalOrganizations/bg608.cfm.

74. It is worth noting that the labor movement has been slow to respond to globalization of production and has made little progress in organizing on a global scale.

75. Kofi Annan, "Address to the World Economic Forum in Davos," United Nations Secretary-General press release, 1999; United Nations Development Programme, *Human Development Report, 1995—Gender and Human Development* (Oxford, UK: UNDP, 1995).

76. Peter Ungphakorn, e-mail, June 14, 2007.

77. De Feyter, *Human Rights: Social Justice in the Age of the Market*.

78. Chomsky, "'Recovering Rights.'"

79. Andrew Linklater, *The Transformation of Political Society* (Cambridge, UK: Polity, 1998).

80. Marcuse, "Repressive Tolerance."

81. Ibid.

82. Pasha and Blaney, "Elusive Paradise," pp. 417–540.

83. Barry Hindess, "Power and Rationality: The Western Conception of Political Community," *Alternatives* 17, no. 2 (1992): 149–163.

84. Universal Declaration of Human Rights, Article 2.

85. Marcuse, "Repressive Tolerance," pp. 92–93.

86. Ibid., p. 82.

87. President George W. Bush was fond of using the word *evildoers* in speeches following the events of 9/11.

88. Tony Evans, "The Limits of Tolerance: Islam as Counter-hegemony," *Review of International Studies* 36, no. 4 (2010).

89. One of President Obama's first decisions was to suspend these operations.

90. Alan Travis, "Anti-Terror Critics Just Don't Get It, Says Reid," *Guardian*, London, August 10, 2006.

91. De Feyter, *Human Rights: Social Justice in the Age of the Market.*

92. Bertil Duner, "Disregard for Security: The Human Rights Movement and 9/11," *Terrorism and Political Violence* 17 (2005).

93. See, for example, The Canadian Human Rights Commission, http://www.chrc ccdp.ca/research_program_recherche/ns_sn/toc_tdm-en.asp.

94. Duner, "Disregard for Security."

95. Amnesty International, "Amnesty International Report, 2008," London, 2008.

96. Kishore Mahbubani, "The West and the Rest," *The National Interest* (Summer 1992).

97. Gearty, *Can Human Rights Survive?* p. 82.

98. Teeple, *Riddle of Human Rights,* p. 12.

99. Gearty, *Can Human Rights Survive?* p. 4.

100. De Feyter, *Human Rights: Social Justice in the Age of the Market,* p. 3.

101. Susan George, "Globalizing Rights?" in *Globalizing Rights: The Oxford Amnesty Lectures, 1999,* ed. Matthew J. Gibney (Oxford: Oxford University Press, 2003), p. 17 (emphasis in original).

102. Ibid., p. 18.

103. Pasha and Blaney, "Elusive Paradise," p. 424.

104. Ibid.

105. James Keeley, "Towards a Foucauldian Analysis of International Regimes," *International Organization* 44, no. 1 (1990).

9

Human Rights
as Political Process

This book has offered an overview of some of the most prominent critiques of the post-1945 project for universal human rights. What is noticeable about these critiques is that few seek to deny that human rights will continue to play a role in global politics. While some claim that the project for human rights is little more than an attempt to exercise continued hegemonic control over countries previously under colonial rule, through disabling any intercultural discourse on the genealogy of human rights,[1] others argue that human rights talk provides the language for and context within which previously excluded cultural ideas that might be used for, imagining new futures.[2] Even when postmodernist thinkers argue that there are no universal truths, the idea of human rights as a pragmatic solution for many human ills retains its appeal.[3] Moreover, the energy applied to the practice of human rights, within formal institutions, civil society, and nongovernmental organizations, attests to a ubiquitous belief in some idea of universal moral standards.

However, the creation of the contemporary human rights regime, which is said to reflect the impact of the idea on the imagination of the world's peoples, has also stimulated trenchant criticism and critique. The regime has expanded to include many forms of human suffering that the founders of the Universal Declaration had not anticipated. Today, there is a "human rights market," including producers, investors, consumers, and traders.[4] While this suggests the "commodification" of rights, it has also provided the momentum for imagining a better world. During the early years of the regime, the European credentials it boasted did not seem to match the imperial powers' view that saw the "imposition of dire and extravagant suffering upon individual human beings as wholly justified" in the colonies.[5] In more recent times, there has been a growing acceptance that human rights are related to particular socioeconomic configurations, suggesting that under conditions of globalization, ideas from non-European cultures about what we mean by dignity, equality, and justice promise to transform our understanding of moral claims.[6] For Baxi, this distinguishes "modern" from "contemporary" human rights talk, where the former operated on exclusionary principles, in the sense that it was others who had to accept the "truth" of European values, and the latter operated on inclusionary principles, inspired by contact with others from non-European cultures.[7] It is a

195

distinction that provides the space for critique by exposing the early years of the regime as an attempt at "closure," including the exclusion of many forms of human suffering not central to the interests of the dominant legal and political order.

What this suggests is that the idea of universal human rights should be understood as a process, rather than an end point to be achieved over time. The observation that in the six decades since the Universal Declaration, the variety, intensity, and extent of violations—seen in daily media reports of ethnic cleansing, civil wars, torture, slavery, racism, starvation, poverty, and a multitude of refugees—remains unchanged, suggesting that not all is well with existing approaches to the promotion and protection of human rights.[8] Despite this depressing and pessimistic news, the idea of human rights continues to inspire optimism and a determination to continue the struggle, exemplified by the cacophony of civil society groups with a human rights focus.

Progress and Process of Human Rights

The Oxford English Dictionary defines "progress" as "advancement to a further or higher stage or to further or higher stages successively" and notes that this is usually understood through the language of growth and development toward a better state or condition. Linked to this is "process," which is defined as the "course of becoming as opposed to static being" or the "passage of a discourse."[9] Both terms suggest movement over time in some specific area of human endeavor (technology, society, standard of living, performance, etc.), which, through the exercise of imagination, is intended to deliver improvements on previous states of affairs. This view is often associated with history, some approaches to political theory (Marx), science (Darwin), and many religious beliefs (perfecting the individual), where progress and change is cast as a relentless march toward some inevitable goal. In this view, particular events can be judged by the contribution made toward the purpose or design of history, politics, science, or spirituality. Progress in this sense is teleological.[10]

Moral discourses are often couched in terms of progress and process. In the case of human rights this is often expressed in the literature, particularly when some new institutional development has taken place, like the creation of the International Criminal Court (ICC), the Human Rights Council, or, indeed, the standard-setting seen in the development of international human rights law. Of course, progress and process in this meaning do not necessarily imply outcomes that further protect human rights but, rather, improvements in the opportunity to measure the actions of governments against pledges to respect the goal of human rights. It is formal progress through the processes facilitated by the United Nations or some other international organization that assumes the focus for such claims. Importantly, progress toward the goal or end point of the process is judged by how new initiatives move toward the realization of the human rights expressed in the Universal Declaration and the major covenants, which continue to provide the fundamental statement of "truth" upon which the regime is built. Challenges to the established foundational claims for the idea of human rights play no role in mainstream human rights talk. For those sympathetic to this view of "progress," understanding human rights as a process threatens to challenge all the major human rights standards and norms enshrined in international law. Human rights process is not therefore on the agenda.[11]

An alternative view that seeks to move away from a vision of some utopian end point is to adopt the idea of process utopianism developed by Joseph Nye.[12] Nye argues against the prospect of ever achieving an imagined utopia, if this means an anticipated, incontrovertible end point, such as that proposed by the "end of history" thesis, Communism, and particular interpretations of scripture. Arguments for sustaining such a view commonly claim that utopia can be realized only when social and political decisionmakers follow the "correct" and "true" path. To accept this view of utopia is to accept that "on the day that these end points are achieved . . . politics as struggle stops, and is replaced by administration and management."[13] End-point utopianism therefore promises to deliver prized social goals, but at the expense of a stagnant, moribund social order in which people no longer feel the need for participation or to exercise political imagination, a world in which we have surrendered our future.[14] In this understanding of utopia, the realization of the values expressed in the Universal Declaration are not recognized as a stage in a dynamic process characteristic of history but a final moral "truth" toward which all societies must work.

As an alterative, Nye proposes process utopianism. In this formulation, imagination is continually applied to the social milieu in ways that generate innovative ways of thinking, knowing, and acting, stimulating new accounts of moral and utopian futures through social and political struggles. It is a process that allows us to dream of an alternative society to the one we currently inhabit: a new society that expresses our reflections on moral motivations and energies within the immediate social order. This is because the actions and decisions made in one period alter the social and political context for thinking about the next. Process utopianism focuses upon progressive but pragmatic processes that are not driven by any ideological blueprint. Rather, process utopianism proposes that the dynamics of social change compel us to engage in reimagining our future, including the moral goals we set ourselves. As McKenna puts it, "there is no disjunction of means and an end . . . each end-in-view achieved eventually becomes the means for achieving new ends-in-view." In this way, concepts like human rights and democracy are "an open-ended process, capable of being reformed and redirected."[15] Through this process, we inherit our moral outlook from the past generation, engage with this outlook in the current generation, and bequeath a revised, reformed, and sometimes transformed outlook to the next generation. As Booth puts it,

> it is especially futile to try to over-manage the long-term future in an era of rapid change. One generation must seek to establish progressive principles and benign conditions for the next, with the hope that if we look after the processes, the structures will look after themselves.[16]

In this view, utopia is a process of discovery,[17] providing no possibility of achieving an imagined end point. Those who continue in the belief that reaching an end point that achieves the perfection of humankind are therefore destined for disappointment.

For Baxi, what this implies is that "in the eye of the future that which we now term 'human rights' may live on only in the ruins of memory."[18] This is especially relevant in an age characterized by the rapid changes that are the focus of globalization theory.[19] While the concept of human rights may be associated with the modern era of the Enlightenment, the industrial revolution, and capitalism, the contemporary, dynamic world of globalization demands that we create new conceptions of human rights that better fit the prevailing socioeconomic order. By presenting human rights as an eternal, unchanging set of values, values that are now entrenched in international law, we substitute human rights as a means to an end for human rights as an end in itself. Human rights become an end point, a "good" that pays no attention to the complex, dynamic processes of social construction, which successive generations seek to create anew. Intellectual and philosophical discourses should therefore stimulate our imagination for generating the "good" we want to assert, not the rights, which are a means to achieving the "good."[20] Expressing this, Douzinas is able to argue that when "apologists of pragmatism pronounce the end of ideology, of history or utopia, they do not mark the triumph of human rights; on the contrary, they bring human rights to an end." Put enigmatically by Douzinas, when the "end of human rights comes then they lose their end."[21]

These remarks reiterate arguments encountered earlier—that we need to realize that the human rights movement is just that: a movement. And as a movement the current generation can always claim that it does not represent a final truth, but remains young, vibrant, and experimental. Something of this movement can be seen in the vestiges of foundational debates on human rights, which have moved from claims based on reason to those based on persuasion. Human rights are "true," not because we can reveal their verity using the tools of philosophy but because so many now say they are "true": a form of democratic majoritarian argument that turns to techniques of argumentation, campaigning, political struggle, and debating for its source of legitimacy.[22] Those who claim that all the most significant aspects of human rights are now accepted ubiquitously and repeat the commonly held mantra that we have now moved from the era of standard setting to that of implementation fail to recognize the dynamic nature of social order and the changing contextual nature in which rights talk is conducted.[23] The consequences of this failure only add to the confusion that surrounds human rights, the tendency to conflate philosophical, legal, and political arguments, and the opposing cultures of pessimism and optimism that are a characteristic of contemporary human rights talk.[24]

It should also be noted that process and utopian thinking are not confined to Western political thought. The Islamic scholar Abdolkarim Soroush, for example, has argued that reason can be understood as both destination and path, where the first is understood as a source and storehouse of truth and the second as a "critical, dynamic, yet forbearing [force] that meticulously *seeks* the truth by negotiating torturous paths of trial and error."[25] As a storehouse, the application of reason does not encourage discourses that include thinking about social contexts and processes that established a particular truth in the first place. As a path, reason can be understood as a process whereby respect for the method of establishing a truth is given as much attention as the truth it claims to have revealed. As Soroush puts it, "it is not enough to attain the truth; the manner of its attainment is equally important."[26] From this take by Islamic scholarship, the idea of destination suggests the rejection of freedoms that enable challenges to the "truth," while the idea of path embraces such freedoms. Thus, for Soroush, without freedom there is no prospect of stimulating a dynamic struggle to find new moral and ethical principles that reflect processes of socioeconomic change at the local, national, regional, and global levels. Structuring human rights talk as "generations" of rights (civil and political rights, economic rights, group rights) might be seen as an example where human rights as process already operates.

The "Problem" with Human Rights Talk

The conclusion that the global project for human rights reflects a particular historic sociopolitical configuration that no longer pertains in the current period leaves critiques in the uncomfortable position of denying one of the most totemic and emblematic symbols of what it means to be "civilized." Although critique has a rationale, what it delivers is far from providing solutions.[27] If in the era of globalization human rights offers a site for contestation, particularly over foundational claims, then it is necessary to develop an account that explains the (re)emergence of social, political, economic, and cultural critiques. In itself, this will not lead to obvious, rational, and inevitable answers or a program for action that will move us further toward delivering human rights universally, but it will provide the space for engaging in a discourse between the subjects of rights, as it responds to the new and dynamic context of the current period.[28] To accept this view is to accept that there is nothing absolute about human rights, but, rather, that the contemporary global injunction to protect human rights is contingent upon historical contexts. The importance we attach to human rights in regard to other issues—the threat of terrorism, sustaining the current global political economy, and technical and scientific discoveries—requires constant reassessment. Only then can we determine where human rights falls in the list of normative, ethical, and material issues with which we are asked to deal.[29]

What are the motivations for engaging in this dynamic debate? Bhikhu Parekh begins by noting that within community we stand in a variety of relationships with others—brother, colleague, neighbor, business associate, friend, religious community, and so forth—relationships that are regulated by particular norms describing particular rights and duties.[30] To act morally is to recognize these norms and respect them. Although there is not much difficulty in accepting this formulation as a central characteristic of community, how we treat the "other"—those we encounter outside our own recognizable community relationships—presents a problem. As Parekh argues, once encounters with the "other" become regular and frequent, we are left "wondering how to respond to them and even whether one may treat them as one pleases including kill or harm them."[31] While such contacts are not a new phenomenon (Parekh cites the Roman Empire as a historic example), the intensity and reach of economic globalization exposes all communities to the politics of difference in ways that call for new reflections upon rights and duties.

Changes in world order since the creation of the Universal Declaration and the major pieces of international law on human rights, particularly the shift to ever-greater levels of economic integration, which leaves no society untouched, provides a very different context in which rights talk is conducted today from that in the past. The global, regional, and local institutions created for the protection of human rights were, and remain, largely built upon an understanding of rights that reflects a past period. The failure to grasp the idea of human rights as process, and to continue to cling to notions of rights from the past, acts as a barrier to taking up new moral challenges that cannot be solved through the precepts of the past. As the technology associated with globalization provides knowledge that awakens us to the suffering of others, including those who suffer as a consequence of socioeconomic planning that supports the material well-being of wealthy communities, an opportunity arises for us to reconsider our moral responsibilities, including rights and duties. Where this will lead remains unclear, but it may see the development of new concerns, not for the individual as reflected in the Universal Declaration, but for communities as they struggle for survival in the face of private interests.

To take up this challenge, there is a need to understand moral and ethical issues by constructing a radical and perpetual dialogue about the central assumptions upon which societal norms and values are built. This should be an inclusive discourse, accessed by all moral agents with an interest in interrogating established moral precepts and institutional machinery designed to protect societal values. Crucially, Parekh notes that we have not reached some end point that permits us to say, with some assurance, that human beings are a finished product, fully formed in every aspect, including our moral values. Instead, society is constantly undergoing change, refinement, reconstruction, and transformation, making all our efforts to define our essential humanity tentative. Human beings are socially constructed and reconstructed over the generations, which in the most recent formulation include many ideas that are peculiar to the age; for example, the individual, choice, and self-realization. While these ideas may have served in the past, there can be no certainty that such values will provide a secure foundation for notions of the moral life in a future world.[32]

Although Parekh's proposal does acknowledge human rights as a process, it does not recognize many of the issues set out in previous chapters. In particular, it does not engage sufficiently with the politics of rights, the values attached to the global political economy, new debates about relativism stimulated by globalization, and the hegemony of international law as the prime tool for defining, promoting, and protecting human rights.

As with all political questions, the politics of rights is concerned with relations of power.[33] While philosophy and law are often discussed in the politics of rights literature, the focus remains on identifying the interests associated with dominant forms of philosophical and legal reason. It is therefore concerned with questions to do with why human rights emerged as a prominent issue in the post–World War II order, why the regime was built upon particular foundations, why the institutional development of the modern human rights regime took the form that it did, and why, in the changed context of globalization, the need to critically reassess human rights receives so little attention. Furthermore, it raises questions about how, in any attempt to engage in processes for reformulating human rights, we can avoid an outcome where dominant interests speak the loudest, dominate the discourse, and develop a new human rights regime that reflects particular interests, rather than the interests of humankind. Put simply, and to place the questions in a wider context of global politics, short of some form of global democracy, how would we know when a consensus has been reached?[34] However, if, as Chomsky contends, two of the pillars of the post–World War II international order (Bretton Woods and the UN Charter) are redundant or irrelevant, and the third, the Universal Declaration, remains to a large extent "a letter to Santa Claus,"[35] there is a need not only to engage in processes for the further development of rights but in the politics of change generally, if we are to respond successfully to the new conditions of globalization.

Taken as a whole, the critiques presented in this book support the argument that the future of human rights is crucially dependent upon our ability to imagine new futures. Our failure to take up the challenges presented by current movements in globalization will, therefore, see human rights become progressively moribund.[36] The success of such a project depends upon some notion that global relations are becoming stronger, more complex, and widespread in a movement toward a less socially, economically, and politically divided and conflicted world. However, the discussion in earlier chapters on the (re)emergence of cultural relativism as a consequence of globalization, feminist arguments that suggest human rights are the rights of men, and conflicts within current institutions for the protection of human rights serve to underline the challenges that confront future human rights talk. Furthermore, the nature of sovereignty has undergone a considerable transformation under conditions of globalization, raising important questions about the state's relationship to human rights, including established assumptions about the subjects of international law. If human rights are to assume a central place in the processes of globalization as a "discipline" that determines our moral future, then many political obstacles must be overcome.[37]

Barriers to Process

The political barriers in the way of reviving a dynamic discourse of human rights cannot, of course, be divorced from the globalization of the political economy. While the accent on normative issues provides a crucial element for debates on creating a future world, such debates cannot "neglect or underrate the role of concrete motivations."[38] The (re)emergence of nationalism, particularly in new states created in the ruins of the USSR, new political struggles stimulated by processes of economic and political inclusion and exclusion, and the rise of international terrorism can all be placed within this context. These movements are characteristic of a "global dialectic of disintegration and integration"[39]—a historic moment when the old has not been replaced by the new and the new has not yet fully emerged.[40] It is an emerging order described by the language of modernity, secularism, and materialism, values that are proselytized throughout the world, dividing communities between those who cling to a known past and those who embrace the promise of an unknown future. The political conflicts that arise over choices between radical social change and tradition often lead to policies designed to marginalize resistance to the "irresistible" forces of modernization. Such policies curtail civil and political rights, disrupt the possibility of delivering economic, social, and cultural rights, and often end in violent clashes between protesters and the military or police. Underlying this phenomenon is the globalization of production, finance, and exchange, where the authority of nonstate actors coalesce with the state, state apparatus, and international organizations to fashion an order that bears little resemblance to that in which the Universal Declaration was created.

The consequences for human rights are several. First, the established human rights regime is widely accepted as built upon a Western tradition of natural rights derived from a state of nature, most eloquently articulated by John Locke. Its more recent articulation is found in the work of John Rawls. Rawls argues that in a state of nature, those possessed of superior strength, intellectual talents, and skills are presented with an opportunity to coerce the weak and less talented and thus undermine any prospect for sustaining a social contract. However, he argues that this overlooks the "original position," which places individuals behind a "veil of ignorance."[41] Unaware of important social markers, like race, ethnicity, sex, and belief system, individuals are thus deprived of knowledge about themselves and others. According to Rawls, under these circumstances rational individuals will seek to construct and maintain a social contract that secures a fair and just society for all citizens, including equal rights, rather than risk an uncertain future. Human beings are thus cast as risk averse.

Although as an intellectual exercise this justification for achieving a rights-based social order appears sound, it should be contrasted with the central assumption of the global capitalist order, which assumes, contra Rawls, that it is within humankind's nature to take risks, albeit within a framework of rational calculations. Without this characteristic feature of the capitalist order, a core incentive for motivating individuals to engage in production and exchange would be removed. This tension between liberal philosophical thought and capitalist values, between the norms and principles for developing a rights-based society and those that are said to sustain market discipline, present a series of contradictions that stand in the path of any attempt to engage fully in proposals to revitalize the process of human rights along Western liberal lines. Not least is the observation that, even while the liberal view of rights was promoted as the central value upon which to construct the postwar order, colonial peoples continued to suffer subjugation. While that form of repression is no longer acceptable today, the structures of economic globalization perform a similar task in many regions of the world.

Second, following the dissolution of what Gill has called the "glue of the Cold War"[42] and the more recent crisis of capitalism seen in the credit crunch of 2008–2009, further questions about the potential for stability within the capitalist world order are raised at the very instant when the virtues of free-market, laissez-faire global competitiveness seemed to have delivered on the promise of generating ever-greater levels of wealth. Such periodic crises point to the unraveling of existing social hegemonies and political consensus that achieved widespread acceptance, first in North America and Western Europe[43] and later in the developed states of the global South, where free-market and private property principles are promoted as the only sure path for economic development. Indeed, the right to development itself assumes a particular conception necessarily associated with Western thought. The imposition of these principles, which see the state's redistributive role emasculated as a condition for receiving economic assistance, complicates the potential for delivering economic and social rights, leading to social unrest and attracting military and police action in violation of civil and political rights.

Third, some scholars have noted that the institutionalization of ideas increases their longevity, allowing them to survive for considerable periods after the material forces that brought them to the fore have changed.[44] Cox, for example, argues that the "universal" values promoted by any hegemonic power in the service of its own interests will attract adherents during periods of transition, characterized by the struggle between newly emerging social forces and those established in the previous period.[45] For human rights, this implies that the struggle to establish a post–World War II moral order that supported human rights in the interests of capital has had to contend with, first, the end of the Cold War, and, second, economic globalization.[46] The reevaluation of human rights during this comparatively short period saw the discourse of rights shift from proclamations of the "end of history"[47] and the triumph of liberal rights to increasing challenges to any claim of universalism, seen, for example, in the work of feminists, neo-Marxists, postmodernists, and social movements. The confusion that this brings to the human rights discourse, as interests associated with past claims for universalism face opposition from a complex of sources, adds further to the complexities of reviving human rights as a process.

Fourth, the global technological revolution of the past two decades has brought to the fore new problems not easily integrated into existing human rights talk. For example, the human genome project could be used to identify disabilities, prospects for ill health, and the longevity of individuals, information that would be of great interest to employers, insurance corporations, banks, and departments of state with an interest in pensions and social services. Such information could also be used to deny reproductive rights as a means to prevent particular health conditions emerging in future generations, reviving the prospect of eugenics associated with nineteenth-century attempts to identify the "criminal classes" and, for that matter, Nazism.[48] Furthermore, the possibility of finding new ways of preventing infectious disease through the genome project may be attractive to many states engaged in developing techniques of germ warfare. Recognizing the human rights implications of this new technology, UNESCO in 1997 prepared a Universal Declaration on the Human Genome and Human Rights, and in 1999 issued guidelines for implementing the Declaration's principles. Article 6 seeks to outlaw "discrimination based on genetic characteristics that is intended to infringe or has the effect of infringing human rights, fundamental freedoms and human dignity." Article 10 states that no research or research applications flowing from the human genome project should "prevail over respect for the human rights, fundamental freedoms and human dignity of individuals or, where applicable, of groups of people."[49] Other examples of new technology with human rights implications are only now being debated; for example, digitalization and claims for environmental rights.

Fifth, although it is now widely accepted that the globalizing order is constructed through the interactions and relations between many different actors, the central actor in the human rights regime remains the state. It is the state that remains central to organizing the institutions for the protection of human rights, the state that is the subject of international law, and the state that takes responsibility for violations of human rights, no matter where they occur. Given the conditions of globalization, including the organization of production and exchange on a global scale, which provides transnational corporations with considerable power and influence over people's lives, it is no longer clear whether the state is the most appropriate, or even the most suitable, agent through which human rights might be negotiated and protected.[50] Corporate Social Responsibility might be seen as an early response to this problem, but so far has failed to convince that it can achieve a real and lasting solution. Indeed, the weakness of the response only serves to highlight problems associated with overcoming entrenched interests before a revitalized process of human rights talk can begin.

Sixth, while reviving the process of human rights talk does not by itself solve the central issues that remain for the existing regime, it will revitalize the politics of rights within the context of globalization. In particular, in a global order where the level of development enjoyed by the wealthy can be maintained only by the exploitation of labor, natural resources, and the environment on a global scale, there is a need to take seriously the rights of the poor and excluded, also on a global scale.[51] While in the past it may have been possible to construct arguments demonstrating that the achievement of economic and social rights depended upon the level of development that a people had achieved nationally, today, when production and labor are organized globally, such arguments are not so easily defended.

Seventh, cultural relativism has long confronted the idea of universal human rights, but has emerged in a different form since the advent of globalization. Eleanor Roosevelt's early experience as chair of the Commission on Human Rights persuaded her that no progress could be made in drafting international law if cultural relativist arguments were given too much space.[52] During the early years of the Cold War, the perceived imperative of military security pushed human rights to the margins, particularly when security demanded building alliances with those who were avowedly anti-Communist, no matter their human rights record, and when ideological differences could be exercised over dissimilarity in the approach to human rights. Although human rights began to assume greater importance in international relations from the late 1970s, debates on the foundations of rights in a multicultural world were rare. However, following the collapse of the USSR and claims of the "triumph of liberalism," relativist challenges have emerged in the intellectual vacuum created by the divergence between human rights discourse grounded in the post-1945 era and the changing structures of the global political economy. The technologies associated with globalization have not only brought an exchange of material goods but have also stimulated interest in the foundational claims for human rights within both Western political thought and that of many other traditions. These critiques of human rights highlight a series of discrepancies between claims of universality and the progressive realization of human rights, on the one hand, and their actual role, institutionalization, and implementation within the global political economy, on the other.

The recent revival of cultural relativism was first signaled in the ambiguities set out in the 1993 Bangkok Declaration of Asian states prior to the Vienna UN conference on human rights.[53] The Bangkok Declaration begins by acknowledging the interdependence and indivisibility of all rights and the progress made in developing institutions for the promotion and protection of human rights. However, it also expresses concern that "these mechanisms relate mainly to one category of rights"[54] and asserts that national, religious, and cultural particularities cannot be ignored, values that are the duty of the state to promote and protect. In recognition that the conditions of globalization present a new context for human rights, the declaration stresses that "the main obstacles to the realization of the right to development lie at the international macroeconomic level, as reflected in the widening gap between the North and South, the rich and the poor" (Art.18). As Weston notes, in the current global milieu, with its "riot of ideological, philosophical, and religious divisions that prevail worldwide, even as the globalization of capital renders us ever more homogenous," the Bangkok Declaration reminded us that cultural relativism remains contentious and promises to become more prominent.[55]

More recently, the conditions of globalization have begun to force a reappraisal of "old thinking" on human rights, which dismissed cultural relativist ideas on grounds that all humankind does, in fact, share a common foundation, which is said to be clearly expressed in the belief systems of all cultures.[56] Against this tradition is Rorty's "ironism," by which he means a reaffirmation and growing confidence in our own values accompanied by radical doubts.[57] While, on the one hand, we are impressed by the development of our own values, and even the values of other cultures, we are also aware that no particular set of values moves us nearer to the "truth." Similarly, but from another cultural perspective, Soroush claims to have identified a trend in Islam for greater doubt and reflection upon the cherished values expressed in Muslim societies, which he argues is of similar kind to that found in the West. The failure to make this move, and to confront the "old thinking" of the Enlightenment, with its belief in an objective human nature and a common set of interests binding all humankind, is a failure to recognize important social, economic, and political changes wrought by globalization. In the current global order, characterized by rapid and intense exchanges of ideas, such an entrenched approach cannot be sustained.

Finally, the hegemony of international law as *the* means for promoting and protecting human rights stands in the way of processes for exploring alternative ways of promoting and protecting human rights and dignity. This is not to argue that international law has nothing to offer to the protection of human rights, but, rather, that the singularity of faith placed in international law masks the potential for taking social, economic, and political action that leads to real improvements in people's lives. In the post–World War II period of international reorganization, where the sovereign state was represented as the only actor of consequence, it seemed unthinkable not to turn to international law for solutions to almost all global issues.[58] While it cannot be claimed that globalization has seen the sovereign state enter into a period of terminal decline—a process that would have serious consequences for international legal principles that place the state as the subject of international law—the sovereign state is widely understood as undergoing a period of transformation. In this sense, as Scholte has noted, the state represents both continuity and change: continuity in that the state and interstate relations persist as the core of global politics, assuming the roles of governance necessary to sustain global order, while the capacities, constituencies, policy-making processes, and content, including those associated with international law, are in flux.[59]

The tension between continuity and change in the role of the state is seen in what Jackson has termed "treaty rigidity," a condition that points to the difficulties of amending, revising, or replacing existing international law that served the interests of dominant states in a particular historic period.[60] This observation assumes greater complexity when we experience changes *of*, rather than *within*, global order, such as the shift from an international order to one more accurately described through the language of globalization. While, in the preceding period, the principles of international law may have reflected the supremacy of the sovereign state within the international order, these principles may no longer offer a system of rules sufficient to organize the current period. What may be required is a new type of law, which includes a multiplicity of actors as its subjects.[61] Something of this can be seen in the creation of the World Trade Organization, which has been given powers to take decisions on trade issues, including the power to overturn state decisions that impede free trade, thus relieving the state of responsibilities that in a previous period were considered a sovereign right. However, while this may provide a form of law more suited to recent changes in global order, and reflect the move to a globalized economy, whether such a model is suitable for moral issues is questionable, particularly where regulation may stand in the way of further advances in economic interests.

* * *

Increasingly, in the legal, philosophical, and political literature on human rights, those who offer critique claim that the project has failed in its current guise. This is not to argue that the postwar human rights regime has failed in every aspect of its aims and objectives. It has undoubtedly offered a focus for those engaged in the struggle to claim their rights. The very idea of rights, which in the past did not receive so much attention, today achieves a level of recognition that places it on many economic, social, and political agendas. If we accept that action is always informed by ideas, then the prominence of human rights talk has surely achieved this significant goal. But to recognize some of the achievements of the past six decades, no matter how limited they may be, does not lead to the conclusion that all is well. The impact of economic globalization needs to be recognized as a vital contextual framework that requires us to look seriously at the many critiques of human rights being voiced currently, some of which have been looked at here. Without accepting this, in the struggle between conservative and radical uses of the term *human rights*, the conservatives will remain in the ascendance.

This is not only because the idea of natural rights or self-evidence cannot be sustained in a world where we are increasingly conscious of other's cultural values, but also because its Western philosophical pedigree marks it as a means for imposing particular values on "other," non-Western peoples. The shift to a globalized world order has impacted many of the principles that sustained the past order in which the international human rights regime was constructed. While the idea of human rights appears to remain strong in the language of global politics and international relations, for reasons associated with transitional periods an approach that centers upon the state and international law is increasingly tested by the emerging order.[62] There is, therefore, a need to engage afresh in the process of human rights, to engage with the cacophony of global voices that seek to enter the debate, and to seek new ways of defining and delivering rights that avoid further human misery.[63]

If we fail to rework what human rights means today, including some concerted attempt to provide the idea with intellectual confidence and theoretical zest in a changing world, "then the time might come when firing the human rights argument will be greeted with neither warmth nor dismay but rather with blank indifference, or (which is worse) mute incomprehension: whatever can that term mean?"[64] While it is clear that we have not yet reached this point, the dissonance and discord that appears to be achieving a wider and deeper place within the politics of human rights will move us closer still to this conclusion. The first step along the path to avoiding this pessimistic outcome is to accept that human rights remain a process, not an end point. Our failure to recognize this can lead only to further confusion and discontent.

By responding to the changing conditions of globalization we recognize that the context within which the current human rights regime was built no longer pertains. Something of this can be seen when Amnesty International argues that the "world needs a new global deal on human rights—not paper promises but commitment and concrete action from governments to defuse the human rights time bomb." And the human rights time bomb, according to Amnesty, concerns the crisis in "shortages of food, jobs, clean water, land and housing, and also about deprivation and discrimination, growing inequality, xenophobia and racism, violence and repression across the world"—in the main, economic and social, rather than civil and political rights.[65]

In the *Analects,* Confucius describes the exemplary person as one who keeps trying, even when it is clear that all is in vain.[66] While it may be foolish to hope that we can ever devise ways of avoiding violation of all human rights, human misery, or lack of economic security for all people, thinking about human rights as a process, and continuing the political struggle to claim rights no matter how remote the chances of success often appear, adds to the politics of hope, rather than the politics of despair.[67]

Notes

1. For example, see Kishore Mahbubani, "The West and the Rest," *The National Interest* (Summer 1992).

2. For example, see Abdolkarim Soroush, *Reason, Freedom, and Democracy in Islam*, trans. Mahmoud Sadri and Ahmad Sadri (Oxford: Oxford University Press, 2002).

3. Richard Rorty, "Human Rights, Rationality, and Sentimentality," in *On Human Rights: The Oxford Amnesty Lectures, 1993*, ed. Stephen Shute and Susan Hurley (New York: Basic Books, 1993); Richard Rorty, "Universality and Truth," in *Rorty and His Critics*, ed. Roper R. Brandon (Oxford, UK: Blackwell, 2000).

4. Upendra Baxi, *The Future of Human Rights* (Oxford: Oxford University Press, 2002).

5. Ibid.

6. Ibid., p. 33.

7. Ibid.; see esp. Chapter 2.

8. Pierre Sane, "Human Rights in the 90s: An Agenda for Action" (London: London School of Economics, Centre for the Study of Global Governance,1993).

9. Oxford English Dictionary online: http://dictionary.oed.com/cgi/entry/ 50065594?single=1&query_type=word&queryword=discursive&first=1&max_to_show =10.

10. Ken Booth, *Theory of World Security*, ed. Steve Smith, Cambridge Studies in International Relations (Cambridge: Cambridge University Press, 2007), pp. 118–129. Of course, the teleological view of Darwinism is not the only possible view of the processes of evolution.

11. Makau Mutua, *Human Rights: A Political and Cultural Critique*, ed. Bert B. Lockwood, Pennsylvania Studies in Human Rights (Philadelphia: University of Pennsylvania Press, 2002).

12. Joseph Nye, "The Long-Term Future of Deterence," in Roman Kolkowicz, ed., *The Logic of Nuclear Deterrence* (Boston: Allen & Unwin, 1987), pp. 245–247.

13. Booth, *Theory of World Security,* p. 252.

14. Erin McKenna, *The Task of Utopia: A Pragmatist and Feminist Perspective* (Lanham, Md.: Rowman & Littlefield, 2001).

15. Ibid., p. 93.

16. Booth, *Theory of World Security,* p. 252.

17. David Kettler, *Utopian as Discovery Process* (2006), at www.cjsonline.ca/ soceye/utopia.html (cited 2008).

18. Baxi, *Future of Human Rights,* p. 3.

19. See, for example, David Held et al., eds., *Global Transformations: Politics, Economics, and Culture* (Cambridge, UK: Polity, 1999); Jan Aart Scholte, *Globalization: A Critical Introduction* (Basingstoke, UK: Palgrave, 2000).

20. Fiona Robinson, "The Limits of a Rights Based Approach to International Ethics," in *Human Rights Fifty Years On: A Reappraisal*, ed. T. Evans (Manchester: Manchester University Press, 1998).

21. Costas Douzinas, *Human Rights and Empire: The Political Philosophy of Cosmopolitanism* (Abingdon, UK: Routledge-Cavendish, 2007), p. 4.

22. Conor Gearty, *Can Human Rights Survive?* (Cambridge: Cambridge University Press, 2006).

23. Mutua, *Political and Cultural Critique.*

24. Tony Evans, *The Politics of Human Rights: A Global Perspective*, 2nd ed. (London: Pluto Press, 2005); see esp. the introduction.

25. Soroush, *Reason, Freedom, and Democracy in Islam,* pp. 89–90 (emphasis in original).

26. Ibid., p. 90.

27. Terrell Carver, *The Postmodern Marx* (Manchester: Manchester University Press, 1998).

28. Simon Chesterton, "Human Rights as Subjectivity: The Age of Rights and the Politics of Culture," *Millennium* 27, no. 1 (1998).

29. Gearty, *Can Human Rights Survive?*

30. Bhikhu Parekh, "Principles of a Global Ethic," in *Global Ethics and Civil Society*, ed. John Eade and Darren O'Byrne (Aldershot, UK: Ashgate, 2005).

31. Ibid., p. 15.

32. Parekh's view on how we should proceed with developing our moral values in the current and future world order, particularly his idea of an inclusive and perpetual

discourse, does offer some way forward when questioning human rights. However, unless the question of power relations is considered, there seems no reason to believe that the outcome in any period would not reflect dominant voices, just as the current human rights regime does today.

33. Evans, *Politics of Human Rights;* Neil Stammers, "Human Rights and Power," *Political Studies* 41 (1993).

34. Mustapha Kamel Pasha and David L. Blaney, "Elusive Paradise: The Promise and Perils of Global Civil Society," *Alternatives* 23, no. 1 (1998).

35. Noam Chomsky, "'Recovering Rights': A Crooked Path," in *Globalizing Rights: The Oxford Amnesty Lectures, 1999,* ed. Matthew J. Gibney (Oxford: Oxford University Press, 2003).

36. Baxi, *Future of Human Rights,* p. 16.

37. Fred Dallmayr, "Cosmopolitanism: Moral and Political," *Politcal Theory* 31, no. 3 (2003).

38. Ibid., p. 428.

39. Stephen Gill, "Reflections on Global Order and Sociohistorical Time," *Alternatives* 16, no. 3 (1991): 276.

40. Chesterton, "Human Rights as Subjectivity"; Jorge Nef, "Globalization and the Crisis of Sovereignty, Legitimacy, and Democracy," *Latin American Perspectives* 29, no. 6 (2002).

41. John Rawls, *A Theory of Justice* (Oxford: Oxford University Press, 1999).

42. Gill, "Reflections on Global Order," p. 277.

43. Ibid., p. 276.

44. For the classic view of this argument, see Robert O. Keohane, *After Hegemony: Cooperation and Discord in the World Political Economy* (Princeton, N.J.: Princeton University Press, 1984).

45. Robert Cox, "Social Forces, Forms of State, and World Orders: Beyond International Relations Theory," *Millennium* 10, no. 2 (1981); Robert Cox, "Democracy in Hard Times: Economic Globalization and the Limits of Democracy," in *The Transformation of Democracy,* ed. A. McGrew (Cambridge, UK: Polity Press, 1995), pp. 49–75.

46. Ankie Hoogvelt, *Globalization and the Postcolonial World: The New Political Economy of Development* (Basingstoke, UK: Palgrave, 2001).

47. Francis Fukuyama, "The End of History," *The National Interest* (Summer 1989).

48. Allyn L. Taylor, "Globalization and Biotechnology: UNESCO and an International Strategy to Advance Human Rights and Public Health," *American Journal of Law and Medicine* 25 (1999).

49. Universal Declaration on the Human Genome and Human Rights, UNESCO Gen. Conf. Res. 29 C/Res.16, reprinted in Records of the General Conference, UNESCO, 29th Sess., 29 C/Resolution 19, at 41 (1997) (adopted by the UN General Assembly, G.A. Res. 152, U.N. GAOR, 53rd Sess., UN Doc. A/RES/53/152 (1999)).

50. Chesterton, "Human Rights as Subjectivity."

51. Charles Jones, *Global Justice: Defending Cosmopolitanism* (Oxford: Oxford University Press, 2000).

52. At a well-reported "tea party" given by Roosevelt following the first meeting of the commission, a heated argument broke out between P. C. Chang and Charles Malik. Chang demanded that Confucius be required reading for all commission members before any progress could be made. See Tony Evans, *US Hegemony and the Project of Universal Human Rights* (Basingstoke, UK: Macmillan, 1996), p. 84.

53. For the Bangkok Declarations, see http://www.unhchr.ch/html/menu5/wcbangk.htm.

54. See http://law.hku.hk/lawgovtsociety/Bangkok%20Declaration.htm, at preamble.

55. Burns H. Weston, "The Universality of Human Rights in a Multicultural World: Towards Respectful Decision-Making," in *The Future of International Human Rights*, ed. Burns H. Weston and Stephen P. Marks (New York: Transnational Publishers, 1999).

56. Dallmayr, "Cosmopolitanism: Moral and Political."

57. Rorty, "Universality and Truth."

58. Within the first two weeks of her appointment as CHR chair, Eleanor Roosevelt made a note on briefing paper that "the job is to complete a draft Bill in two weeks." See papers of Eleanor Roosevelt, Roosevelt Library, Hyde Park, N.Y., box no. 5487.

59. Jan Aart Scholte, "Globalization and the State," *International Affairs* 73, no. 3 (1997).

60. John H. Jackson, "Sovereignty-Modern: A New Approach to an Outdated Concept," *American Journal of International Law* 97, no. 4 (2003).

61. J. Oloka-Onyango and Deepika Udagana, "The Realization of Economic, Social, and Cultural Rights: Globalization and Its Impact on the Full Enjoyment of Human Rights" (Sub-Commission on the Promotion and Protection of Human Rights, 2000).

62. Chesterton, "Human Rights as Subjectivity."

63. Baxi, *Future of Human Rights*.

64. Gearty, *Can Human Rights Survive?* pp. 21–22.

65. Amnesty International annual report, 2009, *State of the World's Human Rights*, http://thereport.amnesty.org/en/introduction.

66. Confucius, *The Analects* (Oxford: Oxford University Press, 1993).

67. Jones, *Global Justice: Defending Cosmopolitanism*.

Bibliography

Aaronson, Susan Ariel, and Jamie M. Zimmerman. "The World Trade Organization and Human Rights: Providing Some Power to the People Some of the Time," ISA Annual Conference, San Diego (2006).

Al-Hargan, Abdulhamid A. "Saudi Arabia and the International Covenant on Civil and Political Rights, 1966: A Stalemate Situation." *International Journal of Human Rights* 9, no. 4 (1995): 491–505.

Alves, Jose A. Lindgren. "The Declaration of Human Rights in Postmodernity." *Human Rights Quarterly* 22, no. 2 (2000): 478–500.

Amnesty International. "Amnesty International Report, 2008." London, 2008.

———. *Amnesty International Urges WTO Members to Respect Human Rights Obligations in Trade Negotiations in Hong Kong* 2005. Cited, http://web.amnesty.org/library/engindex.

Amoore, Louise. "Introduction: Global Resistance—Global Politics." In *The Global Resistance Reader*, edited by Louise Amoore, 1–12. Abingdon, UK: Routledge, 2005.

Angle, Stephen C. *Human Rights and Chinese Thought: A Cross-Cultural Inquiry*. Cambridge: Cambridge University Press, 2002.

Annan, Kofi. "Address to the World Economic Forum in Davos." Press release, edited by United Nations Secretary-General, 1999.

———. "The Secretary General Addresses the World Economic Forum." World Economic Forum, 2002.

———. "Secretary-General's Address to the World Economic Forum." World Economic Forum, 2004.

———. "The United Nations Cannot Stand Still, Because the Threats to Humanity Do Not Stand Still." World Economic Forum, Davos, 2006.

Apodaca, Clair. "The Globalization of Capital in East and Southeast Asia: Measuring the Impact on Human Rights Standards." *Asian Survey* 42, no. 6 (2002): 883-905.

Appiah, K. Anthony. "Citizens of the World." In *Globalizing Rights*, edited by Matthew Gibney, 189–232. Oxford: Oxford University Press, 2003.

Arslan, Zuhtu. "Taking Rights Less Seriously: Postmodernism and Human Rights." *Res Publica* 5 (1999): 195–215.

Ashworth, Georgina. "The Silencing of Women." In *Human Rights in Global Politics*, edited by Tim Dunne and Nicholas J. Wheeler, 259–276. Cambridge: Cambridge University Press, 1999.

Bauer, Joanne R., and Daniel A. Bell. *The East Asian Challenge for Human Rights*. Cambridge: Cambridge University Press, 1999.

Baxi, Upendra. *The Future of Human Rights*. Oxford: Oxford University Press, 2002.

Beck, Ulrich. *What Is Globalization?* Cambridge, UK: Polity Press, 2000.

Berween, Mohamed. "International Bills of Human Rights: An Islamic Critique." *International Journal of Human Rights* 7, no. 4 (2003): 129–142.

Billington, Ray. *Understanding Eastern Philosophy*. London: Routledge, 1997.

Blair, Tony. "Speech at the WTO, 19th May 1998," Geneva (1998), www.wto.org/english/thewto_e/minist_e/min98_e/anniv_e/blair_e.htm

Bluthner, Andreas. "Trade and Human Rights at Work: Next Round Please . . . ?" In *Agreeing and Implementing the Doha Round of the WTO,* 335–375, edited by Harold Hohmann. Cambridge: Cambridge University Press, 2004.

Booth, Ken. *Theory of World Security*, edited by Steve Smith. Cambridge Studies in International Relations. Cambridge: Cambridge University Press, 2007.

Boutros-Ghali, Boutros. "Agenda for Peace." New York: United Nations, 1992.

Broomhall, Bruce. *International Justice and the International Criminal Court: Between Sovereignty and the Rule of Law*. Oxford: Oxford University Press, 2005.

Brown, Malcolm D. "An Ethnographic Reflection on Muslim-Christian Dialogue in the North of France: The Context of *Laicite." Islam and Christian-Muslim Relations* 13, no. 1 (2002): 5–23.

Bruno, Kenny. "Perilous Partners," *Multinational Monitor* 21, no. 3 (2000), www.multinationalmonitor.org/mm2000/00march/economics1.html. Cited April 17, 2007.

Bull, Hedley. *The Anarchical Society*. London: Macmillan, 1977.

Camilleri, Joseph A., and Jim Falk. *The End of Sovereignty? The Politics of a Shrinking and Fragmenting World*. Aldershot, UK: Edward Elgar, 1992.

Carothers, Thomas. "Democracy and Human Rights: Policy Allies or Rivals?" *Washington Quarterly* 17, no. 3 (1994): 109–120.

Carver, Terrell. *The Postmodern Marx*. Manchester: Manchester University Press, 1998.

Cassese, Antonio. *Human Rights in a Changing World*. Oxford: Oxford University Press, 1990.

Cerone, John P. "Dynamic Equilibrium: The Evolution of US Attitudes Towards International Criminal Courts and Tribunals." *European Journal of International Law* 18, no. 2 (2007): 277–315.

Chan, Joseph. "The Confucian Perspective on Human Rights for Contemporary China." In *The East Asian Challenge for Human Rights*, edited by Joanne R. Bauer and Daniel A. Bell. Cambridge: Cambridge University Press, 1999.

Chandler, David. *Constructing Global Civil Society: Morality and Power in International Relations*. Basingstoke, UK: Palgrave, 2004.

———. *From Kosovo to Kabul: Human Rights and International Intervention*. London: Pluto, 2002.

Charlesworth, Hilary, Christine Chinkin, and Shelly Wright. "Feminist Approaches to International Law." *American Journal of International Law* 85, no. 4 (1991): 613–645.

Cheru, Fantu. "The Silent Revolution and the Weapons of the Weak: Transformation and Innovation from Below." In *Innovation and Transformation in International Studies*, edited by Stephen Gill and James H. Mittelman, 153–169. Cambridge: Cambridge University Press, 1997.

Chesterton, Simon. "Human Rights as Subjectivity: The Age of Rights and the Politics of Culture." *Millennium* 27, no. 1 (1998): 97–118.

Chimini, B. S. "Marxism and International Law." *Economic and Political Weekly* 34, no. 6 (1999): 349–359.

Chinkin, Christine. "International Law and Human Rights." In *Human Rights Fifty Years On: A Reappraisal*, edited by Tony Evans, 105–129. Manchester: Manchester University Press, 1998.

Chomsky, Noam. "'Recovering Rights': A Crooked Path." In *Globalizing Rights: The Oxford Amnesty Lectures, 1999*, edited by Matthew J. Gibney, 45–80. Oxford: Oxford University Press, 2003.

———. "The United States and the Challenge of Relativity." In *Human Rights Fifty Years On: A Reappraisal*, edited by Tony Evans, 24–57. Manchester: Manchester University Press, 1998.

———. *World Orders, Old and New*. London: Pluto, 1994.

Chossudovsky, Michel. "World Trade Organisation (WTO): An Illegal Organisation That Violates the Universal Declaration of Human Rights," 1999.

Christie, Kenneth, and Denny Roy. *The Politics of Human Rights in East Asia*. London: Pluto Press, 2001.

Collins, Hugh. *Marxism and Law*. Oxford: Oxford University Press, 1990.

Coomaraswamy, Radhika. "To Bellow Like a Cow: Women, Ethnicity, and the Discourse of Rights." In *Human Rights of Women: National and International Perspectives*, edited by Rebecca Cook, 39–57. Philadelphia: University of Pennsylvania Press, 1994.

Cox, Robert. "Civil Society at the Turn of the Millennium: Prospects for an Alternative World Order." *Review of International Studies* 25, no. 3 (1999).

———. "Democracy in Hard Times: Economic Globalization and the Limits to Liberal Democracy." In *The Transformation of Democracy*, edited by Anthony McGrew, 49–75. Cambridge, UK: Polity Press, 1997.

———. "A Perspective on Globalization." In *Globalization: Critical Reflections*, edited by James H. Mittelman. Boulder, Colo.: Lynne Rienner Publishers, 1995.

Cozens Hoy, David. "Power, Repression, Progress: Foucault, Lukes, and the Frankfurt School." In *Michel Foucault: Critical Assessments*, edited by Barry Smart, 173–191. London: Routledge, 1995.

Dallmayr, Fred. "Cosmopolitanism: Moral and Political." *Politcal Theory* 31, no. 3 (2003): 421–442.

Danino, Robert, Jean-Pierre Chauffour, Daniel Kaufmann, and Ana Palacio. "Human Rights and Development." World Bank Institute, 2006.

Davies, Michael C. "The Price of Rights: Constitution and East Asian Economic Development." *Human Rights Quarterly* 20, no. 2 (1998): 303–337.

De Feyter, Koen. *Human Rights: Social Justice in the Age of the Market*. London: Zed Books, 2005.

Devetak, Richard, and Richard Higgott. "Justice Unbound? Globalization, States, and the Transformation of the Social Bond." *International Affairs* 75, no. 3 (1999): 483–498.

Dietrich, Wolfgang. *A Structural-Cyclic Model of Developments in Human Rights*. Human Rights Working Papers, 2000. At www.du.edu/humanrights/working papers. Cited January 20, 2001.

Dine, Janet, and Andrew Fagan, eds. *Human Rights and Captialism*. Cheltenham, UK: Edward Elgar, 2006.

Dirlik, Arif. "Confucius in the Borderlands: Global Capitalism and the Reinvention of Confucianism." *boundary* 22, no. 3 (1995): 229–273.

Dodds, K. "Political Geography: Some Thoughts on Banality, New Wars, and the Geographical Tradition." *Progress in Human Geography* 24, no. 1 (2000): 119–129.

Donnelly, Jack. "International Human Rights: A Regime Analysis." *International Organization* 40, no. 3 (1986): 599–642.

Douzinas, Costas. *Human Rights and Empire: The Political Philosophy of Cosmopolitanism*. Abingdon, UK: Routledge-Cavendish, 2007.

Duncan, Gary. "World Leaders Are Stuck in Moral Maze." *Times*, London, January 31, 2005.

Duner, Bertil. "Disregard for Security: The Human Rights Movement and 9/11." *Terrorism and Political Violence* 17 (2005): 89–104.

Eagleton, Terry. "Deconstruction and Human Rights." In *Freedom and Interpretation: The Oxford Amnesty Lectures, 1992*, edited by Barbara Johnson, 121–145. New York: Basic Books, 1992.

Economides, Spyros. "The International Criminal Court: Reforming the Politics of International Justice." *Government and Opposition* 38, no. 1 (2003): 29–51.

The Economist, "Asian Values Revisited: What Would Confucius Say Now?" July 24, 1989, 25–27.

Engels, Frederick. *Anti-Duhring: Herr Eugen Duhring's Revolution in Science*. London: Lawrence & Wishart, 1975.

Englehart, Neil A. "Rights and Culture in the Asian Values Argument: The Rise and Fall of Confucian Ethics of Singapore." *Human Rights Quarterly* 22, no. 2 (2000): 548–569.

Evans, Tony. "Citizenship and Human Rights in the Age of Globalization." *Alternatives* 25, no. 4 (2000): 415–438.

———. "Human Rights: A Reply to Geoffrey Best." *Review of International Studies* 17, no. 1 (1991).

———. "International Human Rights Law as Power and Knowledge." *Human Rights Quarterly* 27, no. 3 (2005): 1046–1068.

———. *The Politics of Human Rights: A Global Perspective*. London: Pluto Press, 2001.

———. *US Hegemony and the Project of Universal Human Rights*. Basingstoke, UK: Macmillan, 1996.

———. "US Hegemony, Domestic Politics, and the Project of Universal Human Rights." *Diplomacy and Statecraft* 6, no. 3 (1995): 616–644.

Evans, Tony, and Jan Hancock. "Doing Something Without Doing Anything: International Law and the Challenge of Globalization." *International Journal of Human Rights* 2, no. 3 (1998): 1021.

Falk, Richard. *Human Rights Horizon: The Pursuit of Justice in a Globalizing World*. London: Routledge, 2000.

Farer, Tom J. "Restraining the Barbarians: Can International Criminal Law Help?" *Human Rights Quarterly* 22, no. 1 (2000): 90–117.

Favell, Andy. "Do Blue Chips' Green Reports Show Their Blue Colours?" *Independent*, London, February 19, 2006.

———. "Green Grocers? The Big Chains Talk a Good Game but Their True Ethical Colours Are Hard to Determine." *Independent,* London, September 10, 2006.

Felice, William. "The Viability of the United Nations Approach to Economic and Social Human Rights in a Global Economy." *International Affairs* 75, no. 3 (1999): 563–598.

Fernandes, Leela. "The Boundaries of Terror: Feminism, Human Rights, and the Politics of Global Crisis." In *Just Advocacy? Women's Human Rights, Transnational Feminism, and the Politics of Representation*, edited by Wendy S. Hesford and Wendy Kozol, 56–74. New Brunswick, N.J.: Rutgers University Press, 2005.

Fischer, Willaim F. "Doing Good? The Politics and Anti-Politics of NGO Practices." *Annual Review of Anthropology* 26 (1997): 439–464.

Forrest, Anne. "Securing the Male Breadwinner: A Feminist Interpretation of PC 1003." *Relations Industrielle* 52, no. 1 (1997): 91–111.

Foucault, Michel. *Discipline and Punish*. Translated by A. Sheridan. New York: Pantheon Books, 1977.

———. "Two Lectures." In *Critique and Power: Recasting the Foucault/Able Debate*, edited by Michael Kelly, 1–46. Cambridge, Mass.: MIT Press, 1994.

———. "What Is Critique?" In *Twentieth-Century Questions*, edited by James Schmidt, 383–398. Berkeley: University of California Press, 1996.

Fraser, Nancy. "Rethinking Recognition." *New Left Review,* no. 3 (May–June, 2000): 107–120.

Frean, Alexandra. "Corporate Aid or Plain Hypocrisy?" *Times,* London, February 2, 2004, p. 22.

Freeman, Michael. *Human Rights*. Cambridge, UK: Polity Press, 2002.

Fukuyama, Francis. "The End of History." *The National Interest* (Summer 1989): 3–18.

Furet, F. *Marx and the French Revolution*. London: University of Chicago Press, 1995.

Galtung, Johan. *Human Rights in Another Key*. Cambridge, UK: Polity Press, 1994.

Gearty, Conor. *Can Human Rights Survive?* Cambridge: Cambridge University Press, 2006.

General Assembly. "Draft Resolution (a/60/L.48)." In *Report of the Fifth Committee (A/60/271)*. New York: United Nations, 2006.

———. "Kofi Annan Speech Presenting the Report of the High-Level Panel on Threats, Challenges, and Change, GA Fifty-Ninth Session: Agenda Item 55." New York: United Nations, 2004.

George, Susan. "Globalizing Rights?" In *Globalizing Rights: The Oxford Amnesty Lectures, 1999*, edited by Matthew J. Gibney, 15–33. Oxford: Oxford University Press, 2003.

———. *The Lucano Report*. London: Pluto, 1999.

Gershman, John, and Alec Irwin. "Getting a Grip on the Global Economy." In *Dying for Growth: Global Inequality and the Health of the Poor*, edited by Jim Young Kim, Joyce V. Millen, Alec Irwin, and John Gershaw, 9–43. Monroe, Maine: Common Courage Press, 2000.

Giddens, Anthony. *Modernity and Self-Identity*. Cambridge, UK: Polity Press, 1990.

Gill, Stephen. "Constitutionalizing Inequality and the Clash of Civilizations." *International Studies Review* 4, no. 2 (2002): 47–65.

———. "Finance, Production, and Panopticanism: Inequality, Risk, and Resistance in an Era of Disciplinary Neo-Liberalism." In *Globalization, Democratization, and Multiculturalism*, edited by Stephen Gill, 51–75. Basingstoke, UK: Macmillan, 1997.

———. "Globalization, Market Civilisation, and Disciplinary Neoliberalism." *Millennium* 24, no. 3 (1995): 399–423.

———. "Reflections on Global Order and Sociohistorical Time." *Alternatives* 16, no. 3 (1991): 275–314.

Gills, Barry K. "The Crisis of Postwar East Asian Captialism: American Power, Democracy, and the Vicissitudes of Globalization." *Review of International Studies* 26, no. 3 (2000): 381–403.

Gills, Barry, Joel Rocamora, and Richard Wilson. "Low Intensity Democracy." In *Low Intensity Democracy*, edited by Barry Gills, Joel Rocamora, and Richard Wilson, 3–34. London: Pluto, 1993.

Global Compact. *What Is the Global Compact?* UN Global Compact web pages. Cited March 13, 2007.

Global Compact Office. "The United Nations Global Compact: Advancing Corporate Citizenship." UN Global Compact Office, 2005.

Global Exchange. "The WTO Erodes Human Rights Protection: Three Case Studies." 1999, www.globalexchange.org/campaigns/wto/casestudies.

Goodhart, Michael. "Origins and Universality in the Human Rights Debate: Cultural Essentialism and the Challenge of Globalization." *Human Rights Quarterly* 25, no. 4 (2003): 935–964.

Goodwin, Christopher. "Woman at War with the Mullahs." *Sunday Times*, London, April 7, 2006.

Gramsci, Antonio. "Selections from the Prison Notebooks," edited by Quinton Hoare and Geoffrey Smith. London: Lawrence & Wishart, 1996.

Hall, Mark A. "The Scope and Limits of Public Health Law." *Perspectives in Biology and Medicine* 46, no. 3 (2003): 199–208.

Held, David. "Democracy: From City-States to a Cosmopolitan Order." *Political Studies* 40, special issue (1992): 10–39.

Held, David, Anthony McGrew, David Goldblatt, and Johanthan Perraton, eds. *Global Transformations: Politics, Economics, and Culture*. Cambridge, UK: Polity Press, 1999.

Heller, Agnes. "The Legacy of Marxian Ethics Today." *Praxis International* 1, no. 4 (1982): 346–364.

———. "The Limits to Natural Law and the Paradox of Evil." In *On Human Rights: The Oxford Amnesty Lectures, 1993*, edited by Stephen Shute and Susan Hurley, 149–173. New York: Basic Books, 1993.

Hemingway, Christine A. "An Exploratory Analysis of Corporate Social Responsibility: Definitions, Motives, and Values." Centre for Management and Organisational Learning, University of Hull Business School, Hull, UK, 2002.

Herman, Edward S., and David Peterson. "Morality's Avenging Angels: The New Humanitarian Crusaders." In *Rethinking Human Rights*, edited by David Chandler, 279–309, Basingstoke, UK: Macmillan, 2002.

Hicks, Peggy. "The UN Human Rights Council: Testimony Delivered to the US Senate Foreign Relations Committee," July 7, 2007.

Hirst, Paul, and Grahame Thompson. *Globalization in Question?* Cambridge, UK: Polity Press, 1996.

Hoffman, John. *Sovereignty*. Minneapolis: University of Minnesota Press, 1998.

Hoogvelt, Ankie. *Globalization and the Postcolonial World: The New Political Economy of Development*. Basingstoke, UK: Palgrave, 2001.

Hopkins, Michael. *The Planetary Bargain*. London: Earthscan, 2003.

Hormats, Robert. "Globalization and Human Rights." Public Broadcasting Service, Washington, D.C., 1998.

Howse, Robert, and Makau Mutua. "Protecting Human Rights in a Global Economy: Challenges for the World Trade Organization." Rights and Democracy website, www.dd-rd.ca, 2000.

Human Rights Watch. "New Council Opposed by Unusual Duo: U.S. and Cuba." 2006, www.hrw.org/en/news/2006/03/12/new-council-opposed-unusual-duo-us-and-cuba.

———. *"No Guarantee: Sex Discrimination in Mexico's Maquiladora Sector."* Human Rights Watch: Women's Rights Project, 1996.

Hunt, Alan, and Gary Wickham. *Foucault and Law: Towards a Sociology of Law and Governance*. London: Pluto Press, 1994.

Huntington, Samuel P. *The Clash of Civilizations: Remaking of World Order*. New York: Touchstone, 1997.

Hutchings, Kimberly. "The Idea of International Citizenship." In *The Ethical Dimensions of Global Change*, edited by Barry Holder. Basingstoke, UK: Macmillan, 1996.

Huysmans, Jef. "Post-Cold War Implosion and Globalization: Liberalism Running Past Itself. " *Millennium* 24, no. 3 (1995): 471–487.

International Court of Justice. "Advisory Opinion." 33: ICJ, 1923.

Ivison, Duncan. "The Disciplinary Moment: Foucault, Law, and the Reinscription of Rights." In *The Later Foucault: Politics and Philosophy*, edited by Jeremy Moss, 129–148. London: Sage, 1998.

Jackson, John H. "Sovereignty-Modern: A New Approach to an Outdated Concept." *American Journal of International Law* 97, no. 4 (2003): 782–802.

Jacobs, I., G. Guopei, and P. Herbig. "Confucian Roots in China: A Force for Today's Business." *Management Decision* 33, no. 10 (1995): 29–34.

Jamali, Dima, and Ramez Mirshak. "Corporate Social Responsibility (CSR): Theory and Practice in a Developing Country Context." *Journal of Business Ethics*, no. 72 (2007): 243–262.

James, Stephen A. "Reconciling International Human Rights and Cultural Relativism: The Case of Female Circumcision." *Boethics* 8, no. 1 (1994): 1–26.

Johansen, Robert C. "The Impact of US Policy Toward the International Criminal Court on the Prevention of Genocide, War Crimes, and Crimes Against Humanity." *Human Rights Quarterly* 28 (2006): 301–331.

Jones, Charles. *Global Justice: Defending Cosmopolitanism*. Oxford: Oxford University Press, 2000.

Jones, Peter. *Rights*. Basingstoke, UK: Macmillan, 1994.

Kaufmann, Daniel. "Human Rights and Development: Towards Mutual Reinforcement." Paper presented at the Human Rights and Global Justice conference, New York University Law School, March 1, 2004.

Kaul, Hans-Peter. "Construction Site for More Justice: The International Criminal Court After Two Years." *American Journal of International Law* 99, no. 2 (2005): 370–384.

Keeley, James. "Towards a Foucauldian Analysis of International Regimes." *International Organization* 44, no. 1 (1990): 83–105.

Kettler, David. *Utopian as Discovery Process*, 2006. At www.cjsonline.ca/soceye/utopia.html. Cited 2008.

Kirkup, Alex, and Tony Evans. "The Myth of Western Opposition to Economic, Social, and Cultural Rights? A Reply to Whelan and Donnelly." *Human Rights Quarterly* 31, no. 1 (2009): 221–238.

Krasner, Stephen. *Sovereignty: Organized Hypocracy*. Princeton, N.J.: Princeton University Press, 1999.

Langlois, Anthony J. "Human Rights: The Globalization and Fragmentation of Moral Discourse." *Review of International Studies* 28, no. 3 (2002): 479–496.

Lauren, Paul Gordon. "'To Preserve and Build on Its Achievements and to Redress Its Shortcomings': The Journey from the Commission on Human Rights to the Human Rights Council." *Human Rights Quarterly* 29 (2007): 307–345.

Leite, Sergio Pereira. "Human Rights and the IMF." *Finance and Development: A Quarterly Magazine of the IMF* 38, no. 4 (2001).

Linklater, Andrew. *Man and Citizen in the Theory of International Relations*. Basingstoke, UK: Macmillan, 1990.

———. *The Transformation of Political Society*. Cambridge, UK: Polity Press, 1998.

———."What Is a Good International Citizen?" In *Ethics and Foreign Policy*, edited by Paul Keal. Canberra: Allen & Unwin, 1992.

Lukes, Steven. "Can a Marxist Believe in Human Rights?" *Praxis International* 1, no. 4 (1982): 334–345.

———. "Five Fables About Human Rights." In *On Human Rights: The Oxford Amnesty Lectures, 1993*, edited by Stephen Shute and Susan Hurley, 19–40. New York: Basic Books, 1993.

Lyotard, Jean-Francois. "The Other's Rights." In *On Human Rights: Oxford Amnesty Lectures, 1994*, edited by Stephen Shute and Susan Hurley, 136–147. New York: Basic Books, 1993.

Macfarlane, Sarah, Mary Racelis, and Florence Muli-Muslime. *Public Health in Developing Countries*, 2000. Cited June 2001.

MacIntyre, Alasdair. *After Virtue: A Study in Moral Theory*. London: Duckworth, 1981.

MacKinnon, Catharine A. "Crimes of War, Crimes of Peace." In *On Human Rights: The Oxford Amnesty Lectures, 1993*, edited by Stephen Shute and Susan Hurley, 83–109. New York: Basic Books, 1993.

MacLeod, Sorcha, and Douglas Lewis. "Transnational Corporations: Power, Influence, and Responsibility." In *Global Ethics and Civil Society*, edited by John Eade and Darren O'Byrne, 121–137. Aldershot, UK: Ashgate, 2005.

Madison, G. B. *The Political Economy of Civil Society and Human Rights*. London: Routledge, 1998.

Mahbubani, Kishore. "The West and the Rest." *The National Interest* (Summer 1992): 3–12.

Marcuse, Herbert. "Repressive Tolerance." In *A Critique of Tolerance*, edited by R. P. Wolff, Barrington Moore, and Herbert Marcuse. Boston, Mass.: Beacon Press, 1969.

Marx, Karl. "On the Jewish Question." In *Karl Marx: Selected Writings*, edited by David McLellan, 46–70. Oxford: Oxford University Press, 2002.

——. "Preface to the Critique of Political Economy." In *Karl Marx: Selected Writings*, edited by David McLellan, 424–428. Oxford: Oxford University Press, 2002.

——, ed. *Early Political Writings*. Edited by Joseph O'Malley. Cambridge: Cambridge University Press, 1994.

Marx, Karl, and Frederick Engels. "The Communist Manifesto." In *Karl Marx: Selected Writings*, edited by David McLellan. Oxford: Oxford University Press, 2002.

Mauzy, Diane K. "The Human Rights and 'Asian Values' Debate in Southeast Asia: Trying to Clarify the Key Issues." *Pacific Review* 10, no. 2 (1997): 201–236.

McCorquodale, Robert, and Richard Fairbrother. "Globalization and Human Rights." *Human Rights Quarterly* 21, no. 3 (1999): 735–766.

McGrew, Anthony. "Globalization and Territorial Democracy: An Introduction." In *The Transformation of Democracy*, edited by Anthony McGrew, 1–24. Cambridge, UK: Polity Press, 1997.

McKenna, Erin. *The Task of Utopia: A Pragmatist and Feminist Perspective*. Lanham, Md.: Rowman & Littlefield, 2001.

Mernissi, Fatima. *Islam and Democracy: Fear of the Modern World*. Cambridge, Mass.: Perseus Publishing, 1992.

——. *The Veil and the Male Elite: A Feminist Interpretation of Women's Rights in Islam*. Translated by Mary Jo Lakeland. New York: Basic books, 1991.

Merry, Sally Engle. *Human Rights and Gender Violence*. Chicago: University of Chicago Press, 2006.

Meyer, William H. *Human Rights and International Political Economy in Third World Nations*. Westport, Conn.: Praeger, 1998.

Mieville, China. *Between Equal Rights: A Marxist Theory of International Law*. London: Pluto Press, 2006.

Millen, Joyce V., Evan Lyon, and Alec Irwin. "Dying for Growth: The Political Influence of National and Transnational Corporations." In *Dying for Growth: Global Inequality and the Health of the Poor*, edited by Jim Young Kim, Joyce V. Millen, Alec Irwin, and John Gershaw, 225–233. Monroe, Maine: Common Courage Press, 2000.

Monshipouri, Mahmood. "Islamic Thinking and the Internationalization of Human Rights." *The Muslim World* 84, nos. 2–3 (1994): 217–239.

Monshipouri, Mahmood, Jr., Claude E. Welch, and T. Evan Kennedy. "Multinational Corporations and the Ethics of Global Responsibility: Problems and Possibilities." *Human Rights Quarterly* 25, no. 4 (2003): 965–989.

Moskovitz, Moses. *International Concern with Human Rights*. Dobbs Ferry, N.Y.: Oceana Publications, 1974.

Moss, Lawrence. "New Human Rights Council Requires Greater Political and Diplomatic Effort to Realize Its Potential." In *Commentary*: Human Rights Watch, 2007.

Mutua, Makau. *Human Rights: A Political and Cultural Critique*. Edited by Bert B. Lockwood, Pennsylvania Studies in Human Rights. Philadelphia: University of Pennsylvania Press, 2002.

——. "Human Rights International NGOs." In *NGOs and Human Rights: Promise and Performance*, edited by Claude F. Welch, 151–163. Philadelphia: University of Pennsylvania Press, 2001.

Muzaffar, Chandra. "From Human Rights to Human Dignity." In *Debating Human Rights: Critical Essays from the United States and Asia*, edited by Peter Van Ness, 26–31. London: Routledge, 1999.

Nardin, Terry. *Law, Morality, and the Relations of States*. Princeton, N.J.: Princeton University Press, 1983.

Nash, Kate. "Human Rights for Women: An Argument for 'Deconstructive Equality.'" *Economy and Society* 31, no. 3 (2002): 411–433.

Nef, Jorge. "Globalization and the Crisis of Sovereignty, Legitimacy, and Democracy." *Latin American Perspectives* 29, no. 6 (2002): 59–69.

NGO Coalition. *Coalition Says Global Compact Threatens UN Mission and Integrity.* Corporate Watch, 2000. At www.commandreams.org/news2000/0725-08.htm. Cited April 17, 2007.

O'Brien, Robert, et al. *Contesting Global Governance: Multilateral Economic Institutions and Global Social Movements.* Edited by Steve Smith, Cambridge Studies in International Relations. Cambridge: Cambridge University Press, 2000.

OHCHR. "Human Rights and Trade." OHCHR website, 2003.

Oloka-Onyango, J., and Deepika Udagana. "The Realization of Economic, Social, and Cultural Rights: Globalization and Its Impact on the Full Enjoyment of Human Rights." Geneva: Sub-Commission on the Promotion and Protection of Human Rights, 2000.

O'Neill, Onora. "Agents of Justice." *Metaphilosophy* 32, nos. 1–2 (2001): 180–195.

Opsahl, T. "Instruments of Implementation of Human Rights." *Human Rights Law Journal* 10, no. 1 (1989): 13–33.

Osiel, Mark J. "Why Prosecute? Critics of Punishment for Mass Atrocities." *Human Rights Quarterly* 22, no. 1 (2000): 118–147.

Ouden, den Bernard. "Sustainable Development, Human Rights, and Postmodernism." *Philosophy and Technology* 3, no. 2 (1997): 71–76.

Pae', JoonBeom. "Sovereignty, Power, and Human Rights Treaties: An Economic Analysis." *Northwest Journal of International Human Rights* 5, no. 1 (2006): 71–95.

Paine, Ellen. "The Road to the Global Compact." In *Global Policy Forum*, 2000, www.globalpolicy.org/component/content/article/225/32188.html.

Palacio, Ana. "Human Rights Day 2006." World Bank, 2006.

Panitch, Leo. "Rethinking the Role of the State." In *Globalization: Critical Reflections*, edited by James Mittelman. Boulder, Colo.: Lynne Rienner Publishers, 1995.

Parekh, Bhikhu. "Principles of a Global Ethic." In *Global Ethics and Civil Society*, edited by John Eade and Darren O'Byrne, 15–33. Aldershot, UK: Ashgate, 2005.

Pasha, Mustapha Kamel, and David L. Blaney. "Elusive Paradise: The Promise and Perils of Global Civil Society." *Alternatives* 23, no. 1 (1998): 417–540.

Patton, Paul. "Foucault's Subject of Power." In *The Later Foucault: Politics and Philosophy*, edited by Jeremy Moss, 64–77. London: Sage, 1998.

Peterson, V. Spike, and Laura Parisi. "Are Women Human? It's Not an Academic Quesiton." In *Human Rights Fifty Years On: A Reappraisal*, edited by Tony Evans. Manchester: Manchester University Press, 1998.

Petras, James. "NGOs in the Service of Imperialism." *Journal of Contemporary Asia* 29, no. 4 (1999): 429–440.

Pianta, Mario, and Raffaele Marchetti. "The Global Justice Movement: The Transnational Dimension." In *The Global Justice Movement: Cross-National and Transnational Perspectives*, edited by Donatella della Porta, 29–51. Boulder, Colo.: Paradigm Publishers, 2007.

Pinter, Harold. "Nobel Prize for Literature Acceptance Speech." *Guardian,* London (2005),www.nobelprize.org/nobel_prixes/literature/laureates/2005/pinterlecture.html

Porta, Donatella della. "The Global Justice Movement: An Introduction." In *The Global Justice Movement: Cross-National and Transnational Perspectives*, edited by Donatella della Porta, 1–28. Boulder, Colo.: Paradigm Publishers, 2007.

Power, Gavin. "Who Cares Wins—the Convergence of Global Corporate Citizenship and Financial Markets." Investment Management Institute Conference, 2006.

Prado, C. G. *Starting with Foucault: An Introduction to Genealogy.* Boulder, Colo.: Westview, 1995.

Rao, Araati. "Home-Word Bound: Women's Place in the Family of International Human Rights." *Global Governance* 2, no. 1 (1996): 241–260.

Raphael, D. D. "The Liberal Western Tradition of Human Rights." *International Social Science Journal* 18, no. 1 (1966): 22–30.

Ratner, Steven R. "Corporations and Human Rights: A Theory of Legal Responsibility." *Yale Law Journal* 111 (2001): 443–545.

Robinson, Fiona. "Human Rights and the Global Politics of Resistance: Feminist Perspectives." *Review of International Studies* 29, special issue (2003): 161–180.

———. "The Limits of a Rights Based Approach to International Ethics." In *Human Rights Fifty Years On: A Reappraisal*, edited by T. Evans, 58–76. Manchester: Manchester University Press, 1998.

Robinson, Mary. "Beyond Good Intentions: Corporate Citizenship for a New Century." RSA World Leaders Lecture, 2002.

Romany, Celina. "State Responsibility Goes Private: A Feminist Critique of the Public Private Distinction in International Human Rights Law." In *Women's Human Rights*, edited by Julie Peters and Andrea Wolper. London: Routledge, 1995.

Rorty, Richard. "Human Rights, Rationality, and Sentimentality." In *On Human Rights: The Oxford Amnesty Lectures, 1993*, edited by Stephen Shute and Susan Hurley, 111–134. New York: Basic Books, 1993.

———. "Universality and Truth." In *Rorty and His Critics*, edited by Roper R. Brandon. Oxford, UK: Blackwell, 2000.

Rosemont, Henry. "Human Rights: A Bill of Worries." In *Confuciansim and Human Rights*, edited by William Theodore De Bary and Tu Weiming, 54–66. New York: Columbia University Press, 1998.

———. "Why Take Rights Seriously? A Confucian Critique." In *Human Rights and the World's Religions*, edited by Leroy S. Rouner, 167–182. Notre Dame, Ind.: University of Notre Dame Press, 1988.

Rosenberg, Justin. *The Empire of Civil Society: A Critique of the Realist Theory of International Relations*. London: Verso, 1994.

Rothe, Dawn, and Christopher W. Mullins. "The International Criminal Court and United States Opposition." *Law and Social Change* 45 (2006): 201–226.

Rouse, Joseph. "Power/Knowledge." In *The Cambridge Companion to Foucault*, edited by Gary Cutting, 92–114. Cambridge: Cambridge University Press, 1994.

Ruggie, John G. "Creating Public Value: Everybody's Business." Herrhausen Society, 2004.

———. "The Global Compact and the Challenges of Global Governance—Berlin." United Nations Global Compact Learning Forum, 2002.

———. "Protect, Respect, and Remedy: A Framework for Business and Human Rights." Geneva: Human Rights Council, 2008.

———. "Report of the Special Representative of the Secretary-General (SRSG), Human Rights Council, 4th session, February 9, 2007, UN Doc. A/HRC/4/035.

Rupert, Mark. "Globalising Common Sense: A Marxian-Gramscian (Re)-Vision of the Politics of Governance and Resistance." *Review of International Studies* 29, special issue (2003): 181–198.

Salmi, J. *Violence and the Democratic State*. Oxford: Oxford University Press, 1993.

Sane, Pierre. "Human Rights in the 90s: An Agenda for Action." Address at the London School of Economics, May 1993.

Saunders, Clare. "Using Social Network Analysis to Explore Social Movements: A Rationalist Approach." *Social Movement Studies* 6, no. 3 (2007): 227–243.

Schabas, William A. *An Introduction to the International Criminal Court*. 2nd ed. Cambridge: Cambridge University Press, 2004.

Scholte, Jan Aart. *Globalization: A Critical Introduction*. Basingstoke, UK: Palgrave, 2000.

———."Globalization and the State." *International Affairs* 73, no. 3 (1997): 427–452.

———. "Towards a Critical Theory of Globalization." In *Globalization in Theory and Practice*, edited by Eleonore Kofman and Gillian Young, 43–57. London: Pinter, 1996.

Secretary-General, United Nations. "Globalization and the Impact on the Full Enjoyment of All Human Rights." New York: United Nations General Assembly, 2000.

Sellars, Kirsten. *The Rise and Rise of Human Rights*. Stroud, UK: Sutton Publishing, 2002.

Shivji, Issa. "Constructing a New Rights Regime: Promises, Problems, and Prospects." *Social and Legal Studies* 8, no. 2 (1999): 253–276.

Shue, Henry. *Basic Rights: Subsistence, Affluence, and US Foreign Policy*. 2nd ed. Princeton, New Jersey: Princeton University Press, 1996.

Simms, Chris, Mike Rawson, and Siobhan Peattie. *The Bitterest Pill of All: The Collapse of Africa's Health System*, report for Save the Children Fund, 2001, www.eldis.org/assets/docs/29246.

Soroush, Abdolkarim. *Reason, Freedom, and Democracy in Islam*. Translated by Mahmoud Sadri and Ahmad Sadri. Oxford: Oxford University Press, 2002.

Spybey, Tony. *Globalization and World Society*. Cambridge, UK: Polity Press, 1996.

Stammers, Neil. "Human Rights and Power." *Political Studies* 41 (1993): 70–82.

———. "Social Movements and the Social Construction of Human Rights." *Human Rights Quarterly* 21, no. 4 (1999): 980–1008.

Staples, V. J. "What Are Human Rights?" *The Lancet*, May 8, 1999. At www.sciencedirect.com). Cited November 2001.

Steans, Jill. "Engaging from the Margins: Feminist Encounters with the 'Mainstream' of International Relations." *British Journal of Politics and International Relations* 5, no. 3 (2003): 428–454.

———. *Gender and International Relations*. Cambridge, UK: Polity Press, 2006.

Stoltenbery, Clyde D. "Globalization, 'Asian Values,' and Economic Reform: The Impact of Tradition and Change on Ethical Values in Chinese Business." *Cornell International Law Journal* 33, no. 3 (2000): 711–729.

Takeda, Sachiko. "Individualism, Human Rights, and Modernization: The Case of Japan." Ph.D. diss., Southampton, 2005.

Tamilmoran, V. T. *Human Rights in Third World Perspective*. Ithaca, N.Y.: Cornell University Press, 1992.

Taylor, Allyn L. "Globalization and Biotechnology: UNESCO and an International Strategy to Advance Human Rights and Public Health." *American Journal of Law and Medicine* 25 (1999): 479–541.

Taylor, Annie. "The Significance of Non-Governmental Organizations in the Development of International Environmental Policy: The Case of Trade and Environment," dissertation, University of Southampton, 1998.

Teeple, Gary. *The Riddle of Human Rights*. Aurora, Canada: Garamond Press, 2005.

Tetrault, Mary A. "Regimes and Liberal World Order." *Alternatives* 13, no. 1 (1988): 5–26.

Thomas, Caroline. *Global Governance, Development, and Human Security*. London: Pluto Press, 2000.

———. "International Financial Institutions and Social and Economic Rights: An Exploration." In *Human Rights Fifty Years On: A Reappraisal*, edited by Tony Evans. Manchester: Manchester University Press, 1998.

Thompson, Grahame. "Is All the World a Complex Network?" *Economy and Society* 33, no. 3 (2004): 411–424.

Thompson, Mark R. "Pacific Asia After 'Asian Values': Authoritarianism, Democracy, and 'Good Governance.'" *Third World Quarterly* 25, no. 6 (2004): 1079–1095.

Travis, Alan. "Anti-Terror Critics Just Don't Get It, Says Reid." *Guardian*, London, August 10, 2006.

UNICEF. *The State of the World's Children—1998*. Oxford: Oxford University Press, 1998.

United Nations. "A More Secure World: Our Shared Responsibilities." United Nations, 2004.

United Nations Development Programme. *Human Development Report, 1995—Gender and Human Development*. Oxford, UK: UNDP, 1995.

———. *Human Development Report, 1996—Economic Growth and Human Development*. Oxford, UK: UNDP, 1996.

———. *Human Development Report, 1997—Human Development to Eradicate Poverty*. Oxford, UK: UNDP, 1997.

———. *Human Development Report, 1998—Consumption for Human Development*. Oxford, UK: UNDP, 1998.

———. *Human Development Report, 1999—Globalization with a Human Face*. Oxford, UK: UNDP, 1999.

———. *Human Development Report, 2000—Human Rights and Human Development*. Oxford, UK: UNDP, 2000.

UN Watch. "Dawn of a New Era? Assessment of the United Nations Human Rights Council and Its Year of Reform." Geneva: UN Watch, 2007.

Utting, Peter. "The Global Compact: Why All the Fuss?" In *UN Chronicle* 2. New York, 2003.

Vaezi, Ahmad. *Shia Political Thought*. London: Islamic Centre of England, 2004.

van der Pijl, Kees. *Transnational Class and International Relations*. London: Routledge, 1998.

———. "Transnational Class Formation and State Forms." In *Innovation and Transformation in International Studies*, edited by Stephen Gill and James Mittelman, 105–133. Cambridge: Cambridge University Press, 1997.

Van Ness, Peter. Introduction to *Debating Human Rights: Critical Essays from the United States and Asia,* edited by Peter Van Ness, 1–21. London: Routledge, 1999.

Vincent, R. J. *Human Rights and International Relations*. Cambridge: Cambridge, University Press, 1986.

Wagner, Antonim. "Redefining Citizenship for the 21st Century: From the National Welfare State to the UN Global Compact." *International Journal of Social Welfare* 13 (2004): 278–286.

Walker, R. B. J. "Gender and Critique in the Theory of International Relations." In *Gendered States: Feminist Revisions of International Relations Theory*, edited by V. Spike Peterson, 179–202. Boulder, Colo.: Lynne Rienner Publishers, 1992.

———. "Security, Sovereignty, and the Challenge of World Order." *Alternatives* 15, no. 1 (1990): 3–27.

———. "Social Movements/World Politics." *Millennium* 23, no. 3 (1994): 669–700.

Walzer, Michael. *Spheres of Justice: A Defence of Pluralism and Equality*. Oxford, UK: Blackwell, 1995.

Waters, Malcolm. *Globalization*. London: Routledge, 1995.

Watson, J. S., and vol. 3, Illinois Law Forum, 1979. "Legal Theory, Efficacy, and Validity in the Development of Human Rights Norms in International Law." *Illinois Law Forum* 3 (1979): 609–641.

Weber, Cynthia. *Simulating Sovereignty*. Cambridge: Cambridge University Press, 1885.

Weller, Marc. "Undoing the Global Constitution: UN Security Council Action on the International Criminal Court." *International Affairs* 78, no. 4 (2002).

Weston, Burns H. "The Universality of Human Rights in a Multicultural World: Towards Respectful Decision-Making." In *The Future of International Human Rights*, edited by Burns H. Weston and Stephen P. Marks, 65–99. New York: Transnational Publishers, 1999.

Wheeler, Nicholas, and Tim Dunne. "Good International Citizenship: A Third Way for British Foreign Policy." *International Affairs* 74, no. 4 (1998): 847–871.

Whelan, Daniel J., and Jack Donnelly. "The West, Economic and Social Rights, and the Global Human Rights Regime: Setting the Record Straight." *Human Rights Quarterly* 29, no. 4 (2007): 908–949.

Wight, Colin. *Agents, Structures, and International Relations: Politics of Ontology*, edited by Steve Smith, Cambridge Studies in International Relations. Cambridge: Cambridge University Press, 2006.

Wilson, Richard A. "Human Rights, Culture, and Context: An Introduction." In *Human Rights, Culture, and Context*, 1–27. London: Pluto, 1997.

Wood, Ellen Meiksins. *Democracy Against Capitalism*. Cambridge: Cambridge University Press, 1996.

Woodiwiss, Anthony. *Globalization, Human Rights, and Labour Law in Pacific Asia.* Cambridge: Cambridge, University Press, 1998.

Woods, Ngaire. "Order, Globalization, and Inequality in World Politics." In *Inequality, Globalization, and World Politics*, edited by Andrew Hurrell and Ngaire Woods, 8–35. Oxford: Oxford University Press, 1999.

World Bank. "Equity and Development." In *World Development Report, 2006*. Washington D.C.: World Bank, 2006.

Young, Bill. "Forget Social Responsibility," *Times,* London, April 5, 2005, p. 12.

Young, Gay, Lucia Fort, and Mona Danner. "Moving from 'the Status of Women' to 'Gender Inequality': Conceptualisation, Social Indicators, and an Empirical Application." *International Sociology* 9, no. 1 (1994): 55–85.

Younger, Tessa. "CSR a Heavy Responsibility." *Times*, London, April 5, 2004.

Zurndofer, Harriet T. "Confusing Confucianism with Capitalism: Culture as Impediment and/or Stimulation to Chinese Economic Development." Paper presented at the Third Global Economic History Network, 2004.

Index

About the Book

Tony Evans critically investigates the theory and practice of human rights in the current global order. Evans covers a range of contentious debates as he considers critiques of the prevailing conceptions of human rights. He then explores the changing global context of human rights issues, the nature and status of human rights within that context, and recent institutional responses. With its emphasis on policy and process, his book offers a rich analysis of the politics of today's human rights regime.

Tony Evans is professor of global politics at the University of Southampton. His publications include *The Politics of Human Rights* and *Human Rights Fifty Years On.*